AFRICAN AMERICAN CINEMA THROUGH BLACK LIVES CONSCIOUSNESS

AFRICAN AMERICAN CINEMA THROUGH BLACK LIVES
CONSCIOUSNESS

EDITED BY MARK A. REID

WAYNE STATE UNIVERSITY PRESS
DETROIT

ISBN 978-0-8143-4548-1 (paperback)
ISBN 978-0-8143-4549-8 (hardcover)
ISBN 978-0-8143-4550-4 (e-book)

Library of Congress Control Number: 2018946464

Wayne State University Press
Leonard N. Simons Building
4809 Woodward Avenue
Detroit, Michigan 48201–1309

Visit us online at wsupress.wayne.edu

For Evelyn

CONTENTS

III. PostNegritude Black Film: Pastiche and Race

IV. Black Cinematic Womanist Praxis

V. Sexual and Racial Polyphony in New Black Films

Acknowledgments

THIS ANTHOLOGY AND ITS list of contributors, those still listed and the many others who for many reasons are no longer included, have seen this volume through several years of transitions from its initial publication house to the welcoming arms of Wayne State University Press, a fine academic press that has an important, long-standing, and committed history in the area of black studies as well as other academic area studies. The Wayne State University Press production team, Annie Martin, Ceylan Akturk, Emily Nowak, Kristina Stonehill, Rachel Ross, and Carrie Downes Teefey, efficiently responded to my queries and expertly prepared this volume.

All authors deserve more than my thanks for their patience and trust in the creation of this imaginatively intersectional film studies project. I would like to thank Melba Boyd for her tenacious support as I went through several hurdles with corporate and a few university presses.

Life experiences and academic studies nurtured my transactional and postnegritude womanist thinking and work in film. My interviews with independent filmmakers, producers, and writers in the United States and abroad instilled a fervent desire to view film as an international art form that has no national boundaries in the areas of shared ethical and moral purposes to make the world a more humane place. In similar fashion, my academic mentors and instructors through college and graduate schools have shaped my views on film and the social sciences. Such scholars include historian Dr. Nathan I. Huggins, who first introduced me to Thomas Cripps's *Slow Fade to Black*; Andrew Sarris for his 35 mm screening and lectures on American and European film, and the scholar-teacher Dr. Katherine Stimpson, who furthered my engagement with feminism. After I graduated from Columbia, Dr. Gerald Mast extended my international understanding and theoretical appreciation of film. Dr. Darwin T. Turner, who chaired my dissertation committee and edited what became my first book-length study on African

American film, *Redefining Black Film,* made the most significant impression, since he taught me the importance of black control over their image in literature and film, as well as the importance of critical and theoretical analyses that are appropriate for black creative works. My work with Dr. Phyllis R. Klotman, Guy Hennebelle, the editor of *CinemAction,* and the *Jump Cut* editors Julia Lesage, John Hess, and Chuck Kleinhans, together encouraged me to continue to develop an internationalist-feminist understanding of the film industry and its products. In summation, these encounters with artists and scholars still guide my work, and I thank them for the opportunity to learn from their suggestions and their intellectual demands.

Finally, I would like to thank my personal editor-in-chief, interior decorator, and soulmate, who influences all that I find is crucial to teaching, writing, and being as an African American in a "Hands Up, Don't Shoot" and an "I Can't Breathe" national (dis)order.

INTRODUCTION

THE EARLIEST BLACK-DIRECTED AFRICAN American feature films provide a backdrop to more recent efforts. The challenges these early filmmakers faced, as well as the successes they achieved, highlight key elements in the black filmmaking experience and offered a glimpse of the path forward for those who followed. From their earliest involvement onward, black actors, writers, and directors have attempted to use these films as a way to make visible the issues blacks were experiencing in their lives, challenge the status quo, and suggest a method for moving forward. I begin here by tracing black involvement in feature filmmaking from its beginning in order to provide a background for the essays that will follow. I will then offer a brief introduction to each of these essays, suggesting how each explores contemporary black experience and its psychological and economic challenges as creatively imagined on the silver screen.

From 1912 to 1918, blacks directed short documentaries, comedies, family melodramas, and action films. The films featured African Americans as soldiers, businessmen, political leaders, celebrities, and adventurers seeking their fortunes in the West. The Foster Photoplay Company was the first African American independent film company. According to film historian Thomas R. Cripps, William Foster probably was the earliest black to direct a film. Cripps describes Foster:

> A clever hustler from Chicago, he had been a press agent for the [Bert] Williams and [George] Walker revues and [Bob] Cole and Johnson's *A Trip to Coontown* [1898], a sportswriter for the [*Chicago*] *Defender*, an occasional actor under the name of Juli Jones, and finally a purveyor of sheet music and Haitian coffee. He may have made the first black movie, *The Railroad*

Porter, an imitation of Keystone comic chases completed perhaps three years before *The Birth of a Nation* [1915]. (Cripps 1977, 79–80)

The Johnson brothers—George Perry (a U.S. postal employee) and Noble (a Universal Pictures contract actor)—established the Lincoln Motion Picture Company in 1916. The Lincoln Motion Picture Company excelled in racial uplift and black soldiering movies. The company produced four middle-class melodramas—*The Realization of a Negro's Ambition* (1916), *The Trooper of Troop K* (1916), *A Man's Duty* (1920), and *By Right of Birth* (1921)—and ended producing films with a one-reel documentary, *A Day with the Famous 10th* (1921), about the black Tenth Cavalry stationed at Fort Huachuca, Arizona. Lincoln Motion Picture Company films always featured a black, virtuous hero who was driven by the Protestant work ethic. Lincoln films avoided lengthy dramatizations of criminality or drunk, vulgar, and licentious behavior, and their films promoted racially uplifting narratives in which the black hero reaped material and spiritual rewards for adhering to the Protestant work ethic.

In 1919, Oscar Micheaux wrote, directed, and produced his first film, *The Homesteader*. He made twenty-five more films that are silent during the nearly ten years before his film company went bankrupt in 1928. As Gerald R. Butters Jr. notes, "Monetary gain from filmmaking was always a priority for Micheaux. In February 1928, at the end of the silent era, he was forced to file for bankruptcy. He reorganized in 1929 under the title The Micheaux Film Corporation with an infusion of white capital" (Butters 2002, 149). Micheaux made films that explored such controversial issues as racial lynching, interracial intimacy, racial passing, urban poverty, and criminality.[1]

From their very independent beginnings to the present, African American filmmakers have treated similar black-oriented themes and social issues within popular genre forms. These filmmakers injected black cultural content into the western, musical, family melodrama, detective, and gangster film genres. Admittedly, early black filmmakers used a cinematic style that was limited by the technology of the day and the filmmaker's modest production budget.

From the 1930s through the 1940s, white producers and theater managers, such as Alfred Sack of Sack Amusement and Leo Brecher and Frank

Schiffman, managers of Harlem's Apollo Theater, financed Oscar Micheaux's films and other black-directed or black-written films (Cripps 1977, 251). Since these small companies and individuals were independent of the major Hollywood studios—Fox Film Corporation, Metro-Goldwyn-Mayer, Warner Brothers, and the like—the all-black cast films produced and distributed by the smaller businesses are vastly different from such Hollywood studio–financed black-oriented musical films as *Hearts in Dixie* (Fox, 1929), *Hallelujah!* (MGM, 1929), *The Green Pastures* (Warner, 1936), and *Cabin in the Sky* (MGM, 1942). To this day, major studios attract some of the most talented black stage and screen actors, employ highly skilled technicians, and use the most up-to-date film technology, which independent filmmakers and productions cannot afford unless they have some business affiliation with the majors, as does Spike Lee. Neither the black independent filmmakers nor the white-controlled small companies that produced black-oriented films could afford such an expensive production overhead.

Thus, these white angels provided black filmmakers with a means to continue directing black-oriented film fare and enter the sound film era. This interracial business relationship, which lasted from 1930 through 1948, permitted Oscar Micheaux to make his first sound film, *The Exile* (1931) (Cripps 1977, 323).

Micheaux made sixteen more sound films during this eighteen-year period without support from Hollywood studios. Black-directed and black-oriented films produced between 1912 and the 1940s, commonly referred to as "race films," exhibit distinct differences in technical skill when compared to the post-1970s black films made by university-trained filmmakers and black directors whose projects were funded or distributed by major studios. In most, if not all, instances, whether black filmmakers worked for large companies or worked independently, they wanted their films to entertain and educate their audiences and make a sufficient profit to finance their next film.

The second renaissance in black independent filmmaking occurred during the late 1960s and 1970s and saw the development of the independently produced social documentary and the fiction film. African American documentary film and video were made for the program needs of television news magazines covering such domestic issues as black urban America, the civil rights and Black Power movements, and the anti-imperialist struggles in Africa, the Caribbean, and other parts of the world. During this period, black filmmakers and videographers were employed by television news programs and government agencies or were contracted by not-for-profit agencies to produce a single work. Black documentary filmmakers such as Madeline Anderson, Carroll Parrott Blue, St. Clair Bourne, Kathleen Collins, Charles Hobson, and Stan Lathan worked for television news programs.[2] William Greaves, the most prolific black documentary artist, worked for governmental agencies, not-for-profit agencies, and news magazine programs.[3]

Black independent fiction filmmakers supplied the growing number of independent movie theaters, international film festivals, and educational venues that welcomed black independent cinema and black-oriented films. The first of this group was the novelist-filmmaker-playwright Melvin Van Peebles, who began filmmaking as an independent filmmaker and whose first works were short documentaries, before he garnered international fame at the 1968 San Francisco Film Festival with the feature-length film *The Story of a Three-Day Pass* (1968). As early as 1970, Van Peebles directed and wrote *Watermelon Man* for Columbia Pictures, which was followed by the independently produced *Sweet Sweetback's Baadasssss Song* (Cinemation, 1971). The later film, *Sweet Sweetback's Baadasssss Song*, is covered in the Blaxploitation section of the anthology.

Very different from Melvin Van Peebles, who was not university trained and alternated between work inside and outside of Hollywood, and unlike the 1960s documentary artists, the late-1960s to mid-1970s university-trained black filmmakers Charles Burnett, Julie Dash, Haile Gerima, Warrington Hudlin, and Alile Sharon Larkin chose to work outside Hollywood. In the 1990s, however, Burnett and Dash made several films for major studios and for broadcast on television. Dr. Patricia Hilliard-Nunn, a former MFA student of Gerima, discusses two of his films in chapter 9 of the anthology.[4]

During the late 1970s, many black independent filmmakers received technical training in white educational institutions. As might be expected, Los Angeles seemed to attract the largest group of black filmmakers. The philosophy of black consciousness and the writings and speeches of African leaders such as Ghanaian Kwame Nkrumah, Guinean Ahmed Sékou Touré, and the Republic of Congo's Patrice Émery Lumumba influenced many of these black students. Such filmmakers as Charles Burnett, Larry Clark, Julie Dash, Haile Gerima, Alile Sharon Larkin, and Billy Woodberry, all graduates of Los Angeles film schools or institutes, rejuvenated the then-languishing black independent film movement.

This new generation of West Coast filmmakers, and East Coast contemporaries such as St. Clair Bourne, rejected the imposed conditions of mainstream American cinema because they limited their artistic and political vision of black life and experience. In their rejection of Hollywood, these filmmakers not only rejuvenated black independent film but also created a paradigm shift in the history of black independent filmmaking.

Similar to the first wave of black independent filmmakers such as Oscar Micheaux, the new generation worked in the shadows of mainstream film. Unlike Micheaux and other black independent filmmakers between the two world wars, Gerima and many members of this new generation used abstract and experimental film styles and articulated a politics of Black Nationalism. This separated them from their American contemporaries, black and non-black, who attended the same film schools but opted to speak to mainstream audiences and acquire major studio financing and distribution. This new generation of black filmmakers chose to work outside the production gates of the neighboring studios. They borrowed the politics, film styles, and narrative forms that were being used by African, Latin American, Asian, and European filmmakers who also worked outside of Hollywood conventions and norms.

Clyde Taylor first coined the term "L.A. rebellion," and several other critics have also referred to this West Coast phenomenon as an "L.A. rebellion." One can also view this as a shifting paradigm in which American filmmakers recognized that Hollywood was not the only cinema and, instead, sought to participate in an international film movement that included such filmmakers as Jean-Luc Godard, Alain Resnais, Sarah Maldoror, Gillo Pontecorvo, and Ousmane Sembene. Thus, the so-called L.A. rebellion was not as local as it may have seemed at the time. This generation of black filmmakers was influenced by international trends in cinema as well as by their international student colleagues and teachers. Theirs was an organic rebellion of international proportions that reflected what was going on in Vietnam, the People's Republic of China, and Africa. It was not simply about a racial angst, but race concerns were very much a part of the mix, along with considerations of class, gender, and sexuality inequities.[5]

The first wave of university-trained black filmmakers (Haile Gerima, Charles Burnett, Larry Clark, Billy Woodberry, Julie Dash, and Alile Sharon Larkin) rejuvenated the black independent feature-film movement, which had been languishing since the decade following World War II. These student filmmakers earned their MFA degree in film production at either the University of California at Los Angeles (UCLA) or the University of Southern California. However, Dash "studied film production at the City College of New York and studied directing at the American Film Institute and the University of California, both in Los Angeles." (Donalson 2003, 179)[6] After a quarter century, Haile Gerima and Larry Clark never abandoned their independent beginnings.

This new group of blacks used film styles that were influenced by European and postcolonial film movements, but their films were focused on the African American community, as were the films of the earliest black filmmakers before them. Italian neorealism and the French New Wave cinematic styles inform certain black independent films of this period.[7] The distinguishing characteristics of black independent film are the handheld camera's trembling movement, the urban location for shooting, discontinuous editing, and "bad" lighting quality. This reflects a lack of money, which is, interestingly, the same factor that determined the look of the Italian neorealism and French New Wave film styles. In the area of film content, the films made by the university-trained blacks (as mentioned earlier) are influenced by the works of their African, Latin American, Caribbean, and Asian contemporaries, whose films shared an interest in exploring urban poverty, police brutality, female subjectivity (as portrayed in films by Julie Dash and Alile Sharon Larkin), and the life experiences of black and other developing world communities.[8]

This post-1960s renaissance also included a more mainstream group of black filmmakers whose films were produced and distributed by major

Hollywood studios; these films included Gordon Parks's *The Learning Tree* (Warner, 1969) and *Shaft* (MGM, 1971), Gordon Parks Jr.'s *Superfly* (Warner, 1972), and Ossie Davis's *Black Girl* (Cinerama, 1972). Although there are exceptions, most black Hollywood filmmakers during the 1970s were not university trained. One explanation for this is that the phenomenon of university-trained filmmakers was a new and particularly novel phenomenon for African Americans. Still, both university-trained and black Hollywood filmmakers employed African American actors, used popular black music forms, and borrowed from existing American film genres. Unlike their independent counterparts, black Hollywood films, especially those of the Blaxploitation genre, exploited the more exotic elements of the black American experience, including many of Oscar Micheaux's sound films.

Further reading in African American film and Black Lives Consciousness should include recent black film genre studies in conjunction with critical race theoretical writings. Such reading might include Treandrea M. Russworm's *Blackness is Burning*, Novotny Lawrence and Gerald B. Butters's *Beyond Blaxploitation, and* Addison Nadia Fields's *Uplift Cinema*. These film-centric books must be paired with theoretical studies that engage our present anti-blackness era, such as Christina Sharpe's *In the Wake: On Blackness and Being*, Frank B. Wilderson III's *Red, White & Black: Cinema and the Structure of U.S. Antagonisms*, and Carol Bunch Davis's *Prefiguring PostBlackness*. My recommendation is grounded in the importance that theory provides, if film research has as one of its goals to interrogate the structures of misogyny, racism, homophobia, and other dehumanizing actions that pervade the entertainment industry that recently birthed the #*MeToo* hash tag.

African American Cinema through Black Lives Consciousness employs an interdisciplinary critical approach to discuss a selected group of black-oriented films. Black Lives Consciousness, as a critical praxis, interrogates and dismantles the fictions that support the master's house. Intersectional corruptive forces of homophobia, misogyny, classism, ethnocentrism, and racism buttress these malevolent fictions. The essays included in this collection intervene at different profound crossroads of watching popular and not-so-popular films.

Many of the authors approach their film analyses as an intersectional practice that combines critical race theory, queer theory, feminism/womanism, and class analytical strategies alongside conventional film history and theory. Taken together, the essays invigorate a "Black Lives Consciousness," hereafter BLC, which speaks to the value of black bodies that might be traumatized, and those bodies that are coming into being-ness through intersectional theoretical analysis and every-day activism.

One might ask "What is Black Lives Consciousness? What are its organic roots, what are its philosophic borrowings, and what is its actional practice?" My response will be tentative and offer no guarantees other than an explanation of its modest intentions. The BLC is an organic revolutionary process that is occasioned by social, philosophical, and artistic paradigmatic shifts in the way blacks and nonblacks, as in the contemporary "Black Lives Matter" and "#Me Too" movements, relate to the world that seeks to order their life. This type of paradigmatic shift is illustrated in similar form as previous philosophical shifts, such as W.E.B. Du Bois *The Souls of Black Folk* (1903) and his campaigning for higher learning for African Americans. Twenty years later, another chiasmic shift in Black Lives Consciousness occurred in the literary and artistic movements of the Harlem Renaissance (1920–30) with Alain Locke and Du Bois encouraging black artists to create and distribute their works to international audiences. Langston Hughes's essay "The Negro Artist and the Racial Mountain" signified another paradigmatic black generational shift that indicated a generational shift within the intellectual and art community as illustrated by the publication of the journal *Fire* (1926). *Fire* contained some of the first references to homoerotism in its illustrations, short stories, and poetry. These elements reflect Hughes's understanding of the "Racial Mountain," which I understand as Black Lives Consciousness:

> He argues that the impasse to developing a black aesthetic is the hegemony of American white culture (figured as the "racial mountain") over representations of "race." And he particularly finds middle class black artists, who have been taught through their education and social milieu to emulate white [middle class] culture, denying their racial identity and heritage. (Dawahare 1998)

This was a mere aesthetic proposition on the part of Hughes and later morphed into the Black Arts and Black Power movements of the sixties and late seventies. In 2013, it further morphed into an intersectional Black Lives Consciousness and Black Lives Matter activism. Here, I want to underline the intersectional nature of the two latter paradigms as moves that embrace an awareness of the importance of L.G.B.T.Q. I.+, feminism/womanism, neocolonialism and class struggles as one united front to resist and interrogate through critical analysis what Michel Foucault had as his study of the archaeology of the penal system.

> What I would like to study is the emergence of the power of normalization, the way in which it has been formed, the way in which it has established itself without ever resting on a single institution but by establishing interactions between different institutions, and by the way it has extended its sovereignty in our society. (Foucault 2003, 26)

The philosophical and creative use of BLC underpins the selection of films and the essays in this anthology. The volume intersects with activism in its critical practice. It reflects a black film studies branch in the tradition of Langston Hughes's "The Negro Artist and the Racial Mountain," James Baldwin's *Blues for Mister Charlie* (1964), Angela Davis's *Freedom Is a Constant Struggle* (2016), and the activism spurred by the visually recorded killings of unarmed African Americans.

In "Paralyzed in a Jungle of Racial Torment and Drowning in a Sea of Self-Hate: *Home of the Brave* (1949) and *A Soldier's Story* (1984)," Charlene Regester explores the black soldier and the traumatic experiences that occur when men are sent to battle imagined foreign enemies without recognizing the threatening forces that inhabit their proper national troops. The first film dramatizes institutional racism during the Korean War when black soldiers integrated predominantly white troops. The latter film centers on the murder of a black sergeant during World War II who serves in an all-black company that is stationed in Louisiana at the war's end. The pairing of the two war films permits two types of racial injustices; the first is white on black and the latter, in *A Soldier's Story*, is black on black, though a white soldier is first suspected of the murder until the real culprit is revealed to be a black soldier from the same outfit. Here, Charles Fuller, the author of the Pulitzer Prize–awarded play, criticizes uncorroborated racist conclusions that inadvertently obscure any comprehension of institutional systemic forms of bigotry and racism. Regester traces out the biases that we immediately accept before interrogating the internecine nature of bigotry and racism—national and internal, as in black self-hatred. The two films appeared long before the popularization of the present Black Lives Matter sociopolitical movement. Still, these films articulate an intersectional consciousness that connects diverse races and interrogates unsound reasoning.

My essay "Is There a Doctor in the House?: Poitier in *No Way Out* (1950)" employs an intersectional understanding of BLC that is not associated with the race of the film's director, screenwriter, and producers. BLC is a complex intersectional activism—a philosophical entity that might or might not affect social change. BLC does affect dialogic processes that may result in a spectator's agency regardless of the author's intentions. Thus, the use of such a consciousness is not restricted to a singular group; it is intersectional and as such traverses and connects socially constructed boundaries.

In the essay "Is There a Doctor in the House?: Poitier in *No Way Out* (1950)," I use the terms "the Black Other" and "racialized Otherness," which are partly based on the psychoanalytic theory of Jacques Lacan, especially his lecture notes posthumously compiled in *The Four Fundamental Concepts of Psycho-Analysis* (1978, 203–60). However, my use of the term "Other" is more reflective of the revisions of Abdul R. JanMohamed ("The Economy of Manichean Allegory" 1995, 18–23) and Judith Butler (*Bodies That Matter* 1993, 167–85), which, respectively, theorize the "Other" as racialized and gendered.

In *No Way Out*, Poitier as Dr. Brooks is the sole black physician in a Chicago hospital where one of his medical procedures leads to the death of a lower-class, racist white man. The death inflames the white, lower-class men, who plan a violent invasion of the nearby black community in which Dr. Brooks's extended family lives. The black community gets wind of the plans to terrorize their community. The black men, with the exception of Dr. Brooks, organize and perform a preemptive strike against the white male racists' principal locality but not their homes. After viewing *No Way Out* and studying the motivations of Dr. Brooks, I find that the black physician generates an "aesthetic du cool" that represses or displaces his racial anger. Still, the film permits black agency in a less-than-cool manner. This is dramatized by a black preemptive attack that predates the black-on-white violence of the 1970s Blaxploitation films. Ironically, the Blaxploitation films' violent displays became an obstacle in the path of Poitier's post-sixties film career. The acclaimed novelist Toni Morrison indicates that the Poitier-directed *Buck and the Preacher* (1972) presents instances when black agency is linked with the Native American struggle. She writes, "Now that Mr. Poitier and Mr. Belafonte have shot up all the racists in *Buck and the Preacher*, have they all gone away? Can we move into better neighborhoods and not be set on fire?" (Morrison 2008, 8–9). Morrison's comments reveal the limits of cinematic intersectional actions on the actual politics of political gerrymandering, economic redlining, and police brutality that communities of color experience daily. Still, I would argue that imaginative films such as *Buck and the Preacher* offer pathways to understanding the value of BLC as an intersectional praxis and goal.

Throughout the essays included in this volume, BLC elicits and engages a creative and socio-philosophical praxis. Later in the introduction, I will describe how Melba Boyd's essay invokes the intersectional elements that are also used in Quentin Tarantino's *Django Unchained*.

Karen Bowdre's "Sidney Poitier and *For Love of Ivy*" illustrates how the frequently neglected black genre romance film elicits similar psycho-agentive feelings. *For Love of Ivy* simulates a different, but just as valuable, BLC as that found in films such as *No Way Out* and the two aforementioned war films. The black lived consciousness of *For Love of Ivy* lies in its story of two black individuals and in Sidney Poitier's original story. Poitier performs the role of a trucking firm executive by day and a gambler by midnight, while Abby Lincoln is a timid, attractive, wise maid. It was rare to find a black romance that was sustained in 1968, and it is only more than forty years after the release of this film that this type of black activism is becoming more common. Intersectionality in this film rests in the interracial characters that assist in the generation of the black romance narrative.

Taken together, the three essays that comprise "Postwar Film Treatment of the Civil Rights Era" show how black films express BLC as an intersectional philosophical stance that predates the discourses that surround the present *Black Lives Matter* sociopolitical ways of seeing and praxis. The following sections and essays reflect and in some cases resist *Black Lives Matter* philosophy and activism. In repudiating forms of BLC they inadvertently reproduce, by their resistance, intersectional dialogic processes. This is the case with many of the films covered in "The Blaxploitation Film and Pastiche" section.

For example, Gerald R. Butters Jr.'s "Blaxploitation Film" charts the genre and its uses of violence, sex, and, at times, misogyny to provoke a realization of other philosophical and sociopolitical themes that concern intersectional praxis. Jonathan Munby's "Militant Blax: Screening Revolution in the Films of Oscar Williams, Christopher St. John, and Ivan Dixon" describes how black action films use black proactive resistance strategies. Again, these films realize the detrimental effects when using singular forms of resistance are ineffectual. Finally, Dan Flory's "African American Film Noir" explains the intertextual—fictional and socio-ecological—dynamics of the black action films. Flory illuminates the BLC qualities of the African American noir by underlining that "Both *Menace II Society* and *Clockers* alluringly depict drug dealing and criminality so that audiences may readily understand why some African American youth would see them as viable life choices, as well as why what Cornel West . . . has termed 'black nihilism' might appear to be a reasonable outlook on life. At the same time, these films do not shy away from portraying the ugly and often fatal consequences of such life choices; in fact, like many of their Hollywood predecessors these films' narratives place such outcomes front and center."

"PostNegritude Black Film: Pastiche and Race" includes two essays about films that rework the conventional spectatorial expectations of popular film audiences. The films discussed in this section, *Django Unchained* (2012) and *Medicine for Melancholy* (2008), have similar narrative and political elements to those that are present in the literary social satires of Ralph Ellison's *Invisible Man* (1952), Ismael Reed's *Mumbo Jumbo* (1972), George C. Wolfe's *The Colored Museum* (1986), Paul Beatty's *The Sellout* (2015), and the Dave

Chappelle televised comedy series *Chappelle's Show* (Comedy Central, 2003–6). Together, these black satires are serious satires that articulate contrasting and competing ideas of blackness in an America that advances only when the intersectionality of race, gender, sexuality, ethnicity, and class dynamics is destabilized and questioned. *Medicine for Melancholy* revises the black romantic film as seen in *For Love of Ivy*, and *Django Unchained* performs the same revisionist praxis for the Blaxploitation film genre. The two essays, Melba Boyd's "'Who's that Nigga on that Nag?': *Django Unchained and the Return of the Blaxploitation Hero*" and Mark Cunningham's "Barry Jenkins's *Medicine for Melancholy*: Race, Individualism, and Denisian Influence" enhance this anthology's commitment to BLC as a theoretical praxis.

Melba J. Boyd's essay "'Who's that Nigga on that Nag?': *Django Unchained* and the Return of the Blaxploitation Hero" argues a similar intersectional understanding of BLC agency. Boyd argues that,

> *Django Unchained* provides cultural and historical insight, "signifies" on blackface stereotypes, and chastises Hollywood cinema's misrepresentation of slavery. The film's tragic dimensions convey the horrors of slavery; consequently, the revenge executed against those guilty of profiting from it and enforcing abuse that sustains it, can be exhilarating for the audience and possibly cathartic for African Americans who experience a vicarious sense of satisfaction through the main character's heroic actions. In sync with the Black Power Movement, the Blaxploitation hero is always a macho character, who never backs down and is often in pursuit of revenge for some serious racial transgression, a theme applauded by 1970's audiences. Tarantino further complicates and intensifies this cinematic genre by incorporating excessive violence that is sometimes juxtaposed with humor for comic relief.

The anthology's "Black Cinematic Womanist Praxis" section is comprised of three essays that connect black feminism and intersectional analytical modes. Patricia Hilliard-Nunn's "Black Female Agency in *Bush Mama* and *Sankofa*" studies the developing consciousness of two types of black female protagonists as they arrive at agency through a theatre-of-the-oppressed-like passage. Kimberly Nichele Brown's "Decolonizing Mammy and Other Subversive Acts: Directing as Feminist Praxis in Gina Prince-Bythewood's *The Secret Life of Bees*" examines a black womanist maroon society. The film explores the lives of several black women and an abused white girl, who form a maroon society that guards against any harmful male intrusion into their gynocentric protective space. The film avoids being an essentialist type of female separatist argument. The women allow a young black male who seeks safe passage within the matriarchal community. His presence in this space is based on his sincerity and the fact that he and the women in this community fear similar white hypermasculine threats.

Unlike the first two essays in this section, "Black Women and the New Magical Negro" illustrates how Black Lives Consciousness critical analysis disrupts dehumanizing images of black female savior tropes. In this essay Chesya Burke employs a BLC critical analytical strategy and deconstructs the "Black Macho and the Myth of the Superwoman" film narrative. Thus, Burke offers a BLC agency-process to interrogate elements of BLC and its discontents. Burke finds,

> within the speculative genre it seems that the real life stereotype of the 'Strong Black Woman' is often conflated with the Magical Negro to create a character henceforth called the Negro Spiritual Woman (NSW). This character is endowed with magical powers that are not only used for the good of the broader white society, but that is also not powerful enough to change her status in the world, thus keeping her subdued and contained.

The concluding section, "Sexual and Racial Polyphony in New Black Films" features Anne Crémieux's "From Queer to Quare: The Representation of LGBT Blacks in Cinema" and James Smalls's "The Past, Present, and Future of Black Queer Cinema." The two essays emphasize that Black Lives Consciousness must retain an intersectional sociohistorical critical approach. Nomadic constructions of race, gender, and sexuality and their revolutionary histories are the constituents of the BLC awareness, though it might be unstable. Crémieux notes,

All of this scholarly work points in the same direction, one of greater inclusion and mutual collaboration. In the same way, the study of black queer representation in cinema can only enrich both black film studies and queer film studies and push them both to be more inclusive. This was Mark Reid's attempt in *PostNegritude Visual and Literary Culture* (1997), which features on the cover the famous intertwined black male bodies of *Looking for Langston* (Isaac Julien, 1989) alongside screenshots of Spike Lee's *Jungle Fever* and a photograph of a black gay man by white gay photographer Alex Hirst, bringing together queer and non-queer productions.

James Smalls's "The Past, Present, and Future of Queer Black Cinema" assesses, "the past, present, and possible future of BQC as a filmic genre/theme and proposes to provide some insight into the history and theory of the issues involved. It sets out to examine the continued viability of the genre by bringing together questions of racial and queer identities as these are inextricably linked in our past, present, and future histories." He underlines the BLC critical purpose of this anthology as a study of history, the present, and what seems to be lurking in the future.

In conclusion, this anthology, its essays, and the authors' overriding purposes embrace varied social experiences within a cinematic Black Lives Consciousness intersectionality. Neither is this concept new nor does it lack a history throughout black cultural and theoretical praxis. As Ta-Nehisi Coates, in conversation with Amy Goodman, claims,

> It's not the violence that's new. We are not in the midst of a new wave of anything. We're, you know, in a new technological wave, you know? And this is not unprecedented. You know, the sort of violence that folks saw in the 1960s, in Selma, for instance, or on Bloody Sunday, that sort of violence was not, in fact, actually new. That's what white supremacy, what racism is. It is an act of violence. What was new was the cameras. There was certain technology that was able to take that into the living rooms of America. And we're going through a similar thing right now, but the violence is not new. ("Ta-Nehisi Coates on Police Brutality" 2015)

This physical and psychical violence permeates most of the films discussed in this anthology. As mentioned previously, Black Lives Consciousness, as a critical praxis, interrogates and dismantles the fictions that support the master's house. Intersectional corruptive forces of homophobia, misogyny, classism, ethnocentrism, and racism buttress these malevolent fictions. The essays included in this collection intervene at different profound crossroads of watching popular and not-so-popular films.

Notes

1. For information on the work of Oscar Micheaux, see Reid, *Redefining Black Film*; Green, *Straight Lick: The Cinema of Oscar Micheaux*; and Pearl Bowser, Jane Gaines, and Charles Musser, eds., *Oscar Micheaux and His Circle*.

2. Kathleen Collins received her B.A. in philosophy and religion from Skidmore College and, as a graduate student, did work in French literature and film, for which she earned an M.A. and a Ph.D. from Middlebury Graduate School of French. See Phyllis R. Klotman, ed., *Screenplays of the African American Experience*, 123.

3. For a focused discussion on William Greaves, see Mark A. Reid, *Redefining Black Film*. For a comprehensive list of blacks working in documentary film, see Phyllis R. Klotman and Janet K. Cutler, eds., *Struggles for Representation: African American Documentary Film and Video*.

4. Charles Burnett's nonindependent work includes *TV's America Becoming* (1991) and the major studio works *To Sleep with Anger* (Samuel Goldwyn, 1990) and *The Glass Shield* (Miramax, 1995). Julie Dash's nonindedpendent television work includes *Subway Stories* (1996), *Funny Valentines* (1998), *Incognito* (1998), *Love Song* (2001), and *The Rosa Parks Story* (2002).

5. Haile Gerima chastises black film criticism in a most scornful tone, disassociating himself from the black film critic-scholar: "they took us as perfect filmmakers at that early age, when we were still awkward filmmakers. So there is no dialectical relationship. We gave them birth, but they don't even challenge us as filmmakers. They only want to coexist incestuously. It is a side effect of a general systemic problem. . . . [T]hey were students at the university. . . . [T]hey didn't know what to do with us and they just fantasized us and admired us falsely because they were as hungry as us. We came shooting in all directions. It was chaotic. They said we were masters, 'the LA rebellion,' the LA bullshit, names left and right, the filmmakers were the only people who said

'wait a minute.' . . . Then the critics came. It became a turf. It became a section territory for tenure and Ph.D. degree getting. And the art, the struggle, the revolution was abandoned. So, we are now in our own placenta. We cannot be born again." Anne Crémieux, "Interview with Haile Gerima," Washington, D.C., March 2001. www.africultures.com/actualite/sorties/anglais/gerima.htm.

6. See Klotman, *Screenplays of the African American Experience*, 191. Klotman writes: "After earning her B.A. degree in film production [at City College of New York], Dash moved to Los Angeles and attended the Center for Advanced Film Studies at the American Film Institute. . . . [S]he conceived and directed an experimental dance film, *Four Women* (1977). . . . That same year, as a graduate film student at UCLA, she directed *Diary of an African Nun* . . . [and] it earned her a Director's Guild Award for student film." Thus, Dash can easily be considered part of the West Coast black independent film movement of the late 1970s.

7. For a filmic illustration of Italian neorealism, see Warrington Hudlin's social documentary *Street Corner Stories* (1977) and Charles Burnett's family melodrama *Killer of Sheep* (1977).

8. African American independent fiction films that exemplify this attention to black female subjectivity include, but are not limited to, Haile Gerima's *Bush Mama* (1976); Julie Dash's *Four Women* (1977), *Diary of an African Nun* (1977), and *Illusions* (1983); and Alile Sharon Larkin's *A Different Image* (1981).

References

Bowser, Pearl, Jane Gaines, and Charles Musser, eds. 2001. *Oscar Micheaux and His Circle: African-American Filmmaking and Race Cinema of the Silent Era.* Bloomington: Indiana University Press.

Butler, Judith. 1993. *Bodies That Matter: On the Discursive Limits of "Sex."* New York: Routledge.

Butters Jr., Gerald R. 2002. *Black Manhood on the Silent Screen.* Lawrence: University Press of Kansas.

Crémieux, Anne. March 2001. "Interview with Haile Gerima." Washington, DC, www.africultures.com/actualite/sorties/anglais/gerima.htm.

Cripps, Thomas R. 1977. *Slow Fade to Black.* New York: Oxford University Press.

Dawahare, Anthony. 1998. "Langston Hughes' Radical Poetry and the 'End of Race.'" *MELUS* 23, no. 3 (Fall): 21–41.

Donalson, Melvin. 2003. *Black Directors in Hollywood.* Austin: University of Texas Press.

Foucault, Michel. 2003. *Abnormal: Lecture at the College De France, 1974–1975*. London: Verso.

Green, Ronald J. 2000. *Straight Lick: The Cinema of Oscar Micheaux*. Bloomington: Indiana University Press.

JanMohamed, Abdul R. 1995. "The Economy of Manichean Allegory." In *The Post-Colonial Studies Reader*, edited by Bill Ashcroft, G. Griffiths, and H. Tiffin. New York: Routledge, 18–23.

Klotman, Phyllis R., ed. 1991. *Screenplays of the African American Experience*. Bloomington: Indiana University Press.

Klotman, Phyllis R., and Janet K. Cutler, eds. 1999. *Struggles for Representation: African American Documentary Film and Video*. Bloomington: Indiana University Press.

Morrison, Toni. 2008. *What Moves at the Margin: Selected Nonfiction*. Jackson: University of Mississippi Press.

Reid, Mark A. 1993. *Redefining Black Film*. Berkeley: University of California Press.

"Ta-Nehisi Coates on Police Brutality: 'The Violence is Not New, It's the Cameras That are New.'" 2015. Democracy Now. September 7, 2015. www.democracynow.org/2015/11/27/ta_nehisi_coates_on_police_brutality.

I

POSTWAR FILM TREATMENT OF THE CIVIL RIGHTS ERA

THE FIFTIES THROUGH THE SIXTIES

1

Paralyzed in a Jungle of Racial Torment and Drowning in a Sea of Self-Hate

Home of the Brave (1949) and *A Soldier's Story* (1984)

Charlene Regester

HOME OF THE BRAVE (Mark Robson, 1949) explores the story of a black soldier who seemingly is suffering from postwar trauma yet is later revealed to be suffering from racial trauma. Peter Moss (James Edwards) witnesses his best friend being killed, and this death causes him to develop a temporary state of paralysis as well as amnesia, requiring him to undergo psychoanalytic treatment with a white psychiatrist who administers narcosynthesis to encourage him to regain his ability to walk. When this method of treatment fails, the psychiatrist resorts to a more aggressive strategy as he commands, "You dirty nigger, get up and walk." This command speaks volumes regarding the soldier's psychotic state as well as the methods employed to treat this psychologically impaired black patient. Nearly thirty-five years after the film's release, the black psychotic soldier returned to the screen in *A Soldier's Story* (Norman Jewison, 1984), which features a black officer, Sergeant Waters (Adolph Caesar), who is similarly afflicted with psychosis and descends into alcoholism (another form of paralysis), but in Waters's case no single event triggers his psychotic state, unlike with Moss. Instead, Waters engages in his own self-hatred resulting from a lifetime of racial oppression that is responsible for his demise. Prior to Waters's death he utters the words, "They still hate you," and these words become indicative of his psychotic state and explain how he invites his own death when he taunts the black soldiers who murder him.

Because both films depict black males who are afflicted with psychosis—a psychosis rooted in racial torment—undoubtedly these films are parallel, as the earlier *Home of the Brave* informs the latter *A Soldier's Story*. To demonstrate how these two films are linked, this essay (1) introduces relevant literature, (2) examines how the black male protagonist is mirrored in the soldiers who surround him (to build on Gary Storhoff's views), (3) investigates how both films construct black male psychosis, (4) interrogates how both films employ metaphors to advance the film's narrative, and (5) establishes how the earlier film informs the later film.

Review of the Literature

IT BECOMES GLARINGLY APPARENT that while the literature that focuses on *Home of the Brave* is voluminous, a paucity of literature exists on *A Soldier's Story*, even though both films explore black male psychosis. Of course, this disparity partially can be explained by the fact that *Home of the Brave* has been in existence for a much longer time period than *A Soldier's Story* has been. Furthermore, when *Home of the Brave* was released in the late 1940s, it was considered revolutionary in terms of race relations because it featured a black soldier who is thrust into an all-white environ and becomes the target of racial assaults. Whites are made responsible for the trauma he endures. As for *A Soldier's Story*, when it was released in the 1980s, the film had less of an impact on molding or shaping America's racial attitudes because it featured a black sergeant who is thrust into a predominantly black environ and who engages in self-hate when he projects his internalized racial trauma onto other blacks—a film less likely to influence racial attitudes. Despite the differences between these two films, as well as the time periods in which they were produced, it seems necessary to address the literature devoted to these films.

Following the release of *Home of the Brave*, early scholars such as V. J. Jerome note this was "the first Hollywood film to attempt full-length treatment of the thesis of anti–Jim Crow and of Negro-white fraternity . . ."(Jerome 1950, 43). He claims that "instead of presenting the Negro question as grounded in economic and political solution through the collective liberation movement of the Negro people, [the film] reduces it to an abstract, psychic, moral issue, to a personalized problem of adaptation to the status quo" (Jerome 1950, 45). In a similar vein, black playwright Lorraine Hansberry charges that the film neutralized racism because it diverted attention away from oppressed blacks to disabled whites (symbolized when white character Mingo loses an arm). Hansberry elaborates, "When the black hero suggests that a partnership with himself would not be easy because of racism in this country, the white man's answer is to lift an empty sleeve and say that he too knows something of this kind of a problem" (Hansberry 1992, 459). Ralph Ellison, critical of the white psychiatrist's dismissal of Moss's racial conflict, extrapolates, "for it is here exactly that we come to the question of whether Negroes can rightfully be expected to risk their lives in an army in which they are slandered and discriminated against. Psychiatry is not, I'm afraid, the answer. The soldier suffers from concrete acts, not hallucinations" (Ellison 1964, 278). Targeting the film's sexual politics more so than its racial politics, James Baldwin comments on the film's homoerotism, asserting that, "the late James Edwards, and Lloyd Bridges . . . love each other, as friends must, and as men do. But the fact that one is black and one is white eliminates the possibility of the female presence. . . . But why is the price of what should, after all, be a simple human connection so high? . . . A man can fall in love with a man: incarceration, torture, fire, and death, and still more, the threat of these, have not been able to prevent it, and never will" (Baldwin 1976, 67, 68). These early critics were followed by a later generation of critics such as Peter Roffman and Jim Purdy, who argue that because *Home of the Brave* was released during an era when blackness was deemed problematic, Hollywood in response created, "the self-effacing black who embodied white values which was the perfect expression of the prevalent integrationist belief that all men are the same under the skin" (Roffman and Purdy 1981, 245). In comparison, Krin and Glen O. Gabbard contend that when Moss is cured of his psychosomatic disorder, it encourages white audiences to confront racial prejudice and fosters the belief that "something can be done to heal the wounds" racial hatred causes (Gabbard and Gabbard 1987, 39).

Michele Wallace, recalling Baldwin's insightful critique, proposes a feminist reading and makes note of the absence of women in the film. Furthermore, she insists, "what fascinates me about [this film] is the superimposition of a narrowly psychoanalytic Oedipal drama upon the otherwise reckless vagaries of 'race'" (Wallace 1993, 268). Shifting to an evaluation of the film's masquerades, Michael Rogin, widely known for his work on blackface performance, ascertains that the Jewish psychiatrist who treats the black protagonist engages in a form of masquerade. Specifically, the psychiatrist "is making the black face and body," according to Rogin, "perform emotions forbidden to his (male, Jewish) self. In turning Moss into an infant and mammy, he also joins the doctors who invade women in innumerable postwar psychological films, doctors who heal women's divided identities, as this doctor heals Moss" (Rogin 1996, 235). Rogin continues, "As [the film's] message deprives Moss of his difference as caused by racial prejudice, by a compensatory logic the story restores his racial difference as less than whole" (239). Consistent with Rogin's and Wallace's views, E. Ann Kaplan affirms how Moss is feminized, in that "he stands in awe of the white psychiatrist, and his transferential position is similar to that of the female patient" (Kaplan 1997, 107). Moreover, Kaplan claims, "the alteration of the story from one about a homosexual in the army to that of a black man is telling in its exposure of the unconscious structure of a white, male dominant norm around which congeal 'differences' all made equal, the same" (106). Gwen Bergner, like Rogin, critiques the psychoanalytic methods and argues that the film utilizes psychoanalysis "as a mechanism of assimilation and suppression" (Bergner 1999, 226). Martin F. Norden, reverberating the views of Roffman and Purdy, suggests the "film implies that a disabled white man and able-bodied African-American are on the same social footing (in other words, that a disabling injury to a white man abruptly 'reduces' him to the status of an African-American man)," demonstrating how Moss's trauma is substituted for white male trauma (Norden 2001, 344). Expanding this discussion, Kelly Oliver and Benigno Trigo declare that when the black character refuses to ignore racism, he is characterized as pathological. In their opinion, reducing Moss to his pathology neutralizes the film's racial politics in its assertion that "there is no such thing as institutional or cultural racism; rather, it is just a few white bullies needling a few oversensitive head cases" (Oliver and Trigo 2003, 13). John Nickel, in his examination of white male suffering onscreen and race message films, proposes that because Moss is strategically inserted in *Home of the Brave* to personify the "'missionary complex'" where whites rescue him from his psychological disorder, this rescue alleviates white guilt for the racial torment projected onto the black subject (Nickel 2004, 36). More recently, Jay Garcia reads *Home of the Brave* through the lens of Frantz Fanon, whom he claims attended the European screening of the film; a film that "brought together subjects . . . directly relevant to Fanon's life . . ." (Garcia 2006, 53). Garcia parallels Fanon's military career with Moss's career, claiming, "Fanon takes on a dissenting, combative, position in relation to . . . *Home of the Brave* in particular, because he is interested in doing something other than merely saying that racism is wrong" (54). Garcia admits at the film's end, "Fanon finds the finale disquieting because Moss is in a sense back where he started—negotiating the racial codes of the prevailing social order—though by the end he appears to assent to the racial regulations that surround him" (56).

In comparison, although the literature on *A Soldier's Story* is not as extensive as is the literature on *Home of the Brave,* it is equally important in terms of depicting black male psychosis onscreen. In fact, prior to the film's production and after Charles Fuller (playwright for *A Soldier's Play,* 1983) won a Pulitzer Prize for his play, black scholar Amiri Baraka provided the historical context from which this film evolved. Baraka reveals that Fuller produced two earlier plays that may have impacted the latter play and the film—one is *Brownsville Raid,* based on the 1906 real-life case where black soldiers were wrongly accused of retaliating after confronting discrimination in Brownsville, Texas, and the second is *Zooman: The Negro Consciousness*—a play where "the consciousness of the black people" is so erased by white supremacy that blacks no longer believe whites are the problem but instead believe blacks are the problem (Baraka 1983, 52). Incorporating themes from these earlier productions into *A Soldier's Play,* Baraka argues, "The negro captain proves his right to be among white officers by uncovering the militant. Despite white supremacy, he has proved his mettle, his ultimate worth. He is a soldier, and it is a soldier's play" (53). Following the film's release, Don Kunz explored how sound functioned in and echoed the film's murder mystery. Kunz observes that the sound overlaps "prior to the climax [and] . . . disturbs the audience's comfortable, stereotypical thinking by intruding new and even threatening information from the past which demands interpretation. Paradoxically, the sound overlap reveals the incongruity between past and present which is at the heart of the mystery. . . . When the mystery has been solved correctly, the reverberation symbolizes the logical consistency between the facts of the past and the perception of the present" (Kunz 1991, 28). Employing a different approach to reading this film, Gary Storhoff examines "the pattern of reflection" that occurs throughout the film and suggests "black bigotry is a reflection of white racism, just as Waters himself—the hated sergeant—is a refracted image of what the black soldiers fear and hate in themselves: that they will lose their own identity by being defined by white ideals and ambitions" (Storhoff 1991, 22). Examining the intersectionality of race, spectatorship, and identification, Manthia Diawara insists that "the black male subject always appears to lose in competition for the symbolic position of the father or authority figure. And at the level of spectatorship, the Black spectator . . . fails to enjoy the pleasures which are at least available to the White male heterosexual spectator positioned as the subject of the film's discourse" (Diawara 1993, 216). Diawara continues, "The surprise twist at the end of the narrative, which sacrifices one more Black man in order to show that justice exists, fails to satisfy the expectation, on the part of the Black spectator, to find the Klan or a White soldier responsible for the crime" (217). Critiquing how the play/film equates southern blacks with a lack of sophistication and northern blacks with the antithesis, Riche Richardson argues that "Although Fuller succeeds in illustrating the complexity of African American identity by highlighting internal racial conflict and debunking stereotypes, he ultimately falls short of offering an inclusive model of black identity in terms of geography and gender and links the most desirable blackness with an economically privileged and educated urban elite" (Richardson 2005, 15). The present essay intends to expand this ongoing discussion and offer alternative ways of reading these films.

Mirror Images of the Protagonists

Expounding on Storhoff's views, it is conceivable that the black male protagonists in both films are surrounded by males with whom they interact and who on some level mirror their personality traits, despite how these males either contribute to their psychotic demise or become victims of their psychotic state. For example, in *Home of the Brave*, Moss (a surveyor and former high school basketball player) is sent on a special intelligence mission to a Japanese-held island with a group of white soldiers. His comrades include: TJ (Steve Brodie—who refuses to shake his hand when first introduced because of his race, who refers to Moss as a "boogey," and who engages in deprecation when he imitates a black janitor's dialect with "I ain't lazy, I'se just tired"); Finch (Lloyd Bridges—an old high school friend with whom he played basketball and whom he admires); Mingo (Frank Lovejoy—who is "looking for the powder room," writes poetry, is divorced, loses an arm, and invites Moss to join him in a business venture after leaving the military); and Major Robinson (Douglas Dick—who possesses his own insecurities as a young officer in command of more experienced soldiers). These males become signifiers of Moss's own psychodynamics because when Finch is killed in combat he represents the death of the Self later exemplified in Moss's immobilization. TJ, who issues a number of racial assaults targeted toward Moss and engages in racial harassment, becomes a signifier of Moss's internalized racial trauma. Mingo represents Moss's feminization when he becomes physiologically ill and has to be cared for. Finally, Major Robinson, who is insecure because of his age and lack of experience relative to the other soldiers on the special mission, represents the insecurity that Moss himself possesses and that contributes to his psychotic demise. These characters reify the failings and flaws that Moss possesses—a mirroring that similarly emerges in *A Soldier's Story* with Sergeant Waters, whose character flaws are reflected in the men who surround him.

In particular, Sergeant Waters is surrounded by black soldiers—CJ Memphis (Larry Riley—a name not so different from TJ), a soldier who plays the guitar and sings the blues, is an outstanding baseball player, practices voodoo, and is a marker of the "Southern Negro." Peterson (Denzel Washington) is a soldier who exhibits bravery because he challenges Waters's denunciation of black soldiers and resorts to physically fighting the older Waters. Wilkie (Art Evans) is a soldier who is demoted when he has his stripes taken away, and he resents Waters for this reprimand. Smalls (David

Harris) is a soldier who allies himself with Peterson and advises Peterson not to fight the Sergeant. Ellis (Robert Townsend) is a soldier who chauffeurs Captain Davenport (Howard E. Rollins Jr.) around the military base as Davenport attempts to solve the murder mystery. Captain Davenport is a soldier who has ascended the military ranks to become captain, is trained as a lawyer, and is recruited to solve the murder mystery. Finally, Captain Taylor (Dennis Lipscomb) is a white military officer who initially leads the investigation but whom Davenport displaces as the chief investigator. As with *Home of the Brave,* these characters (with the exception of Smalls and Ellis), in some instances, according to Storhoff, "all reflect some aspect of Waters, positively or negatively" (Storhoff 1991, 22). My intent is not necessarily to make a distinction between the positives and negatives these characters share with the protagonist but instead to identify parallels in personality traits between the protagonist and the men who surround him. For example, CJ, whom Waters targets for his virulent racial hatred, becomes a signifier of the "Southern Negro" who is believed to be inept, backward, unprogressive, and responsible for the inability of blacks to elevate themselves, and therefore, CJ becomes a symbol of Waters's hatred, which justifiably has its origin in white racial oppression. In comparison, Wilkie represents Waters's desire to ascend the military ranks, yet when his stripes are taken away, this could mirror Waters's demise and inability to obtain the level of respect and honor desired when he begins to unravel psychologically. Contrastingly, Peterson, who challenges Waters and is one of the few who lacks a fear of Waters, becomes an embodiment of the black militant, and reflects Waters's own courage as well as his fearlessness as an army officer. Symbolizing what Waters would like to become, Captain Davenport represents the ideal soldier who has proven that he is "qualified to be an officer in 'the man's army,'" but because of Waters's own internalized self-hatred, he knows that he will never ascend to Davenport's stature (Baraka 1983, 52). Captain Taylor, the white captain, becomes symbolic of the white ideal that Waters secretly desires but knows he can never achieve. Because both films portray protagonists whose personality traits are signified in the men who surround them, this demonstrates how these films intersect, but most indicative of their parallels is their depiction of black male psychosis.

Black Male Psychosis

In *Home of the Brave*, Moss develops a temporary state of paralysis in response to his best friend's death. He undergoes psychoanalytic treatment for his condition, which has been diagnosed as primarily mental. The psychiatrist claims that when Finch was killed and Moss was unable to save him, Moss felt guilty about his death. The psychiatrist relates that most soldiers who survive war trauma feel guilty that they have survived when their fellow comrades did not, and he claims this is a normal reaction. But while subjecting Moss to psychoanalysis, the psychiatrist discovers that the patient suffers not only from war trauma but racial trauma characterized as a "collective catharsis," to use Fanon's term, of racial assaults (Fanon 1986, 145). With this discovery, the psychiatrist informs Moss that he has a sensitivity disease whereby a lifetime of racial torment has been projected onto him. Moss now possesses an illness manifested in self-guilt and oversensitivity, both of which make the spectator believe that Moss is responsible for his temporary state of paralysis. Therein, the psychiatrist's diagnosis and explanation can seamlessly substantiate Moss's psychosis as internal rather than the result of external racist acts. In treating Moss, he orders him to walk, but when Moss fails to respond to this treatment, he then uses a racial epithet to arouse Moss when he commands: "You dirty Nigger get up and walk"—a "trick . . . to rouse his wilted manhood . . ." (Bergner 1999, 230). This method of treatment seemingly is the only tactic that the psychiatrist has in his "arsenal" to startle Moss out of his psychotic state and force him to walk. In this instance, the psychiatrist is both enslaving and liberating because he engages in deprecations to arouse his patient. While whites project racial epithets onto Moss in *Home of the Brave*, in *A Soldier's Story*, the black Sergeant Waters internalizes his racial oppression and projects these racial assaults onto black soldiers. The racism whites appropriate in *Home of the Brave* that manifests in Moss's psychotic state shifts to the black Sergeant Waters in *A Soldier's Story*, who is the agent of racial attacks when he engages in equally denigrating behavior toward his black soldiers and, as a result, participates in his own psychotic demise.

To critique Waters's psychosis it is necessary to return to Fanon, who suggests that "the young Negro subjectively adopts a white man's attitude. He invests in the hero, who is white, with all his own aggression—at that age closely linked to sacrificial dedication . . . permeated with sadism" (Fanon 1986, 147). If we apply Fanon's views to Waters when the protagonist remarks, "ya'll always talking about what you gonna do when the white man gives you an opportunity," Waters insinuates that blacks are inadequate and are incapable of taking advantage of such opportunity, demonstrating how he reverses roles with whites yet remains black. Because he hints at black inferiority and because of his own blackness, he cannot extricate himself from such feelings of inferiority. This remark reflects the sadistic self-hatred and belief in black inadequacy that he then projects onto his soldiers. Waters's internalized racial hatred is rather evident when he suggests that even though his father was not educated, his father made sure his children were educated. When one soldier challenges Waters's views, he retorts, "not having is no excuse for not getting." In this instance, Walters's self-hatred reflects Fanon's view that in some cases, like that of Waters, some believe that the "Negro makes himself inferior," when in reality he is made inferior by others (149). Waters then rejects his blackness to appropriate whiteness while at the same time, rendered unable to escape blackness, he adopts a white disposition built on black inferiority, which launches a vicious cycle of self-hatred. If whites possess a sadistic aggression toward blacks and then experience guilt because of their behavior, Waters, who masquerades as white trapped in a black body, convinces himself of the mythology of blackness and then experiences guilt, all the while remaining black. Waters, according to Fanon, "lives an ambiguity that is extraordinarily neurotic" (192). Moreover, "Waters's genocidal project of racial purification is an example of racial uplift gone horribly wrong," implying that Waters adopts the ideological views of those such as Nazi leader Adolf Hitler, who appropriated racial cleansing and engaged in the extermination of Jews (Richardson 2005, 18). Because *A Soldier's Story* focuses on soldiers during World War II, the association between Hitler and Waters is certainly plausible, particularly when we consider that Waters wears a moustache like Hitler, he employs a demagogic leadership style, and descends into psychosis, much like Hitler. Affirming Waters's association to Hitler, *New Yorker Magazine*'s Pauline Kael refers to Waters as "A black Hitler—on a small scale [who] wanted to purge the Negro race of its lazy shuffling clowns" (Kael 1984, 117–18).

Furthermore, because both Moss and Waters endure racial trauma from the past, Freud suggests that reproductions of the past are connected to an infantile sexual life and the Oedipus complex. Thus, Moss is castrated or, as Michael Rogin suggests, he is turned into "half man"—a similar and yet also different position that he shares with Waters. While Moss represents the castrated male, Waters represents the castrating male as he emasculates the black soldiers whom he commands with his continual reprimands and deprecations. And if we consider the relationship between Sergeant Waters and Peterson as simulating a father/son relationship, in view of the Oedipus complex, the son has to eliminate the father in order to achieve subjectivity, which bears resemblance to the religious parable of Noah and Ham. In this parable, when Ham laughed at his father's drunkenness and nakedness, the son was punished for disrespecting his father. In this instance, although Waters punishes Peterson when he forces him to engage in a fist fight, the curse that Peterson endures, in much the same manner as Ham, is that Peterson ultimately murders Waters (his symbolic father). The Hamitic Curse proposes that it is a curse to be black and thus Ham is cursed in that he has descendants who are marked as black. Peterson, however, is cursed through the erasure of his (symbolic) father, a curse that Waters also suffers because of the hatred he possesses for blacks and blackness.

Further indicative of the psychosis that manifests in these films is that blacks are blamed for the racial trauma that is projected onto them. For example, *Home of the Brave* undermines the racism Moss has been subjected to in its implication that he is overreacting to the racial attacks he endures. In fact, Bergner claims that "Although the film suggests that American society bears some responsibility for Mossy's psychic wounds, the denouement ultimately locates the problem of racism within the black, male psyche itself" (Bergner 1999, 229). In comparison, in *A Soldier's Story*, "Waters's genocidal scheme to eliminate black Southerners reflects the blame he misplaces onto black Southerners like 'Moonshine King of the Monkeys'" (Richardson 2005, 27). When he denigrates CJ, whom he blames for being ignorant and backward, rather than blaming the society or the military, "where it belongs," for the racial ostracism endured, he instead blames black Others (27). Because both films blame the victim and make the protagonist the scapegoat for racial oppression, this demonstrates how these films share in their racial politics.

Moreover, because both films feminize the protagonists, it is through their emasculation that they become feminized. For instance, Moss's feminization is evident when he cradles Finch in his arms prior to Finch's death; when the psychiatrist in a position of power hovers above him while he lies below, disempowered, while undergoing psychoanalytic treatment; when white soldiers come to rescue him after he refuses to leave the island; when he desires to remain with his dead friend rather than leave the island; and when he is "wracked with guilt and a sense of impotence as he hears Finch scream" when the Japanese torture him (Bergner 1999, 228). That Moss is made to feel different, is eroded of his self-esteem because of the racial attacks leveled against him, and has to be cared for or protected are markers of his feminization. In fact, Bergner suggests that Moss takes up the "wife's position in relation to Mingo in an interracial, homoerotic suturing of the wounds of war" (230). She continues that because Moss assists Mingo, whose arm is amputated, to lift his duffle bag, he offers "help not from a position of masculine sufficiency superior to Mingo's, but rather from the castrated, feminized position of the black man masquerading as the white woman . . ." (231). Expounding on these views, Rogin contends: "Tying Moss to the disabled veteran, the movie intends to dissolve the stigmas attaching to racial difference and amputation (and, subliminally, homosexual love), but in proclaiming that two damaged men could make a postwar life together, the movie was allying the black man with the cripple" (Rogin 2005, 88). Although both Bergner and Rogin (among others) hint at a homosexual relationship between Moss and Mingo, despite the implications of this pairing, Moss's feminization, as previously noted, is "made emotion-ridden and female at the low level of body. . . . In forcing words and tears from the black face, the Jewish doctor, imitating the jazz singer before him, is effectively putting on blackface. He is making the black face and body, perform emotions forbidden to his (male, Jewish) self . . . turning Moss into an infant and mammy . . ." (84–85). Yet, it is conceivable that Moss manages to reverse his feminization to some extent when he regains the ability to walk. In comparison, Waters's feminization is apparent when the white soldiers wrongly accused of his murder taunt and knock him to the ground, when he engages in a fight with Peterson and his small stature as well as weak body is contrasted to Peterson's stronger and more masculinized body, and when he walks in a drunken stupor because he is inebriated, indicating a lack of control. Such weaknesses indicate how Waters is feminized. When he meets his tragic death, becoming a tragic figure (similar to the tragic mulatto), this marks his feminization. While the feminization of these protagonists explains how these films parallel, because both employ metaphors that reverberate the film's racial complexity, these metaphors become further indicative of their intersectionality.

Metaphors

HOME OF THE BRAVE utilizes the jungle as a metaphor for the convoluted state as personified by Moss's mental condition, and as the jungle setting for which Moss is seemingly best suited. When the soldiers are sent on a special mission they are thrust into a Pacific island jungle and utilize maps to both locate the enemy and assess their own position. While located in the jungle, they hear noises (either animal noises or enemy noises) that evoke a sense of terror, and they are surrounded by dense brush designed to complicate their journey as well as to protect them from the encroaching enemy or make it difficult for them to discern the enemy, who remains hidden from view. The jungle terrain, then, reflects the complexity of race and serves as the locale for Moss's racial assault when his white friend Finch nearly calls him a yellow-bellied "nigger" but substitutes the term "nit-wick" instead prior to his death despite the fact that Moss holds a genuine affection for him, evinced when he protects and refuses to abandon his friend. At the same time, Moss reacts to the racial assaults TJ projects onto him—assaults that erode his sense of self. So, the jungle becomes a signifier of the racial complexity Moss confronts and also symbolizes the racial confusion embodied in his mental state. Finally, the primitive setting of the jungle becomes a signifier of his primitive black self: since blackness is associated with animalism and the jungle, Moss is an extension of the jungle. If we consider his name, Moss, which also refers to vegetation associated with the jungle terrain, then the film undoubtedly plays on this metaphor to advance its racial thematic.

As for *A Soldier's Story*, water is the metaphor utilized to both advance the film's narrative and reflect on the film's complicated racial politics. Water is derived from Sergeant Waters's name and is a subtext to the film's thematic, which conceivably reflects attributes associated with murky, muddy, and muddled waters. In particular, murky water is caused by a heavy dimness or obscurity apparent in overhanging fog and is applicable to the film in that who actually killed Waters remains unclear. The film poses the question of whether it was black soldiers, white soldiers, or society that caused blacks to engage in the self-hate that led to Waters's death. Muddy waters refers to that which is covered in mud or is morally impure. In the case of Waters, he dies lying on the ground in a puddle of mud. Additionally, because CJ's singing style is derived from the blues singer Muddy Waters, this gives further credence to the use of water as a metaphor. Added to this, when blacks question how one of their own could have committed the murder of this black officer when it was assumed that whites killed Waters and given that "muddy" refers to that which is morally impure, the film then hints at the murder mystery as being consistent with muddy waters. Finally, muddled waters refer to that which is mixed confusedly, as in a state of mental confusion. This is exemplified in Waters's own confused mental state when he has internalized his racial oppression to such an extent that he hates himself and forces CJ to commit suicide. But more than this, if we read Waters as drowning in a sea of self-hate, the metaphor of water is further applicable. Additionally, if Waters engages in racial cleansing and purification, the association with water as a metaphor is rendered plausible. Giving legitimacy to this metaphor, when Captains Davenport and Taylor lean against a rail above a river prior to solving the murder mystery, while black and white children play together on a raft below, it is at this moment that Davenport has an epiphany regarding Waters's murderer. So, water, in this instance, gives Davenport the impetus to solve the murder mystery. Finally, when the real killers, Peterson and Smalls, are arrested, they are caught in pouring rain—a marker of troubled or turbulent waters. Therefore, the jungle in *Home of the Brave* and water in *A Soldier's Story* serve as metaphors to advance the films' narratives and reify the racial thematic demonstrating how *Home of the Brave* informs *A Soldier's Story*.

Conclusion

DESPITE THE TIME SPAN between the two productions and the numerous parallels that exist between these films, the similarities do not end. For instance, both films unfold through flashbacks, a process that not only serves to advance the films' narratives but allows the protagonists to relive the racial trauma endured. For Moss, when the psychiatrist interrogates him, he returns to his early years when he was subjected to racial trauma. As for Waters, he similarly returns to his early years and relates how black soldiers were humiliated in France, given that many white soldiers believed black soldiers had tails. Furthermore, both films are based on plays, as Arthur Laurents's 1946 Broadway play (where a Jewish protagonist is depicted) provided the basis for *Home of the Brave* and Fuller's prize-winning play provided the basis for *A Soldier's Story*. Further evidence of their linkage is that both films and plays utilize character names that have significance, as when Stanley Kramer adapted *Home of the Brave*, he named the protagonist Moss based on the black journalist Carlton Moss, who wrote and starred in *The Negro Soldier* (1944)—an army documentary designed to center the black soldier, demonstrate race pride, promote racial tolerance, and recruit soldiers for the military (Cripps 1993, 114). As for *A Soldier's Story*, both the film and the play are set in the fictional Fort Neal, located in Tynin, Louisiana, with the fort's name designed to pay tribute to Larry Neal, who, along with Amiri Baraka, was instrumental in founding the black theater arts movement. But more importantly, these films depict the black male soldier as psychotic, nearly defusing him of the heroism desired, and since the military symbolizes liberation for some black soldiers, these films suggest that the black soldier can never really be liberated because he will forever be mentally enslaved or deemed pathological, as Moss is paralyzed in a jungle of racial torment while Waters drowns in a sea of self-hatred.

References

Baldwin, James. 1976. *The Devil Finds Work*. New York: Dial Press.

Baraka, Amiri. 1983. "The Descent of Charlie Fuller into Pulitzerland and the Need for African-American Institutions." *Black American Literature Forum* 17, no. 2 Black Theatre Issue (Summer): 51–54.

Bergner, Gwen. "Politics and Pathologies: On the Subject of Race in Psychoanalysis." In *Fanon, Frantz: Critical Perspectives*, edited by Anthony C. Alessandrine. New York: Routledge, 1999, 219–34.

Cripps, Thomas. 1993. *Making Movies Black: The Hollywood Message Movie from World War II to the Civil Rights Era*. New York: Oxford University Press.

Manthia Diawara, Manthia. 1993. "Black Spectatorship: Problems of Identification and Resistance." In *Black American Cinema*, edited by Manthia Diawara. New York: Routledge.

Ellison, Ralph. 1964. *Shadow and Act*. New York: Random House, 211–20.

Fanon, Frantz. 1986. *Black Skin, White Masks* (London: Pluto Press).

Gabbard, Krin, and Glen O. Gabbard. 1987. *Psychiatry and the Cinema*. Chicago: University of Chicago Press.

Garcia, Jay. 2006. "*Home of the Brave*, Frantz Fanon and cultural pluralism." *Comparative American Studies: An International Journal* 4, no. 1: 49–65.

Hansberry, Lorraine. 1992. "The Case of the Invisible Force: Images of the Negro in Hollywood Films." In *Celluloid Power: Social Film Criticism from The Birth of a Nation to Judgment at Nuremberg*, edited by David Platt. Metuchen: The Scarecrow Press: 72–89.

Jerome, V. J. 1950. *The Negro in Hollywood Films*. New York: Masses & Mainstream.

Kael, Pauline. 1984. "*A Soldier's Story*." *New Yorker Magazine* 60 (November 26, 1984): 117–18.

Kaplan, E. Ann. 1997. *Looking for the Other: Feminism, Film, and the Imperial Gaze*. New York: Routledge, 1997.

Kunz, Don. 1991. "Singing the Blues in *A Soldier's Story*." *Literature/Film Quarterly* 19, no. 1: 27–34.

Nickel, John. 2004. "Disabling African American Men: Liberalism and Race Message Films." *Cinema Journal* 44, no. 1 (Fall): 25–48.

Norden, Martin F. 2001. "Coward, Take My Coward's Hand": Racism, Ableism and the Veteran Problem in *Home of the Brave* and *Bright Victory*." In *Classic Hollywood, Classic Whiteness*, edited by Daniel Bernardi. Minneapolis: University of Minnesota Press: 339–56.

Oliver, Kelly, and Benigno Trigo. 2003. *Noir Anxiety*. Minneapolis: University of Minnesota Press.

Richardson, Riche. 2005. "Charles Fuller's Southern Specter and the Geography of Black Masculinity." *American Literature* 77, no. 1 (March): 7–32.

Roffman, Peter, and Jim Purdy. 1981. *The Hollywood Social Problem Film: Madness, Despair, and Politics from the Depression to the Fifties*. Bloomington: Indiana University Press.

Rogin, Michael. 1996. *Blackface, White Noise: Jewish Immigrants in the Holly-wood Melting Pot.* Berkeley: University of California Press.

Rogin, Michael. 2005. "*Home of the Brave.*" In *The War Film*, edited by Robert Eberwein. New Brunswick: Rutgers University Press: 82–89.

Storhoff, Gary P. 1991. "Reflections of Identity in *A Soldier's Story.*" *Literature/Film Quarterly* 19, no. 1: 21–26.

Wallace, Michele. 1993. "Race, Gender and Psychoanalysis in Forties Film: *Lost Boundaries, Home of the Brave*, and *The Quiet One.*" In *Black American Cinema*, edited by Manthia Diawara. New York: Routledge: 257–71.

2

Is There a Doctor in the House?

Poitier in *No Way Out* (1950)

Mark A. Reid

SIDNEY POITIER'S FORTY-PLUS FILMS provide a visual history of America's postwar racial relations. The characters that Poitier chose to play and the themes treated in most Poitier vehicles dramatize the politics of race, class, and gender. Since his leading role in Joseph Mankiewicz's *No Way Out* (20th Century Fox, 1950) as Dr. Luther Brooks, Poitier has been the lead or costar in most of his Hollywood films. His acting career covers westerns, comedies, romance films, detective thrillers, war films, and social melodramas. Poitier's film beginning was concurrent with the postwar civil rights movement. His eminence as a film star results from his acting skills, his handsome physiognomy, and, most importantly, the social environments in which he appears, both filmic and real. Poitier's compassion, tolerance, and fortitude are what the postwar period demanded of integrationist-type black film heroes and heroines. He performed exceptionally well as both an artist and a citizen. In commenting on this social period and what it called on Poitier to perform, Thomas Cripps writes: "Poitier's character worked the centers of the American ethos; [Harry] Belafonte's played its rim lands [borderlands]. If this seems to reassert a determinism at the core of popular culture, that dooms it to promote the status quo, it must also [have] been seen that the racial status quo, or its ideology at least, had been transformed by war" (Cripps 1993, 251).

Outpatients of an Exclusive White Circle

In 1947, Jackie Robinson worked the center of the American ethos when he became the first African American to play in the major leagues. He was one of the many skilled black baseball players of his time. By the end of World War II, there were such talented African American film actors as James Edwards, Juano Hernandez, and the blacklisted Canada Lee. Postwar African American theater offered a rich source of seasoned actors ready for Broadway and American feature films. In 1950, for example, Ossie Davis and Sidney Poitier had their Hollywood film debut in *No Way Out*. It was Poitier, not Davis, who received leading roles. In understanding Poitier's extraordinary film career, one has to admit that chance and accident mattered. Thomas Cripps recognizes this while he also finds that Poitier was technically readier for his role than Belafonte was for his, the latter not yet having used his loosely worn singing style to free his tense acting style. So, it was Poitier who dominated the racial politics of the ensuing quarter of a century of black movies (Cripps 1993, 251–52).

Following the end of World War II, America in general, and the film industry in particular, adjusted to the social and economic demands for equal employment, nonsegregated housing, education, and the right to vote. Blacks and whites sought changes in the nation's conventional attitudes toward its African American citizens. During the same postwar period, Sidney Poitier arrived at a most opportune time. The country was undergoing a reevaluation of its racist beliefs and practices in employment, housing, public transportation, and education. Hollywood studios chose Poitier to perform America's new racial awareness. Years later, Poitier would report that the racist practices that his performances in films condemned remained inconvenient social truths about the American experience. In his autobiography, *The Measure of a Man* (2000), Poitier writes: "Only in my sixties, did I fully absorb my outsider status and begin to settle into some kind of comfort with it. I'd been on the fringes for fifty-odd years whether I knew it or not, so at last I accepted the likelihood that I would always be an outsider" (Poitier 2000, 84).

Since Poitier was born in 1927, his self-discovery comment refers to the years between 1987 and 1997 and after his *Buck and the Preacher* (1972) directorial debut. Poitier, in the above quotation, acknowledges that his artistic successes, nine directed films, and career longevity did not make him a Hollywood insider. Though the film industry honored him with their highest artistic and financial awards, he remained at the margins, and tentatively accepted "the being of blackness" as a fact. Thomas Cripps's earlier comments state that Poitier played in the political center. His roles were neither as social marginal, political activist, or passive victim of institutional racism. Nonetheless, both Cripps and Poitier acknowledge that his award-winning screen performances did not translate into his offscreen social existence, which kept him in the same rimlands that contained his fellow black actors—Harry Belafonte, Canada Lee, Paul Robeson, and the lesser-known black Others.

My use of the term "the Black Other" and "racialized Otherness" is partially based on the psychoanalytic theory of Jacques Lacan, especially his lecture notes compiled posthumously in *The Ethics of Psychoanalysis 1959–1969: The Seminar of Jacques Lacan Book VII*. However, my use of the term "Other" is more reflective of the revisions of Abdul R. JanMohamed (1995, 18–23) and Judith Butler (1993, 167–85), who, respectively, theorize the "Other" as racialized and gendered.

On July 17, 2009, Poitier's outcast sentiment was made even more valid when Cambridge police sergeant James Crowley arrested Henry Louis Gates Jr. as Gates entered his own Cambridge home. For more information on the misadventure, there is a redacted police docket, two arresting images of Henry Louis Gates, and Lucia Whalen's brief description of viewing two men trying to gain access into a two-story Cambridge home. Initially, Whalen neither used racial descriptors nor stated that the men were attempting illegal access. When goaded by the police dispatcher on the race question, she was unsure about one of the men. To Lucia Whalen's merit, she resisted the "always be an outsider" trope, and the Fanonian determined psychosocial discourse "Look a Negro" (Fanon 1967, 109).

I include the Gates incident only to advance Poitier's feeling that in all likelihood he would "always be an outsider." Professor Gates became an outsider to his Cambridge house when police suspected that he was a burglar. Crowley's racist deed was to arrest Gates who, quite understandably, admonished the officer who mistreated and emasculated him. Crowley's thoughts and deeds made Gates an outsider. Unfortunately, America treats blacks psychologically, socially, and juridically as outsiders. The Fanonian cry of "Look a Negro" connected Poitier's existentialist reflection with Gates's surrealistic pas de deux with officer Crowley. Additionally, the Fanonian yell connected Poitier and Gates. In explaining the anxiety over Henry Louis Gates Jr.'s encounter with a white Cambridge police sergeant, President Obama recognized that his election to the presidency did not mark the beginning of a postracial America.

When President Barack Hussein Obama commented on the Gates-Crowley encounter, he acknowledged that racial profiling exists. He described how it confines black and brown people to a criminal typology based on their physiognomy. In responding to a reporter's question about the arrest of Henry Louis Gates, President Obama maintained, like the Hollywood social problem film *No Way Out*, that blacks are targets of racism. The thought or utterance "Dirty nigger!" or simply, "Look, a Negro!" is the first impulse when recognizing an "aberrant" physiognomy that deviates from the "white" norm (Fanon 1967, 109).

After the Gates-Crowley ordeal, the South Carolina representative Joe Wilson greeted President Obama with "You Lie!" when Obama convened the US Congress to discuss the National Health Bill. The congressional representative's utterance, Crowley's arrest of Gates, and Poitier's thoughts on "the blackness of being" reveal that Obama's presidency, Gates's academic fame, and Poitier's prestigious acting awards provided no shelter from the storm of racism in thought and deed. Too many black *Others* remain outsiders regardless of their economic success, artistic talent, and academic accomplishments. The actor Poitier, the scholar Gates, Sergeant Crowley, Congressman Wilson, and President Obama are inextricably connected to "the fact of blackness" and the many verbal and nonverbal ways to utter it as expressed in Fanon by "Dirty nigger!" and "Look, a Negro!" and in Representative Wilson's "You Lie."

Black achievements in industry, politics, entertainment, and academic life have not created a postracial America. A postracial America requires a postracial world in which blacks and nonblacks psychologically and socially dismantle the Fanonian "fact of blackness" wherever it rears its ugly head.

Frantz Fanon's critical race theory provides tools for analyzing the psychological aspects of institutionalized racism as they appear in art, cinema, and everyday social reality. Sidney Poitier's film roles and his political activism have always been an actional effort to dismantle the hateful stare as mirrored in American films and registered in the peculiar institution of slavery and racism. One need only recall Senator Obama's path to the White House, which was laden with monkey imagery and questions about his citizenship and his faith: Is he a Christian or a Muslim? Moreover, his proofs of US citizenship and Christian faith were met with a Joe Wilsonian "You Lie!" In 2010, this is unfortunately a prime topic and question for Americans who regret President Barack Obama's election to the American presidency.

In performance after performance, Poitier's roles resist the deterministic discourse of "Dirty nigger!" or "Look, a Negro." Film historians and aficionados need only review Poitier's roles in such films as *No Way Out* (1950), *The Defiant Ones* (1958), *Pressure Point* (1962), *In the Heat of the Night* (1967), *They Call Me Mr. Tibbs!* (1970), and *The Organization* (1971) to conclude that Poitier is a doctor searching for a cure against the contagion of American racism, which can easily turn to fascism, as described in Antonio Negri's collection of essays *Negri on Negri*:

> The multitude can become fascist only when it has been emptied
> of its specificity, which is to say of the fact that it is an ensemble
> of singularities, a multiplicity of irreducible activities. Just like
> evil, fascism is always a negation of power, a withdrawal from
> the common Being. The fascist encourages hatred of the other,
> sanctifies violence as the remedy for the vices of the world,
> obliterates differences, and exalts the order of a bygone world.
> Fascism—all fascism—reacts destructively against the move-
> ment of life, against the joyous and multiple manner in which
> it invents itself. . . . Fascism is terrified, then, by the emergence
> of differences; scandalized by interbreeding, exasperated by
> alternatives to sexual pseudo-normality. (Negri 2004, 73–74)

The film *No Way Out* and Poitier's role as Dr. Luther Brooks challenge the hatred of the "Other" and the sanctity of violence. Still, the film does not deny the use of retaliatory violence against fascist threats. However, throughout the film Dr. Brooks resists retaliatory violence because he is the doctor in the house of multiplicity and change that has no way out. The film supports a philosophical stance that embraces multiplicity and interracial action. As Antonio Negri states, "One encounters a discovery, deepening, and development of another heritage of modernity; a heritage that, instead of hiding difference behind identity and repetition, exalts it through the diversity of life" (74).

"Is There a Doctor in the House?"

THE TITLE OF THIS essay, "Is There a Doctor in the House?" refers to America and its irreconcilable racial problems. In addition, the title is a trace of the many examples of blacks, like Dr. Luther Brooks, who try to cure a *"huit clos"* (Jean-Paul Sartre's play *Huis Clos* [No Exit] circa 1943–45) of American racial hatred. Sidney Poitier, in the role of Dr. Brooks, performs the hopes of liberal white professionals. Sidney Poitier and the role he performs in this film create a lonely example of the black striver who must contend with racism and the questioning of his professional skills. Admittedly, this is the nature of the 1949 social problem film genre, as seen in such race-focused films as *Home of the Brave* (a visibly black soldier in a predominantly white Army unit), *Pinky* (a racially passing black nurse), and *Lost Boundaries* (a racially passing black doctor in a predominantly white northern community). In 1950, writers Joseph L. Mankiewicz and Lesser Samuels received a nomination for Best Story and Screenplay from the Academy of Motion Picture Arts and Sciences for *No Way Out*. The film expands the problem film genre by its dramatization of a black doctor in a predominantly white-staffed big-city hospital, Cook County. Like Private Peter Moss (James Edwards) in *Home of the Brave*, Dr. Brooks suffers a momentary psychological setback when he questions his acquired professional skills and diagnosis. Like Moss, Brooks is an exception to the black working-class characters that are more inclined to be the targets of white violence and take the pacifist route. Their educational success as soldier and medical doctor, respectively, becomes a razor that psychologically wounds their black self-worth. They are no longer protected by a racial ghetto and now become easy targets of cutting racial slurs.

In *No Way Out*, male members of the black working class, however, are also more inclined to violently retaliate against white male violence and racism. Dr. Brooks represents the wishful nonviolence of America liberalism, as Dr. Martin Luther King Jr. and the Student Nonviolent Coordinating Committee (SNCC) would channel ten years later. The film espouses a transracial, not postracial, idea that once the educated and skilled African Americans attain professional parity with their white counterparts, the nation as a whole will reach the mountaintop envisioned by Dr. Martin Luther King Jr. The post-Obama reality is far from this colonial fantasy.

The title of this essay also refers to the Obama era when people of color arrived at the summit of their professional careers but remained contained in a *huit clos* of American racial hatred. Simultaneous with post-Obama successes, the *huit clos* of racial containment demands a centrist albeit pacifist political strategy. It is this modus operandi that Poitier, in the role of Dr. Brooks, generates in his first feature film and in those that follow throughout his first twenty years in Hollywood. Ironically, this strategy would fuel the movement led by Dr. Martin Luther King Jr. and, apparently, was adopted by President Barack Obama during his presidential bid and as the first African American president of the United States of America. I am stressing the *performative* nature of this strategy and do not mean to construe it as an essential quality of either of the two leaders. In citing Louis Althusser's notion of interpellation and discussing the "performative," Judith Butler explains:

> There is the policeman, the one who not only represent the law but whose address "Hey you!" has the effect of binding the law to the one who is hailed. This "one" who appears not to be in a condition of trespass prior to the call (for whom the call establishes a given practice as a trespass) is not fully a social subject, is not fully subjectivated, for he or she is not yet reprimanded. The reprimand does not merely repress or control the subject but form a crucial part of the juridical and social *formation* of the subject. The call is formative, if not *per*formative, precisely because it initiates the individual into the subjected status of the subject. (Butler 1993, 121)

The interpellation of "Hey you" by the policeman is very similar to Fanon's description of "The thought or utterance 'Dirty nigger!' or simply, 'Look, a Negro!' [which is] the first impulse when recognizing an 'aberrant' physiognomy that deviates from the 'white' norm" (Fanon 1967, 109). The film's narrative emphasizes this in its formation of Dr. Luther Brooks and is implied in the homebound black female characters.

In most of Poitier's film roles, the characters he portrays are progressive in their social activism and writings, which tend to politically differ from their centrist public performances. In *No Way Out*, certain visual and oral elements resist racism and interracial sexual fears. Ironically, the film's repression of these elements also creates subtle transgressions, which I will discuss later in the chapter.

No Way Out is set in Chicago, and most of the scenes are confined to interior shots of Cook County Hospital's prison ward. The film introduces Sidney Poitier in the role of Dr. Luther Brooks. The role establishes Poitier as an educated and demur black icon whose historicity is shaped during the House Un-American Activities Committee (HUAC, 1938–69)–inspired Communist witch hunts. "Through its power to subpoena witnesses and hold people in contempt of Congress, HUAC often pressured witnesses to surrender names and other information that could lead to the apprehending of Communists and Communist sympathizers. Committee members often branded witnesses as 'red' if they refused to comply or hesitated in answering committee questions" (Black et al. 2003). HUAC also targeted such civil rights activists and performers as Paul Robeson, Eartha Kitt, Harry Belafonte, Canada Lee, and Marlon Brando. Interestingly, HUAC considered Sidney Poitier "a person of interest" but they did not pursue him as they did his contemporaries who were active in the 1950s–1960s civil rights movement and regularly spent time with Poitier.

Dr. Brooks undermines deterministic forces that would justifiably lead blacks to retaliatory violence. Brooks navigates between two racial poles and remains in the middle by remarkably avoiding racial hatred and violence. He is the middle-class black medical doctor par excellence. Ray Biddle (Richard Widmark) represents white working-class Beaver Canal men who plan to attack the neighboring black working-class community. They believe

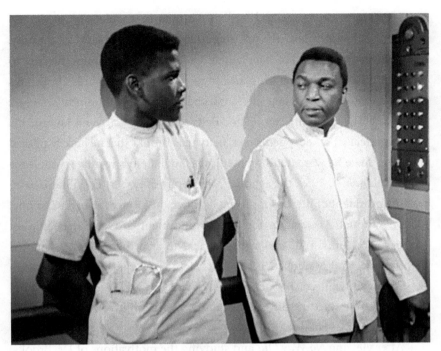

Two Black political stratagems: Dr. Brooks's (Sidney Poitier's) passive resistance and Lefty's (Dots Johnson's) retaliatory violence.

that Dr. Brooks intentionally killed Ray's brother and Edie Johnson's (Linda Darnell's) former husband, Johnny (Dick Paxton) when Brooks administered a spinal tap. A white police officer shot Ray and Johnny as they were robbing a gas station. Ray is an unashamed racist whom Dr. Brooks treats while ignoring Ray's unending racial slurs.

Lefty Jones (Dots Johnson), the film's second most important black character, is the hospital's elevator operator. At the beginning of the film, Brooks warmly greets Lefty as if they are social equals. Lefty is proud of his position and demands respect for both Dr. Brooks and himself. The first example of this occurs when Ray Biddle mistakes Brooks for a maintenance worker. Lefty quickly corrects Biddle with "You're talking to a doctor." In the same scene, Lefty tells Ray to stop his racist slurs as Dr. Brooks looks on in silence. Here is the hyperlink to a film clip that show the hospital setting as a film noir–like, psychologically uncanny scene where Lefty, Dr. Brooks, and the Biddle brothers are inescapably contained: http://youtu.be/7ItsP_QWbdM.

Later, Lefty organizes and leads black men in a violent attack on the Beaver Canal white men, who are preparing to attack the black community. When Brooks gets wind of the planned violence of both groups, he tries to persuade Lefty to abandon his plans. In response, Lefty reminds Dr. Brooks that the white Beaver Canal men attacked the black community six years previously. The racist attack rendered Lefty with a scar across his jaw and his sister physically handicapped. Next, Lefty tells Brooks that he luckily missed the event since he was attending medical school. Lefty's retaliatory violence would become, in 1959, the actional philosophy of Robert F. Williams, who was the president of the Union County branch, in Monroe, North Carolina, of the National Association for the Advancement of Colored People. In *Negroes with Guns*, Williams advises blacks to arm themselves (as quoted in Broderick and Meier 1965, 321–33). Here is a hyperlink to a montage that interlaces white racist men who plan violence and black men who are motivated to protect the black community by pre-emptive violence (http://youtu.be/mnjPC1Eb8dk).

After viewing *No Way Out* and studying the motivations of Dr. Brooks, I find that the black physician generates an "aesthetic du cool" that represses or displaces his racial anger. Still, the film permits black agency in a less than cool, visually violent eruption that predates the black-on-white violence that appears in Blaxploitation films. Ironically, the Blaxploitation film's violent agency would become an obstacle that pursued Poitier throughout his post-sixties film career. Yet and still, Toni Morrison's wise comment, "Now that Mr. Poitier and Mr. Belafonte have shot up all the racists in *Buck and the Preacher*, have they all gone away? Can we move into better neighborhoods and not be set on fire?" (Morrison 2008, 8–9). Morrison notes that it is ludicrous for anyone to think that progressive works of art result in social and economic progress. She feels that real change comes by people not by art though artists and their works may assist in real social change.

In the prison ward of Cook County Hospital and handcuffed to his hospital bed, Ray Biddle conspires to avenge the death of his brother Johnny because Ray believes that Dr. Brooks killed Johnny with the spinal tap procedure. Unfortunately, the procedure causes Johnny's death and results in Ray's desire to seek revenge by organizing a white-on-black riot.

Dr. Luther Brooks and Dr. Dan Wharton (Stephen McNally) visit Edie Johnson (Linda Darnell) to entreat her to permit an autopsy on Johnny Biddle, her deceased lover, whom Brooks had treated.

Scenes that are located outside the hospital are mostly limited to the exteriors and interiors of racially exclusive working-class neighborhoods. The interior shots of the Brooks family's large apartment introduce the film audience to Dr. Luther Brooks's wife, Cora (Mildred Joanne Smith), and three members of his extended family who share the modest but spacious living quarters. The other members of the Brooks family include Luther's brother, John (Ossie Davis), his mother (Maude Simmons), and his sister, Connie Brooks (Ruby Dee). In the street near their apartment, we see children at play.

Diverging from the previous scene of an extended black family in a comfortable but modest apartment, white Edie Johnson resides in a one-room tenement apartment located in a white working-class neighborhood. Edie's neighborhood borders the white lower-class neighborhood of Beaver Canal, where she was born. Again, we see children are at play in the street. The two street scenes express the shared humanity of the two racially different but similar working-class communities. Edie plays a central role in the film because she will be the interracial bridge to black women. She will also help to balance the overall racial tensions between black Dr. Brooks and white Ray Biddle, who is her former brother-in-law and past lover.

The proximity of Edie and Dr. Brooks in the setting of Edie's studio apartment, shot in a medium shot where he seems to be angered and then in a close-up where Edie gives him a slippery, uncanny look, momentarily usurps how previous Hollywood scenes have dealt with the frame space between black men and white women. The scene introduces issues that concern the way American films position educated black men and white women. Dr. Brooks is the sole black who peacefully crosses the racial threshold of Edie's white, working-class neighborhood and her home. Accompanied by Dr. Wharton, Dr. Brooks enters Edie's walk-up studio apartment, where she greets them in a housecoat. One can view the scene as simply an integrationist element that reflects the film's liberal racial attitude and its film noir sources. *No Way Out* exhibits the marginal qualities of film noir characters in the way a thinly clad white female, Edie, is framed within the same space as a black male, Dr. Brooks. In commenting on film noir's transgressive elements that unhinge middle class respectability, Eric Lott writes:

> Noir's crossings from light to dark, the indulgence of actions and visual codes ordinarily renounced in white bourgeois culture and thereby raced in the white imaginary, throw its protagonists into the predicament of abjection. Noir characters threaten to lose themselves in qualities that formerly marked all the self was not and that unsettle its stable definition. Antisocial acts of lawlessness and passion, deceit and recklessness signify the state that . . . makes borders irrelevant, repression inoperative, and the ego and *Other.* With stable demarcation (moral, visual, racial) replaced by fluidity, straining, "going all the way to the end of the line" (as *Double Indemnity* has it), noir's abject selves meet the world without boundaries—no mere moral failing, since it involves disturbances around the disavowal of the mother in the formation of (principally masculine) gender definition and of the racial Other in the formation of white self-identity. (Lott 1997, 549)

The scene in Edie's studio apartment is an atypical example of visually imbricating race, gender, and class boundaries because of the presence of middle-class black Dr. Brooks. Unlike the whiteness of Dr. Wharton, the blackness of Brooks emits a tinge of antisocial lawlessness, a possibility of passion that disrupts fixed racial borders. This is truly a psychological threat for southern viewers and northern spectators who reside in urban cities that have recently witnessed postwar race riots. When Dr. Brooks mounts the stairs to Edie's apartment, her female neighbors show anxiety over the imagined threat due to Brooks's blackness.

A few film scholars find that *No Way Out* exhibits several stylistic elements of the film noir genre. For instance, in Andrew Spicer's *Historical Dictionary of Film Noir*, he states that "The African American experience was only very occasionally broached, as in *No Way Out* (1950), in which Sidney Poitier . . . plays a young, idealistic intern at a metropolitan hospital whose encounter with a bigoted, racist crook . . . is seen as part of a wider black-white confrontation" and confirms that "*No Way Out* is the only film noir in which a black man is the hero" (Spicer 2010, 1). Ryan De Rosa finds that the storyline of *No Way Out* outlines "the complexity of the dark psychological film noir; particularly the kind that entangles the hero . . . in a threatening world in which he must prove his innocence of a crime" (De Rosa 2012, 56).

The lower-class setting, its mise-en-scène, and the figure of a woman dressed in bedroom attire in the presence of men is reminiscent of film noir images that express a latent "non-normative" sexuality. Additionally, this scene in Edie's apartment has a psychologically threatening mise-en-scène that includes the presence of a black man sharing the same film space as a partially clad white female who is of dubious moral character. Local censor boards and individual spectators alike might find that the scene challenges social conventions and taboos against images that might be seen to support the possibility of miscegenation.

Moreover, the scene predates similar scenes found in pre-1950s major studio productions that feature black leading men. In quieting such fears, the script directs Wharton and Edie to have most of the dialogue. Brooks observes the two from a safe but interested distance. Wharton entreats Edie to authorize an autopsy on Johnny Biddle, her former husband. Later in the scene, Brooks expresses his belief that an autopsy will prove that the spinal tap he gave Johnny was necessary, though it led to his death. It is at this point in the scene that Edie and Dr. Brooks enter into the same frame and emotional space. The scene threatens contemporary racial and sexual taboos because Brooks's black masculine presence occupies the private space of a white woman dressed in bedclothes. Still, the scene is one of two sexually transgressive moments when the mere physical presence of Dr. Brooks upends the sexual status quo without recourse to violence. The other scene that heavily and heatedly expresses these subliminal sentiments is the final scene that takes place at Dr. Wharton's home, where Ray shoots Brooks as Edie witnesses the brutality and eventually saves Brooks from Ray, who plans to kill him. Before this scene, however, the film shows interracial harmony between Cora Brooks, Gladys, and Edie as Wharton looks admiringly on the women.

Dr. Daniel Wharton's (Stephen McNally's) large home manifests upper-middle-class white racial exclusivity. Neither wife nor children inhabit the Wharton home. It does not have the lively images of family that are seen in Dr. Brooks's home. However, Wharton's black housemaid, Gladys (Amanda Randolph), provides the bachelor and his home with care. Both Dr. Wharton and Edie Johnson admire Dr. Brooks. Suggestively, Johnson resides in the same black neighborhood and has the same sort of maternal relationship with her white employer as, later in the film, Dr. Brooks has with his white patient, Ray Biddle. Gladys's caring attitude toward the white liberal Wharton and, later, Edie, mirrors that of Brooks. Such altruism is mirrored in Brooks's care of Ray, though Edie thinks that Ray does not deserve it.

EDIE—Gladys, what do you do on your day off, like today?

GLADYS—Oh, go sit in the park. Maybe go to church, maybe to a movie. Come suppertime, I go somewhere and cook.

EDIE—Where?

GLADYS—Friends. I fix 'em a good supper.

EDIE—Some day off.

GLADYS—[Chuckles] I like it. I'm a good cook. It's somethin' I can do better than other people. It makes me a somebody. Gives me a reason to be alive. Everybody gotta have that (D'Ambra, "*No Way Out* (1950): Is it a question or an answer?").

Dr. Wharton's home: left to right: Cora Brooks (Mildred Joanne Smith), Dr. Brooks's wife; Gladys (Amanda Randolph), Dr. Wharton's housekeeper; Edie Johnson, the wife of deceased Johnnie Biddle; and Dr. Wharton.

The antithesis of interracial group camaraderie begins with the vigilante pursuits of working-class men. First, there is Rocky Miller (Burt Freed) at the Beaver Canal Social Club, who organizes a few white men and attempts to enlist a reluctant Edie, the sole female present. Rocky tries to persuade Edie to support not only his racist plans but also his carnal desires. She leaves the social club in fear but promises to meet him at his junkyard, where the other white men will gather before they invade the black community. The two racially exclusive nonhospital locations of the club and the junkyard convey a hot racial anger shared between white working-class men. First, in the darkly lit interior of the white Beaver Canal Club, whites plan to organize and meet at Andy's Junkyard to collect scrap iron and chains for their attack on the black community. There are only a few white women in the junkyard scene. The junkyard mise-en-scène shows Edie's and the other women's fear. Again, Edie is a reluctant but passive participant, as are the other women, in a scene in which white homosocial rage dominates. Edie struggles to attain agency, as do black men, like Lefty, who organize to protect their community.

Lefty's retaliatory violence organizational meeting.

In the darkly lit, high-contrast scene at Andy's junkyard, white men prepare the final stages of their planned attack. The two scenes present racist epithets that reveal the source of their hatred is the white fear that the social betterment of the black community threatens the existing racial hierarchy and white masculinity. The Beaver Canal Club and the junkyard are marked by race, class, and gender. The men seem to fill out their hypermasculine dreams in the dark but white homosocial working-class setting. The scene recalls, at least for this viewer, documentaries that feature Nazis storming Jewish businesses, places of worship, and homes. Such scenes, not much later, would appear in fiction films with angry white motorcycle gangs. With the exception of Edie, who is present in the Beaver Canal Club, and Edie and two other white women who are present at Andy's junkyard, the furious white men determine the scenes. The white working-class men, driven by hatred and seeking vengeance, plan another violent attack on the black neighborhood where the Brooks extended family, Lefty, and Dr. Wharton's housekeeper, Gladys, live.

Unlike in the two settings that feature working-class white men, a group of black working-class men meet at Lester Peabody's poolroom. The scene

At Dr. Wharton's home, Dr. Brooks is alone with his racist nemesis, Ray Biddle (Richard Widmark), who plans to avenge his brother Johnny's death.

presents a crowd of black men who are determined to protect their community from another white racist attack such as the one that scarred Lefty's face, crippled his sister, and brought death to members of the black community. The blacks avoid using racial slurs that would uncritically demean all whites. They merely organize to ward off an attack and pursue retaliatory violence against a specific and limited target—Andy's junkyard. The poolroom scene visually and orally expresses a quality of black agency that was rarely if ever dramatized in pre-1970s American cinema. Tony D'Ambra, in "Race and Film Noir: Black and Noir," argues that during the forties and fifties, progressive Hollywood screenwriters and directors made noirs that deal sympathetically with race as important elements of the story. This is more than can be said of the body of Hollywood output for the period. *No Way Out* demonstrates this type of progressive filmmaking, and its black male lead marks it as a notable example.

In the film's final scene, a gun-toting Ray lures Dr. Brooks to Dr. Wharton's house while Wharton is away. Tellingly, the interior and exterior of

Dr. Brooks cares for the injured Ray Biddle.

Dr. Wharton's spacious upper-middle-class house is the setting for the pivotal last scene. Wharton and Mrs. Johnson are not present, which permits dramatic tension to be focused on Dr. Brooks, Ray Biddle, and Edie Johnson. Ray pistol whips Dr. Brooks and plans to kill him. Edie arrives and tries to persuade Ray to let Brooks live. When she finally realizes that Ray is intent on killing Brooks, she turns off the living room lights. Shots are fired in the dark. Edie turns the lights on and views Brooks, with a grazing wound, holding Ray's gun. Ray screams in pain from his worsening leg wound, which he received earlier in the film. In this last scene, Edie entreats Brooks to avenge Ray's racism, which led to the riots and Ray beating and shooting Brooks.

Now, Ray needs Dr. Brooks to save his life and relieve his pain. Brooks refuses to act as Ray and the other Beaver Canal white men did. Unlike Lefty, the elevator operator, his brother-in-law John, and many of the working-class blacks that organized to ward-off the white racist attack, Dr. Brooks remains a "human" and tells Ray, "Don't cry, white boy, you're gonna live." He also counsels Edie that she should abandon her hatred for Ray.

Dr. Brooks works on the injured Ray, over the objections of Edie.

EDIE—You all right?

LUTHER—[Wounded] My arm. Maybe my shoulder. I can't tell.—It's not so bad.

RAY—[Gasping] My leg! [Crying] It tore. Somethin' tore in my leg. [Crying continues] It's bleedin'. It's bleedin' hard. Please!

EDIE—Let it bleed.

RAY—[Groaning]

EDIE—Tear it some more. Let it bleed fast.

LUTHER—You'll have to help me.

EDIE—To do what?

LUTHER—Whatever I can to keep him alive.

EDIE—Why? What for? A human being's gotta have a reason for bein' alive. He hasn't got any. He's not even human. He's a mad dog. You kill mad dogs, don't ya?

LUTHER—Don't you think I'd like to? Don't you think I'd like to put the rest of these bullets through his head?

EDIE—Then go ahead.

LUTHER—I can't.

EDIE—Why not?

LUTHER—Because I've got to live too.

EDIE—Then give it [the gun] to me.

LUTHER—You've got to live.

EDIE—I will, believe me—happy as a bird with him dead.

LUTHER—Please help me. No. Look, he's sick. He's crazy. He's everything you said. But I can't kill a man just because he hates me.
(D'Ambra 2010, "No Way Out")

Film critic Donald Bogle succinctly describes Brooks's motivation as the integrationist discourse of Hollywood scriptwriters who constructed his film
persona for most of his career:

> When one thinks of how much Luther Brooks was to remain
> with actor Poitier, he is tempted to ask if scriptwriters
> Mankiewicz and Lesser Samuels should not be credited with
> creating the most important black actor in the history of motion
> pictures. . . . He lived out Hollywood's fantasy of the American
> Black man. (Bogle 1994, 179)

This fantasy did not include Lefty, nor did it include or seriously imagine the black men (similar to such activists as Robert Williams, Stokely
Carmichael [1941–98], H. Rap Brown [1943–Present], and Eldridge Cleaver
[1935–98]) who gathered to protect the African American community from
a racist attack. Their fantasy also constructed the black women of the Brooks
household to be as equally nonexistent as Dr. Brooks, since they did not participate in the exterior scenes of the poolroom and the retaliatory violence.
Strangely, there was one white woman in the public spaces of the Beaver
Club, and a few white women in the junkyard scene.

In conclusion, *No Way Out* and similar contemporary sociopolitical
existential realities underline the sad but true reality that there seems to be
no exit from them.

> Existentialism is an outlook, which begins with a disoriented
> individual facing a confused world that he cannot accept. It

places its emphasis on man's contingence in a world where there are not transcendental values or moral absolutes, a world devoid of any meaning but the one man himself creates. . . . The special affinity of the film noir is nowhere better evidenced than in a random sampling of some of its most suggestive titles: *Cornered, One Way Street, No Way Out, Caged, The Dark Corner, In a Lonely Place.* (Porfirio 1976, 212)

Still, we should not grin and bear it. As the existentialist character Joseph Garcin exclaims at the end of Jean-Paul Sartre's *Huis clos* (1947): "Alors, c'est ca l'enfer. Je n'aurais jamais cru. . . . Vous rappelez: le soufre, le bucher, le gril. . . . Ah! Quelle plaisanterie. Pas besoin de gril: l'enfer c'est les Autres" (*Huit clos 1947*, 93). An English translation of Joseph Garcin's words would be "So this is hell. I'd never have believed it. You remember all we were told about the torture-chambers, the fire and brimstone, the "burning marl." Old wives' tales! There's no need for red-hot pokers. HELL IS—OTHER PEOPLE!" (http://vtheatre.net/script/doc/sartre.html). Ironically, *Huit clos* predates *No Way Out*, which is very close to the English translation of the title of the play, *No Exit*.

Throughout this chapter, I have argued that that the character of Dr. Luther Brooks is a measure of a certain kind of man—a pacifist. Still, Dr. Brooks evokes self-determinism, racial pride, and a strategic masculinity that competes with white primitivism, as is manifest in scenes of the black retaliatory violence and the atavistic white sexuality of the Beaver Club men. White primitivism, as performed in this film, would later morph into the recipe for the seventies Blaxploitation films. Critics celebrated Blaxploitation films for their retaliatory violence, oversexed black heroes, and submissive white and black maidens. In demeaning Poitier's film roles as less than a measure of a black man, critics and audiences deny the multiple forms that black humanity can take. They also ignore the various strategies blacks use to resist, compromise, and sometimes acquiesce to fascism. In the main, Dr. Brooks espouses an altruism that is morally Judeo-Christian and politically liberal, rather than radically disruptive, a way of sustaining the film's strategy for racial peace. White Dr. Daniel Wharton, the chief medical resident, shares this magnanimity, as do the film's major black female characters: Cora Brooks and Gladys, the maid. Gradually, Edie Johnson, the white, working-class, former sister-in-law of the unabashed racist Ray Biddle, arrives at this humanity. As earlier noted in the Antonio Negri quotation, "The multitude can become fascist only when it has been emptied of its specificity, which is to say of the fact that it is an ensemble of singularities, a multiplicity of irreducible activities" (Negri 2004, 73).

The film depicts a racial reality that could easily have existed in Chicago, but possibly not at Cook County Hospital in 1950. Dr. Brooks anticipates the professional advancement of people of visible color in America. There are many examples of this. In academia, the Harvard scholar Henry Louis Gates Jr. is as renowned in his field as Poitier is in Hollywood. There have been three U.S. Supreme Court Justices of color—Thurgood Marshall, Clarence Thomas, and Sonia Sotomayor. Former US senator for Illinois Carole Moseley-Braun and Oprah Winfrey (Harpo Productions) are two examples of black women who excelled, respectively, in government and corporate America. The dramatist August Wilson and the eight African American Academy Award recipients for Best Actor or Actress in a Leading Role from 1963 to 2006 exemplify black achievement in fields where white men have exclusively dominated. Still and even now, Frantz Fanon's words ring true:

> It was always the Negro teacher, the Negro doctor; brittle as I was becoming, I shivered at the slightest pretext. I knew, for instance, that if the physician made a mistake, it would be the end of him and all of those who came after him. What could one expect, after all, from a Negro physician? As long as everything went well, he was praised to the skies, but look out, no nonsense, under any conditions! The black physician can never be sure how close he is to disgrace. (Fanon 1967, 117)

Fanon's comments are applicable to the 1950s images of race relations in America as depicted in *No Way Out*. The film also confirms the contemporary world of Supreme Court Justice Sonia Maria Sotomayor, President Barack Hussein Obama, Sir Sidney Poitier, and the many colored Others who have made tremendous advancements.

References

Bogle, Donald. 1994. *Toms, Coons, Mulattoes, Mammies, & Bucks: An Interpretive History of Blacks in American Films.* 3rd ed. New York: Continuum.

Broderick, Francis L., and August Meier, eds. 1965. *Negro Protest Thought in the Twentieth Century.* New York: Bobbs-Merrill Company, Inc.

Butler, Judith. 1993. *Bodies That Matter: On the Discursive Limits of "Sex."* New York: Routledge.

Cripps, Thomas. 1993. *Making Movies Black: The Hollywood Message Movie from World War II to the Civil Rights Era.* New York: Oxford University Press.

D'Ambra, Tony. 2010. "No Way Out (1950): Is it a question or an answer?" http://filmsnoir.net/film_noir/no-way-out-1950-is-it-a-question-or-an-answer.html.

D'Ambra, Tony. 2010. "Race and Film Noir: Black and Noir." http://filmsnoir.net/film_noir/race-and-film-noir-black-and-noir.html.

De Rosa, Ryan. 2012. "Historicizing the Shadows and the Acts: *No Way Out* and the Imagining of Black Activist Communities." *Cinema Journal* 51 (3): 52–73.

Fanon, Frantz. 1967. "The Fact of Blackness." In *Black Skin, White Masks*, 109–40. New York: Grove Weidenfeld,

JanMohamed, Abdul R. 1995. "The Economy of Manichean Allegory." In *The Post-Colonial Studies Reader*, edited by Bill Ashcroft, Gareth Griffiths, and Helen Tiffin, 18–23. London: Routledge.

Lacan, Jacques. 1978. *The Four Fundamental Concepts of Psycho-Analysis*, edited by Alan Sheridan, New York: W. W. Norton 203–60.

Lott, Eric. 1997. "The Whiteness of Film Noir." *American Literary History* 9(3): 542–66.

Miller, Jacques-Alain. 1997. *The Ethics of Psychoanalysis 1959–1969: The Seminar of Jacques Lacan Book VII.* Translated by Dennis Porter. New York: Norton.

Morrison, Toni. 2008. *What Moves at the Margin: Selected Nonfiction.* Edited by Carolyn C. Denard. Jackson: University of Mississippi Press, 2008.

Negri, Antonio. 2004. *Negri on Negri: Antonio Negri in conversation with Anne Dufourmantelle.* Translated by M. B. DeBevoise. New York: Routledge.

No Way Out. 1950. 20th Century-Fox. Directed by Joseph L. Mankiewicz.

Poitier, Sidney. 2000. *The Measure of a Man: A Spiritual Autobiography.* New York: HarperCollins.

Porfirio, Robert G. 1976. "No Way Out: Existential motifs in the film noir." *Sight and Sound (Monthly Film Bulletin)* 45(4): 212–17.

Sartre, John Paul. 1947. *Huis clos suivi de Les mouches.* Paris: Éditions Gallimard.

Sartre, John Paul. 2007. *No Exit*. http://vtheatre.net/script/doc/sartre.html.

Spicer, Andrew. 2010. "African American Film Noir." In *Historical Dictionary of Film Noir*, 1–3. Lanham, MD: Scarecrow Press, Inc.

Van Pelt, T. 2000. "Otherness." *Postmodern Culture* 10(2): 3–4.

Williams, Robert F. 1998. *Negroes With Guns*. New York: Marzani and Munsell; repr. Detroit: Wayne State University Press.

3

POITIER'S CINEMATIC INTERVENTION IN *FOR LOVE OF IVY*

Karen Bowdre

THOUGH NOW AN ELDER statesman for actors and feted because of his pioneering acting achievements as well as his diplomatic and charitable work, Sidney Poitier was not always the recipient of such high praise. During the mid-1960s, many of Poitier's roles sparked debate over what many critics considered the excessively accommodating portrayals Poitier performed in relation to white characters; critics contended that many of the actor's depictions tended to reinforce rather than challenge US racial politics. These writers posit that Poitier had a great deal of creative control over his roles and that he had the leverage to significantly alter Hollywood's portrayal of African American men. However, this critique of Poitier, though popular, is misguided in both the oversimplification of the complex nature of Poitier's relationship with Hollywood and the fact that it ignores Poitier's contributions to cinema. I argue that the cultural capital Poitier had accumulated over the years of playing roles that placated white fears about black men enabled him to capitalize on this favor and later in his career create movies such as *For Love of Ivy* (1968). Moreover, *Ivy*, a film that Poitier wrote the story for and I posit is the first black romantic comedy, examines racial issues in ways far more complicated than the simple binary of black and white.

Released in 1968, *Ivy* is the first romantic comedy with African American leads. Sidney Poitier and Abbey Lincoln play Jack Parks, the co-owner of a trucking company, and Ivy Moore, the live-in maid for the Austins, an upper-middle-class European American family. At the start of the film, Ivy quits her job in order to attend secretarial school. The family panics at the news and offers her a raise and vacations. The son and daughter, also concerned about Ivy leaving the family, decide that her real need is a man and set her up with Jack because he is one of the few black men they know and his dubious secondary job, running a gambling casino on his truck, ensures he isn't marriage material.

Ivy and Poitier's other work completed after the various criticisms levelled at him in 1967 can be perceived as a response to those critiques (Mason 1967).Jack Parks is not an "ebony saint"; though he co-owns his trucking company, he runs a gambling casino. Jack having both good and bad qualities, I argue, is a reflection of the fact that Poitier created Jack and not European American screenwriters, who typically seem unable to see complexity in characters that are not white males. In addition to having more complicated African American characters, *Ivy* makes innovative changes that are rarely seen in contemporary film. One of the things that stands out in the film is that it is far more integrated than most in the twenty-first century. Throughout the film, Jack moves in both European American and African American circles; his business colleagues are all black, though they are rarely seen in exclusively all-black settings. As a live-in maid, Ivy is constantly with the Austins, but the audience is also aware that she goes to New York City on her days off, is a member the NAACP, and attends civil rights rallies. Thus the film casts Poitier as a shady character and gives both Jack and Ivy dimensionality with friends and acquaintances from black communities.

Movie critics' reviews at the time of the film's release label *Ivy* as a romantic comedy, with most noting that Poitier is finally able to play a "Cary Grant role." Roger Ebert jokes that Poitier doesn't just have dinner with his love interest, he stays for breakfast (Ebert 1968). Unlike Poitier's previous roles, Jack has romantic relationships with women, and it is implied that he is quite the ladies' man. His ability to embody this role is closely attached to his star status and the gentlemanly portrayals, derided by many, that made his stardom possible. Furthermore, his own role in creating this film—he is credited with the original story—should not be diminished and was also noted in Ebert's review. Hollywood seemed unable to create black male roles having a sexuality of any sort, and it took both Poitier's celebrity and his story to bring the first African American romantic comedy into being. The irony lies in the fact that the earlier sexless characters in his career were stepping stones that enable Poitier to become a romantic lead.

Though *Ivy* is a romantic comedy, it is not a sex comedy, something Bogle insinuates in his evaluation of the film (Bogle 2001, 217). For most scholars of romantic comedy, the term itself is the genre with a series of subgenres—screwball and sex comedies, nervous and new romances (McDonald 2007, 5; Neale 1992, 289). The subgenres are often understood as specific to particular time periods and being the predominant type of romantic comedy released at that time. *Ivy* was release at the tail end of the sex comedies, which were popular during the late 1950s through the 1960s.

The sex comedy, a term coined after these films were released, typically centers around a battle of the sexes, whereby both women and men desire sex yet quibble over gendered differences vis-à-vis sexual desire and romantic expectations (e.g., timing), with men wanting immediate gratification without marriage and women desiring sex within the confines of marriage (Krutnik 1990, 62; McDonald 2007, 38–54). In spite of its name and because of the Production Code, sex was only implied or alluded to in these movies.[1] The sex comedy's key characters were the virginal career girl and the predatory playboy bachelor. Though Jack does have traits of a playboy—he does not desire marriage, has a very nice apartment, and claims to have had a bevy of women—he does not engage in the masquerade ritual for the purposes of seduction, where the sex comedy male protagonist tries to seduce the female by pretending to be someone who is the opposite of himself (awkward around women and inexperienced in the ways of love). Ivy is an aspiring career girl and, though initially nervous after her date with Jack at his apartment, she does not appear uptight, as do the characters portrayed by Doris Day or Natalie Wood.

Because Jack and Ivy are African Americans, their bodies disrupt genre conventions because of the historic expectations of black bodies in American cinema. Both African American men and women were typically portrayed as individuals without sexualities—for example, the desexualized mammy and the rastus, tom, and coon characters. At the other extreme exist oversexualized characters, such as the Black Buck and Jezebel that have far fewer screen appearances. The producers of the film appear to want audiences to view Jack and Ivy as part of the romantic comedy genre without the racial and cultural baggage of cinematic sexual black bodies. Hence the characters embody roles that do not allow a simple mapping of past images. Though Ivy is a maid, she wants to leave this job for one that gives her more autonomy. And while Jack has a dark side (his gambling enterprise), his actions, along with Poitier's portrayal of him, serve to make him a rogue with a heart of gold, as many rom-com male leads are.

In the context of genre analysis, both *Ivy's* labeling as a romantic comedy and its release date mark it as transitional, between the sex and nervous comedies, and not only because of its African American leads. Leger Grindon, who posits there are nine cycles or subgenres of romantic comedy, calls films released during the period 1967 to 1976 "the transition through counter-culture cluster"; though Grindon does not include *Ivy* in his rather extensive list of films, the film does fit his definition of overturning and revising genre conventions (Grindon 2011, 50–53). *Ivy* does not have sex as the centerpiece of the film, and many of its characters talk about and sometimes engage with contemporary issues and popular culture in ways nervous romances would be praised for doing nine years later (McDonald 2007, 50–78). And, not surprisingly because of Jack and Ivy being the central protagonists, the film has racial elements that both work as a source of conflict and provide an insightful view of race relations at the time.

Analysis of the Film

WHILE ON THE SURFACE Ivy's initial circumstances as a domestic seem very pedestrian, her desire to leave her job as well as the fact that her narrative is central to the story should have let audiences know this was not going to be a typical Hollywood film. Ivy giving her notice at the start of the film provides a revealing look at power and racial dynamics, which were probably read very differently by African American and European American audiences. The person hardest hit by Ivy's news is Doris Austin, businesswoman, wife, and mother. But Doris's reaction to Ivy's announcement, though well intended and possibly perceived that way by white audiences, is misguided and self-serving. Her

Tim Austin (Beau Bridges) sets up Ivy for a date with Jack Parks (Sidney Poitier), the owner of a traveling gambling casino housed in a tractor trailer in *For Love of Ivy*.

voice rises considerably initially and then she presumes to know what Ivy really needs—a raise or a vacation. She also states that Ivy is family but unfortunately without recognizing the falseness and condescension of her comment. After Ivy explains that it's not the money or the amount of work, Doris assumes Ivy is pregnant, a comment the latter laughs off. Doris then fondly remembers how they "found" Ivy and asked the latter's grandmother for permission for Ivy to work for the family. During this conversation, Ivy refers to Doris as Mrs. Austin or Ma'am. Ivy has worked for the family for nine years and now suddenly Doris is suggesting Ivy call her by her first name or as "Mother."

Though some European American audiences at that time may have read Doris's actions from her standpoint of privilege as well as her attempt to control Ivy, African American audiences would have been familiar with these racial and hegemonic relations. Doris seems unable to comprehend that Ivy wants to do things other than being a maid. She also does not think Ivy knows the difference between needing time off and wanting a life change when Ivy clearly seeks the latter. It is this type of infantilization that keeps Doris from seeing Ivy as an equal despite the former's saying she views Ivy as a member of the family.

Not surprisingly, Doris isn't the only member of the Austin family who thinks she or he is progressive and yet often demonstrates otherwise. Son Tim views himself as one knowing the youth culture and having business savvy. His interactions with Jack prove otherwise. In his initial conversation with Jack, he tries to negotiate Jack dating Ivy as a favor that Jack should perform out of the goodness of his heart. This might have been a realistic tactic if Tim and Jack were personal friends, but they know one another only because Tim's father uses Jack's trucking company. Since their relationship to one another is only as businessmen, with Jack rarely dealing with Tim, this appeal seems all the more ludicrous. However, when you consider race, it sadly makes sense that Tim believes that Jack, though older than he and actually running his own business and not the son of the owner, as Tim is, would date Ivy. It demonstrates that though Tim does not want to be a part of the establishment, when he is dealing with African Americans he expects to have control as if he were "the man."

Prior to resorting to blackmail, Tim continues to expose his racial insensitivity. When Jack questions why he was the "stud" chosen to date Ivy, Tim says, "All spades are superior at that kind of thing." While Tim is clearly trying to be cool and hip by making this statement, he reveals his shallowness and ignorance about African Americans. He assumes all black men are potential partners for all African American women. Moreover, his "compliment" to Jack is merely a reinforcement of the black rapist stereotypes, but in this case all black men are Casanovas. The only thing he knows that Jack and Ivy have in common is their color and he believes that is enough for them. Returning to the "one of the family" idea, while Tim wants to see Ivy date, his motives in selecting Jack, whom he calls a "good-looking no-good-nik," are dishonest—he believes Jack's shady business will prevent Jack and Ivy from becoming serious—and his selection criteria is solely race; he did not consider social factors such as education, class, or income and whether Ivy and Jack have any of these elements in common. Yet, he would be cognizant of these issues if he were setting up his sister on a date.

The final well-meaning but off-base member of the Austin family attempting to keep Ivy from leaving their employment is daughter Gena. She informs her brother Tim of Ivy's resignation and colludes with him on the dating scheme. She is against Tim using blackmail to achieve their goal and naively believes that through persuasion Jack can be convinced to date Ivy. Her awkward first encounter with Jack demonstrates her similarity to her mother and brother—they all believe that what they say to either Ivy or Jack should be followed, which is because they are oblivious to their white privilege and the expectations it places on those who are not European American. Gena brings Ivy to the store, as she and Tim had planned. The foursome encounter one another in the Austin's department store immediately after Tim and Jack's meeting.

Aspects of this first meeting for Jack and Ivy are awkward; the addition of their matchmakers only heightens the discomfort. Ivy is unaware of Gena and Tim's machinations, and their actions reveal that they don't really know her. When Gena tries to innocently explain that she brought Ivy to the store to look for shoes, Ivy challenges this comment because she wants to make a good impression on Jack. During the introductions, Gena makes another false claim, that she told Ivy about Jack and his trucking business. Ivy's response and facial expressions demonstrate that this is the first time she has ever heard of Mr. Parks. She also reiterates that she does not need shoes. In an attempt to keep Jack from leaving, Tim tries to suggest they all have lunch, but Ivy reminds Gena that she just fed her charge. Gena counters by inviting Jack to dinner and again this conversation falters. A dinner of pot roast had been planned for Tim but Jack balks at this choice. Tim suggests another meal option and Gena, who was going out for the evening, volunteers to help Ivy with the meal. Jack begrudgingly accepts the invitation and playfully threatens Tim afterward.

Throughout this antithesis of a meet cute, a romantic comedy term used to describe the often serendipitous meeting of a future couple, Tim and Gena add a tense dimension because of their positions as blackmailer and employer. While Ivy does seem interested in Jack, she clearly does not appreciate the chicanery that brings them together and she does not know about Tim's blackmail scheme. Jack is clearly annoyed and resentful of Tim forcing him into this situation. Yet, he is a gentleman, as many Poitier characters are, and he puts on a civil front for both Ivy and Gena. Tim and Gena are variables that bring an element of doubt to Jack and Ivy's relationship.

Though Ivy appears attracted to Jack, he is not interested in having a relationship, and the reality of his coercion adds an aspect of insincerity to any interaction between the two. This deception hovers over Ivy and Jack and could be loosely linked to the idea of masquerade or deception found in romantic comedies.

A character presenting him- or herself as someone he or she is not is a popular plot in many romantic comedies and can involve one or both partners. These deception scenarios became prevalent during the sex comedy cycle and, as McDonald posits, later were incorporated into the larger romantic comedy genre, with male characters typically perpetuating the fraud. Frank Krutnik observes that in the 1990s female protagonists like Lucy in *While You Were Sleeping* (1995), Abby from *The Truth about Cats and Dogs* (1996), and Gwen from *Housesitter* (1992) deceive their potential mates (Krutnik 2002, 135; Lent 1995, 322–23). Though Jack is not paid, he is blackmailed, and his situation is similar to that of the male suitors in films such as *Deliver Us from Eva* (2003) and *10 Things I Hate About You* (1999), who are paid to date the female protagonist. Typically in these narratives the deceiver needs to go through a maturation process and realize that serial monogamy is not the best choice.

Tim and Gena complicate Jack's deception because of their ulterior motives. If their desire to see Ivy in a relationship with a good man was sincere, their actions could be viewed as similar to those of children who try to set up their parents in romantic comedies like *The Courtship of Eddie's Father* (1963), *Sleepless in Seattle* (1993), and *One Fine Day* (1996) (Gehring 2002, 84–85). However, Gena and Tim do not want Ivy to leave their employment and set her up with a man Tim believes is not the marrying kind. Here their insincerity shows their selfishness and inability to see Ivy as a human being and peer. Thus for all their posturing as being Ivy's friend or regarding her as one of the family, their actions are similar to those of their mother and indicate that their need for Ivy as their maid far outweighs Ivy's agency.

Clearly this layered deception will have to be exposed if Ivy and Jack are to have a legitimate relationship, but this does not happen during their second interaction at dinner that evening. Again Gena and Tim's presence stunts Jack and Ivy's interaction because of the false pretenses that bring

Jack and Ivy together. He thinks he's going to the Austins' home to discuss business with their parents and she thinks he's a client that Tim needs to impress. Since Tim is blackmailing Jack, the latter does not appear shocked that Mr. and Mrs. Austin are not present at this dinner. However, the lies Tim and Gena have told Ivy make their dating plot harder to maneuver around. They quickly realize that Ivy will not break out of her role as maid without significant coaxing from them. Hence, they temporarily take over Ivy's usual function and encourage her to sit down with Jack.

Once the foursome is seated, Gena tries to encourage conversation. Her attempt to foster verbal exchange humorously exposes an important problem with their matchmaking scheme: she and Tim brought Ivy and Jack together because they are the only black people they know. Though they imagine they are knowledgeable about the world, they don't know a great deal about African American people. Their familiarity with black people and culture is limited to current events of the day, including the Black Power movement, civil rights rallies, and Ralph Bunche. Hit with the realities of Gena and Tim's ignorance, an embarrassed Ivy politely excuses herself to check on dinner. When Gena joins her, Ivy reprimands the former for thinking that African Americans only talk about black issues as well as for the fact that the two forced her to sit with Jack. Gena tries to change Ivy's focus by confirming that Jack likes her. Ivy does not fall for this distraction but agrees to help Tim by serving the meal.

The next scene depicts Jack and Ivy eating with Tim and Gena serving. It seems Tim and Gena have orchestrated the situation in their favor, which gives Jack and Ivy a moment to interact with one another without their "chaperones." Ivy and Jack's initial exchange gives viewers an inkling that the couple might actually be compatible. When he asks why she wants to leave, her honesty and straightforwardness are refreshing changes from his dealings with Tim. Ivy voices that her job with the Austins is too comfortable and she wants to enrich her life so it won't end with her being uneducated or alone. As she is articulating her desire for self-improvement and fulfillment, she elaborates her feelings in ways the viewer has not observed to this point. In her earlier conversation with Doris, the latter could not comprehend Ivy's dreams and desires. Jack, on the other hand, understands Ivy's dissatisfaction.

Another moment that shows the potential that Ivy and Jack may have together is when they are discussing where they are from. Ivy mentions she's from Florida and observes Jack is from the West Indies. This statement elicits a laugh from Jack, and it's the first time in the film the audience sees him letting his guard down and relaxing with Ivy. To this point in the film, Jack's smile has been formal and courteous and not spontaneous, as was his laughter. He responds by asking her if she can detect his accent; she relays that, to some degree, she can. Though this exchange is interrupted when Tim and Gena return, it reveals the possibility that Jack and Ivy can play or have fun together, which is a significant marker for couples in romantic comedies (Neale 1992, 291; Krutnik 1990, 65).

His jovial exchange with Ivy leads Jack to "play" with Tim and Gena. However, unlike in his interaction with Ivy, Jack intends to frighten the two meddlers. They have recently coerced Jack into another date with Ivy, so once she leaves the table, he begins to manipulate them. His motivation could also be read as anger at their continuous manipulation of both he and Ivy. After laughing with them about the next forced date, he then suggests that the four of them really swing—he'll take Gena and Tim can have Ivy. He implies that his aspirin are drugs; they should all get very high and have an orgy. Throughout this conversation, whenever Tim or Gena attempt to rebuff his statements, he counters and continues to say things to unnerve the two busybodies. This particular scene should also be understood with reference to the criticism about earlier Poitier characters. While Jack is being blackmailed, he is not being compliant. He is fully aware of the impression he is making on Tim and Gena with his references to drugs and sex and continues to make them regret that they have embroiled him in this situation. It is also a demonstration of his anger in a way consistent with Jack, and by extension Poitier. He may not ever be a Black Panther, but he menaces Gena and Tim in ways that recall notions of scary African American men. Hence, by the time his car comes for him, the siblings jump to hurry him out of their house because they are so anxious that he leave.

In spite of Jack creating this ominous air, the audience also learns that Jack is concerned about engaging in this "game" of romancing Ivy. When he and Tim are left alone, Tim tries to gauge whether Jack likes Ivy. Jack states that she is not his type because she is the type of woman you marry. Though it is clear neither Jack nor Tim want marriage as an outcome, Jack broaching the topic is reminiscent of the playboy sex comedy hero who wants to avoid marriage at all costs (McDonald 2007, 38–54; Mortimer 2010, 49–53). His reluctance to manipulate Ivy exposes his desire not to harm her or get involved with someone who may cause him to rethink his life, specifically marriage. His ability to have fun with her even while being forced to be there makes her a liability and yet Jack seems enticed by the danger she represents. Therefore, in spite of his statements to the contrary, Jack is attracted to Ivy and fearful this attraction could lead to matrimony. Moreover, he does invite her to dinner at his favorite restaurant, and this will be their first real date.

First Date

IVY AND JACK'S FIRST real date marks a transition in the narrative because it is the first time the audience encounters Ivy alone and outside of the Austin home. The audience walks with her as she goes to meet Jack at a Japanese restaurant in New York City. This is Ivy's first time eating Japanese food or engaging with Japanese culture. As she walks to the room where she and Jack will dine, she takes everything in with curiosity. When she finally meets Jack, she notes the place is "wild."

This scene also stands out because two African Americans are in a setting and circumstance that are not common. In the past, black characters usually stayed in all-black environments or were portrayed working for European Americans. Their date breaks the black/white binary while simultaneously showing African Americans as partakers in other cultures outside of the binary as well as being similar to people of other races and ethnicities who eat ethnic foods. While consumption of others' cultures does not necessarily demonstrate racial unity or transgression of racial norms, it exposes a dimensionality to the protagonists. Ivy desires to learn more about new and different things, and her date becomes an opportunity to expand her horizons. The audience finds out Jack's exposure to Japanese food and his knowledge of the language is the result of his service in the Army. Hence, this date, while mundane in terms of romantic comedy as well as other genres that contain romantic genre conventions, is anything but

Jack (Sidney Poitier) makes his biggest gamble and introduces Ivy (Abbey Lincoln) to Japanese cuisine in *For Love of Ivy*.

typical because of the humanity Ivy and Jack can exhibit that had not been given to black characters prior to this film.

During their date, the protagonists continue being frank with one another. Jack addresses the waitress in Japanese, and Ivy asks if the servers speak English. He responds that they do but he wants speak Japanese. Though he remarks that he's trying to be pretentious, she states that if you know a foreign language you should use it as often as you can. She insightfully notes that his real pretense is acting like he has not worked for what he has, and he responds by letting her know he does not want marriage. In an interesting change from the attitudes of most romantic comedy female heroines, Ivy declares that she does not want to be married either, but Jack doubts this. She assures him she wants to be free to date, even if that one date does not lead to anything more. When she tells him she went out with him knowing there would be nothing more but she would have an interesting evening, her statement moves him. Though her revelation could be read as a ploy for sympathy, it can also be understood as showing Jack how desperately Ivy wants to enrich and change her life.

Since Ivy thinks this date is an obligation Jack has to improve his standing with the Austins, she reminds Jack during the meal that he does not have to be taking her out on a date. She expects that their evening will be over after dinner, but Jack then takes her to a club. Continuing their intercultural experience, Jack takes Ivy to a hippie club with performance artists. Most of those at the club are European American, and, like the restaurant, this club is not the expected place Jack would take Ivy. Many audience members would have thought Ivy and Jack would go to a club with jazz music with most if not all of the clientele being African American. Though Jack's choices in entertainment may be out of the ordinary, Ivy appears to enjoy these "wild" experiences. She considers them part of learning and experiencing new things. Their dinner and dancing gives audiences, particularly those of European descent, an expanded view of the recreational activities in which African Americans participate. And though some critics could view their date as pure fantasy or completely unrealistic, Ivy and Jack's date as a multicultural experience takes the focus off of them being an African American couple. They are getting to know one another like other romantic comedy couples do, and this makes their story universal.

Second Date

AFTER A VISIT TO Jack's illegal second job, Ivy and Jack return to his place. Initially it appears that his plan is to have sex with her, and she is a bit nervous. The two play an interesting game of cat and mouse, with Ivy asking various questions about his apartment and business in an effort to postpone him finally kissing her. Once they have kissed, however, it seems to transform each of them. Jack realizes he does not want to continue his seduction, while Ivy clearly is desirous of a sexual encounter. Again, *Ivy* does not conform to romantic comedy expectations. This is Ivy and Jack's second date and they are still getting to know one another. Both have had bad relationships: he is divorced and she has not been able to find a steady boyfriend. Neither of the two has mentioned a desire to fall in love, and neither want to consider marriage at this point in their lives. These aspects of the film make it more akin to the nervous romances of the late 1970s. In addition to the potential of their relationship being of a short duration, Ivy is not the typical sex comedy heroine striving to retain her virtue until she is married. She is perfectly content to have sexual pleasure with Jack without the commitment

Jack falls in love with Ivy and offers a warm caress.

of marriage, a fact that characterized many female protagonists of nervous romances.

Though Ivy's sexual agency can be read as progressive within the context of romantic comedies, her black body can complicate this reading. Since African American women have historically been understood as being hypersexual, her acceptance of sex without marriage could be viewed as being consistent with the sexually aggressive black female stereotype. However, I argue that to read Ivy in this way discounts all the other elements of her character up to this point in the film in ways similar to how critics of Poitier have continuously read his characters as compromised. Ivy dresses conservatively and has not been the aggressor in the relationship. Moreover, her desire to improve herself through education demarcates her middle-class aspirations. Finally, the producers appear to want audiences to understand Ivy and Jack as regular (read white) people that have the same fears and desires as anyone else.

Returning to their intimate moment, though Jack tries to rebuff Ivy's advances by taking her home, it appears his passion overwhelms him (and her) as they kiss good-bye. The screen fades from the kiss to Jack's piranha. The camera then shifts to Ivy walking around the spacious apartment in

Jack's robe and smiling. Her smile and his robe are signals Ivy and Jack have had sex, and this is an unexpected surprise. It's also a deviation from most romantic comedies of this era because the lead couple has sex. Their intimacy comes as a pleasant and unforeseen situation and an enjoyable experience for each. Furthermore, the sexual aspect of their relationship makes the film a more realistic portrayal of adult relationships at this time. The choice to have Ivy and Jack interact in this manner not only builds upon Jack's character not being perfect, it also addresses the lack of realism in his films, a charge often leveled at Poitier as well as the romantic comedy genre.

Once Jack wakes up, the two continue to flirt and play. This is the most relaxed we've seen either of them, and their playful banter encourages the audience to hope for their union to become more permanent. Initially it seems as if that will happen, but true to romantic comedy conceits, Jack's deception must be revealed. Ivy returns to the Austins to get her things and Jack sends his limousine to wait for her, as he has to work. The family is in disarray because Doris is trying to fix dinner and handle the other household duties. Doris pretends to be happy for Ivy but her frazzled emotions due to her inability (or lack of desire) to maintain her home demonstrate something is amiss. She feels the dinner she is fixing is a disaster, and upon learning that Ivy has another date with Jack, Doris reveals the deception of her children and Jack. Though it is not surprising that Doris is the culprit, the timing of her revelation simply demonstrates her ultimate goal of keeping Ivy as her maid as well as her vindictiveness.

Jack learns from his driver that Ivy terminated their relationship, and he goes to the Austins' home. His presence in this "family" argument is complicated because he is literally chasing Ivy around the house as the family members follow, which is reminiscent of the farcical car chase sequence at the close of the sex comedy *Sex and the Single Girl* (1964). However, the farcical elements are undercut by Frank Austin. Once Jack arrives, Frank keeps stating that he will call the police because Jack is trespassing. His threats could be menacing, but throughout the film Frank has been excluded from the family's machinations, making him similar to many situation comedy fathers: he is the last to know what is going on in his home. He and Ivy learn about the dating hoax simultaneously, and he is very sympathetic to Ivy's

Jack asks Frank and Doris Austin (Carroll O'Connor and Nan Martin) to bid farewell to Ivy because he wishes to marry her.

anger. His "firing" of his family for their actions is an attempt to sustain a type of solidarity with Ivy. From the first time Ivy put the family on notice, Frank understood her need to leave and that the family would have to get a new maid. While his family read his reaction as pragmatic and cold, his viewpoint, whatever the motives, was respectful of Ivy's wishes. Frank can be considerate of Ivy because, unlike the rest of his family, he holds no illusions about her being the maid. His fondness for her does not blind him to the reality of their relationship.

The final scenes of the film continue and complete Jack's maturation process. This is consistent with other romantic comedy males, who must realize and correct their behaviors that are not conducive to a long-term commitment. In addition to confessing his fondness for Ivy, he tells the Austins that they need to come to grips with Ivy's departure. Furthermore, because he deceived Ivy, he does most of the talking during their reconciliation. His final actions are to take control of the legitimate part of the trucking business and take Ivy to New York. Though this type of narrative is out of the ordinary for most romantic comedies from the 1930s to the 1960s that typically center on both the male and female characters, this is another instance where *Ivy* is a precursor to nervous romances and their male protagonist focus. Poitier is the biggest star in the film, and *Ivy* is clearly his vehicle.

Though overlooked as part of Poitier's oeuvre and as a romantic comedy, *For Love of Ivy* is an important film to both categories. *Ivy* can be read as an answer to Poitier's critics who believed he had sold his soul for celebrity. The fact that Poitier wrote the story and that it portrays an African American romance that concludes with marriage means that the film presents an alternative to the "revolutionary" black films of the 1970s. The film celebrates black masculinity and black female self-determination. As a romantic comedy, the film examines issues and situations that would not be explored in other films for almost another ten years. Hence the fact that it is ignored, as most black romantic comedies are in genre studies, exposes the problem of situating films with African American protagonists as black films and not genre films. The film is not just the first African American romantic comedy, it is a forerunner to one of the more acclaimed eras of rom-com films, the nervous romance.

Notes

1. The Production Code started to weaken in the 1950s with films like *The Moon Is Blue* (1953) and continued to lose its control over film content until the ratings systems replaced it.

References

Bogle, Donald. 2001. *Toms, Coons, Mulattoes, Mammies & Bucks: An Interpretive History of Blacks in American Films.* New York: Continuum.

Ebert, Roger. 1968. "For Love of Ivy." Review of *For Love of Ivy. Chicago Sun-Times*, July 26, 1968.

Gehring, Wes. 2002. *Romantic vs. Screwball Comedy: Charting the Difference.* New York: Scarecrow Press.

Grindon, Leger. 2011. *The Hollywood Romantic Comedy.* Malden, MA: Wiley-Blackwell.

Krutnik, Frank. 1990. "The Faint Aroma of Performing Seals: The 'Nervous' Romance and the Comedy of the Sexes," *The Velvet Light Trap* 26 (Fall): 57–72.

Krutnik, Frank. 2002. "Conforming Passions?: Contemporary Romantic Comedy." In *Genre and Contemporary Hollywood*, edited by Steve Neale, 130–47. London: BFI.

Lent, Tina Olsin. 1995. "Romantic Love and Friendship: The Redefinition of Gender Relations in Screwball Comedy." In *Classical Hollywood Comedy*, edited by Kristine Brunovska Karnick and Henry Jenkins, 315–31. New York: Routledge.

Mason, Clifford. 1967. "Why Does White America Love Sidney Poitier So?" *New York Times*, September 10, 1967.

McDonald, Tamar Jeffers. 2007. *Romantic Comedy: Boy Meets Girl Meets Genre*. London: Wallflower Press.

Mortimer, Claire. 2010. *Romantic Comedy*. London: Routledge.

Neale, Steve. 1992. "The *Big* Romance or *Something Wild*?: Romantic Comedy Today." *Screen* 33, no. 3 (Autumn).

II

THE BLAXPLOITATION
FILM AND PASTICHE

4

BLAXPLOITATION FILM

Gerald R. Butters Jr.

BLAXPLOITATION IS THE TERM used to describe a cycle of black films made specifically for African American audiences in the mainstream and independent sectors of the US film industry in the period from 1970 to 1976. Julius Griffin, president of the Beverly Hills-Hollywood chapter of the NAACP, is often attributed with coining the word in 1972. The descriptor "Blaxploitation," as related to this body of films, is contentious because it was originally designated to denigrate these films, with the assumption being that African American audiences were being exploited; it is reductionist because it fails to assign individual films to their respective genres; and it is amorphous because the films that "belong" to this cycle often differ, based upon who is doing the defining (Lawrence 2008, 20). Stephanie Dunn has argued that "Blaxploitation has long been a contested label, raising questions about how it denotes exploitation, who and what is being exploited, who gets to name the genre as such, and whether it is an adequate or appropriate label for this body of films. (2008, 46) Amy Obugo Ongiri has argued that the "the films that fall within the genre category of Blaxploitation are in some senses as varied and uneven as the conditions of their production." (2010, 159–60) Some films that garnered the Blaxploitation label were major productions that had the marketing power of the Hollywood studios behind them, while others filmed were by fly-by-night production companies that struggled to find theaters to exhibit them. Between 1970 and 1976, African American actors, writers, and directors were employed in record numbers in the film industry. Yet the concept of blacks being "exploited" remains one of the root concepts of the genre. In the past two decades, the term has taken on a less negative meaning and has come to represent the more than two hundred films that are often attributed to this genre and the era in which these films were produced.

Scholars have argued that a number of social, economic, and institutional factors created the environment in which the Blaxploitation genre could develop. The first condition was the dismal economic state of the American film industry by the late 1960s. Studios had witnessed the loss of two-thirds of their audience since 1946, and this precipitous decline was often blamed on television. Box office revenue continued to plummet throughout the 1960s, and a number of major studios were on the brink of bankruptcy. (Onigiri, 279) The industry turned to a number of niche genre cycles—beach party, biker, and soft-core porn—in order to cash in on the youth market and to bring audience members back into theaters. Industry heads simultaneously became interested in the box office potential of African American audiences, who made up as much as 40 percent of the box office in some urban locations. Industry leaders recognized that there was an untapped audience who desired more black-themed motion pictures.

The second factor was the rapidly changing dynamic of racial politics due to the civil rights movement. Between 1965 and 1968, the United States had witnessed four summers of racial riots and four prominent political assassinations, including those of Malcolm X and Martin Luther King Jr. The nonviolent direct action techniques of King and the Southern Christian Leadership Conference (SCLC) were falling out of fashion within the African American community and were being replaced with Black Power. In 1968, Charles S. Hamilton, an advocate of Black Power, claimed that the movement was "concerned with organizing the rage of black people" (1969, 181). Black Power and its attributes of Black Pride, meeting violence with violence, and economic and political Black Nationalism, embodied in organizations such as the Black Panthers, were gaining increased appeal within some sections of the African American community. As racial politics made dramatic shifts, the entertainment field was bound to be impacted. Hollywood increasingly began to take chances with African American directors and actors. Gordon Parks Sr. (*The Learning Tree*, 1969) and Melvin Van Peebles (*Watermelon Man*, 1970) both directed major Hollywood releases, and films such as *Uptight* (1968), *Slaves* (1969), . . . *tick* . . . *tick* . . . *tick* (1970), and *The Liberation of L. B. Jones* (1970) featured prominent African American actors. The studios' hiring of African American talent indicated change, but Hollywood had not yet figured out how to financially capitalize on the potential black market.

The film credited with firmly establishing the box office clout of the African American community was *Cotton Goes to Harlem* (1970). *Cotton* illustrated that black-themed pictures did not have to merely be a weekend phenomenon but that they could have "staying" power and play in theaters for weeks, if not months. *Cotton Goes to Harlem* was adapted from the popular comedy-adventure novel by black author Chester Himes and was directed by black actor Ossie Davis. The advertising team for *Cotton* made a concerted effort to demonstrate the African American origins of the film and to appeal to Black Pride with its location and stars. The film centered on the antics of Coffin Ed Johnson and Grave Digger Jones. Ed Guerrero has argued that *Cotton* had a real influence on the Blaxploitation genre with protagonists operating on the periphery of the law and that the film "influenced the pacing and the formal visual-musical elements that would go into the construction of the crime-action-ghetto Blaxploitation features to follow" (1993, 81). *Cotton*'s urban setting, predominantly black cast, and iconography established an important precedent for the Blaxploitation genre.

Cotton Goes to Harlem was a unique Hollywood product, in that it addressed social, political, and economic issues that were connected to past and present contemporary black life. "Cotton" in the title referred to a staple crop that was inextricably linked to black southern life. A Back-to-Africa movement, which makes up part of the narrative, is modeled after the career of Marcus Garvey. The soundtrack of the film included a number of popular musicians of the day performing classic gospel and rhythm and blues numbers of the early twentieth century. *Cotton* used motifs of the past and present to connect to a contemporary audience successfully in a way that had eluded previous black-themed films.

While many of the black-themed films of the 1960s had less-than-stellar box office, *Cotton* bucked this trend, making over $8,000,000 in rentals. In its seventh week of release, the film was the number two box office draw in the United States. Film historian Christopher Sieving argues that the failure of 1960s black-themed motion pictures was their art house pedigree and the fact that they failed to have African Americans in top creative positions. *Cotton* was designed as a commercial product, a crime thriller with comic overtones about the exploits of two Harlem detectives. The film also had black creative talent behind the production that audiences fully recognized (2011, 203). Yvonne D. Sims claims, "on many levels, the movie was unprecedented" (2006, 130). As a result of the success of *Cotton Goes to Harlem*, Hollywood looked to make more money from its newly "discovered" audience.

Sweet Sweetback's Baadasssss Song (1971) is universally recognized as the germinal film in the Blaxploitation genre. The film was written, directed, produced, scored, and edited by and also starred Melvin Van Peebles. Van Peebles was denied entry into film directing through the Hollywood system, so he made his debut film in France. This film, *The Story of a Three Day Pass* (1967), garnered positive critical attention, and Hollywood took notice. Columbia Pictures signed him to a three-picture deal and his first studio project was *Watermelon Man* (1970). The film challenged racism in the United States but the film was clearly designed as a comedy. Increasingly politicized by rapidly changing conditions in the United States, the director decided that he wanted his next motion picture to make a serious revolutionary statement (Lawrence 2008, 41).

Sweet Sweetback begins by depicting a young African American boy (Mario Van Peebles) living in a brothel in Los Angeles in the 1940s. The film then cuts to the boy as an adult (Melvin Van Peebles) running beneath a city bridge. As an adult, Sweetback works as a sex performer in a theater/brothel, entertaining customers with his physical "gifts." The importance of black sexual identity is reinforced in this opening sequence. The sex performance, though, is aimed to be decadent but not erotic, as demonstrated by Sweetback's total lack of emotion. During one performance, a team of LAPD officers come to the show and inform Sweetback's boss, Beetle (Simon Chuckster), that a black man has been murdered and that there is pressure from the black community to bring a suspect to justice. The police arrest Sweetback and blame him for the murder, yet plan to release him in a few days due to a lack of evidence. All of this is designed to placate the African

American community. As the police drive Sweetback to their station, they receive a report of a public disturbance over the car transmitter from a dispatcher. The "disturbance" is a black political rally. The police attempt to break up the rally and disperse the crowd. Chants of "Black Power" and commotion are heard off camera as the focus is placed upon Sweetback's face and his reaction (or lack thereof) to the rally. The police arrest one of the young black political leaders, Mu (Hubert Scales), and handcuff him to Sweetback. When Mu Mu insults the officers on the way to the station, they stop the car in an undisclosed location and begin beating him. Sweetback, meanwhile, who has remained apolitical and unemotional to this point in the film, apparently becomes stirred, saves Mu Mu from the assault, and releases him from the handcuffs, allowing him to escape. Mu Mu is clearly emblematic of the Black Nationalist approach to race relations. Sweetback, who has never met Mu Mu before this encounter in the police car, is moved into action in order to save his black brother, and thus, the revolutionary ideology of the narrative with its exposure of a corrupt law enforcement system is made personal. Sweetback actually beats the officers with the handcuffs that had imprisoned him, emblematic of hundreds of years of slavery and subhuman status.

The bulk of the film chronicles Sweetback's escape and flight from Los Angeles to the United States-Mexico border. The sequence of Sweetback's escape as filmed by Van Peebles is in cinema verité style, and he uses a number of late-1960s psychedelic motifs to illustrate this. A black anti-hero, Sweetback does what is necessary to survive, including sexually performing with a motorcycle moll, stabbing a police officer with a pool cue, and, while in the desert, drinking his own urine and biting the head off a lizard. Sweetback finally makes it across the border, with police dogs chasing him to the end. A final title warns, "A Baad Asssss Nigger is coming to collect some dues. . . ."

Van Peebles argued, "I wanted a victorious film. A film where niggers could walk out standing tall instead of avoiding each other's eyes, looking once again like they'd had it" (Lawrence 2008, 41). He produced his film outside the studio system so that he would not have to compromise the revolutionary tone of the film. He worked with a nonunion crew and received money from black entertainment figures such as Bill Cosby in order to complete the film. Van Peebles refused to submit *Sweetback* to the Motion Picture Association of America, so it automatically received an X rating. The director then used this decision as a marketing tool by using the advertising tagline "Rated X by an all-white jury."

Sweetback was released on April 23, 1971, at two theaters in Detroit and Atlanta. The film was an immediate success, drawing in overflow crowds, and was soon distributed nationally. It broke records at a number of urban theaters. *Sweet Sweetback* gave African Americans a unique experience—one that was both communal and personal at the same time. Crowds cheered on *Sweetback* to victory and booed the cops. *Sweetback* also set off a wave of controversy because of its violence, raw sexuality, and political rhetoric. The film almost immediately became one of the most controversial and talked about African American films of all time.

One of the most noted characteristics of *Sweetback* was that the protagonist—a sex performer, criminal, and escapee—emerged victorious at the end. The film was embraced by many in the Black Power movement and became required viewing for members of the Black Panther Party. Huey P. Newton devoted an entire issue of *The Black Panther* to the film and declared that Sweetback was "the first truly revolutionary Black film made." Sam Worthington, black critic for the *Chicago Sun-Times*, claimed, "for the first time in cinematic history in America, a movie speaks out of an undeniable black consciousness" (Bennett 1971, 112).

The reaction from critics, political and religious leaders, and the moviegoing public was far from positive, though. The Kuumba Workshop, a Chicago Black Arts organization, condemned the film. The board of directors for Kuumba included historian Lerone Bennett Jr., poet Gwendolyn Brooks, and editor and theoretician of the Black Arts Movement Hoyt Fuller. Kuumba immediately began picketing theaters that showed *Sweetback* and drafted a sophisticated position paper condemning the film. Throughout the summer of 1971, the heated discussion over *Sweetback* continued unabated, culminating in a groundbreaking article by Lerone Bennett Jr. in *Ebony* entitled "The Emancipation Orgasm." Bennett elevated the discussion to a national platform. He argued that "the reasons for the movie's appeal, apart from the sex and violence . . . was that it shows a black man thumbing his nose at society and getting away with it." He argued, though, that *Sweetback* was "a trivial and tasteless negative classic" and that it was "neither revolutionary nor black." In his strongest statement against the film, Bennett argued, "nobody ever fucked his way to freedom" (112, 118).

The success of *Cotton Goes to Harlem* and *Sweet Sweetback* demonstrated to Hollywood that African American audiences would patronize black-themed motion pictures. *Sweetback* also illustrated to independent producers that a minimal amount of money in production costs could reap huge financial rewards, thus leading to dozens of creative teams eager to capitalize on the success of these two films.

Shaft further demonstrated that a new cinematic era had begun. A release from Hollywood stalwart MGM, the film opened to the public in July 1971, two months following the release of *Sweet Sweetback*. The film was a huge hit and confirmed that black-themed motion pictures could be enormously successful. The film's title character is John Shaft (Richard Roundtree), a New York City private detective who successfully traverses the worlds of Harlem, midtown New York, and Greenwich Village. Shaft works effectively in both black- and white- dominated worlds, using his cool masculinity and assertiveness to fight against organized crime and sexually attract women of all races (and one man). Shaft is able to negotiate with shady racketeers, black revolutionaries, and the police department but remain his own man.

The film's black credibility was satisfied by the fact that not only the major characters were African American but the director (Gordon Parks Sr.) and composer (Isaac Hayes) were also black. The source material for the film was Ernest Tidyman's 1970 novel of the same name. The film was one of the most profitable that year for MGM, grossing $13,000,000 on a $500,000 budget. Several factors contributed to the film's remarkable success. First, the star power of Roundtree was undeniable. He fully embodied the no-nonsense private detective, and his popularity was such that his wardrobe of turtleneck sweaters and leather coats set off a fashion revolution in the African American community. Second, Parks's direction and his ability to capture the gritty realism of early-1970s New York City made the film appear current and relevant. Third, Isaac Hayes's song "Theme from Shaft" and the soundtrack to the motion picture were enormously popular and critically well received, culminating in Hayes winning the Academy Award. The rhythm of the theme dovetailed brilliantly with Shaft's swaggering walk through the mean streets of New York City. Within the first sung lyric of the opening title, Hayes identifies Shaft's personae—"Who's the black private dick that's a sex machine to all the chicks?" Shaft is black, he's a sex machine, and the use of the word *dick* as it relates to Shaft doubles the phallic nature of the protagonist. The film sold the soundtrack and the soundtrack sold the film, demonstrating to a generation of filmmakers the impact that music could have on the box office potential of a motion picture. Fourth, *Shaft* continued the narrative resolution of *Sweetback,* in that a powerful black man wins in the end. He was a character that could easily be cheered on by urban audiences. Finally, even though 70 to 80 percent of *Shaft*'s audience was African American, the film demonstrated that some white people would be willing to see a motion picture in which the majority of the characters were black and one in which a black man could be victorious. The success of *Shaft* led to two sequels.

The "Blaxploitation" genre exploded in 1971 and demonstrated the box office potential of the African American community. While *Sweet Sweetback* and *Shaft* dominated the genre in terms of sheer dollars, a plethora of other films emerged that year in which the majority of the characters in the film were African American. There are differences between a Blaxploitation film and a black-themed film. While Blaxploitation films were, by their nature, black-themed, not all black-themed motion pictures of the period 1970 to 1976 were Blaxploitation. A number of motifs and plot devices have been used in order to attempt to categorize the genre. These include the presence of a black hero or heroine (or antihero); organized crime; black revolution-aries or radicals; prostitutes and their pimps; the drug dealers, the drug trade, and addiction; violence in the form of fist fights, gunplay, and revenge killing; car chases and stolen cars; explosions; the use of racial slurs; and the latest, most current, and trendiest fashions. Not all Blaxploitation films nec-essarily had all of these characteristics but if a film embodied three or four of them then it was usually placed in this genre. A black-themed film (*The Great White Hope*, 1970; *Lady Sings the Blues*, 1972; *Sounder*, 1972) revolved around an African American protagonist but did not have the tropes of a Blaxploitation feature.

In 1972, Blaxploitation and black-themed films flooded the market and demonstrated the continued profitability of the genre. Clearly, the Blaxploitation film event of the year in terms of critical attention and box office revenue was the release of *Superfly* in the summer. *Superfly*, like *Shaft*, was a technically polished film that was produced and distributed by a major studio, Warner Brothers. *Superfly* also solidified both *Sweetback*'s and *Shaft*'s plot strategy of black triumph. Like *Shaft*, the film deemphasized the role of Black Power revolutionary thought and even castigated a group of Black Panther–like radicals. The film was directed by Gordon Parks Jr. with a landmark soundtrack by Curtis Mayfield. The film exemplified the commercialization of the new trope of black heroics and celebrated the notion of "Black is Beautiful" through its black cultural aesthetics and its black personnel behind the camera.

Superfly's protagonist is Youngblood Priest (Ron O'Neal), a stylish and successful cocaine dealer who attempts to leave behind a life of crime. Priest finds that leaving "the life" is much more difficult than anticipated. Priest does not live like a petty dope dealer; he drives a fancy car, controls a contingent of street salesmen, and lives the comfortable life of a black bourgeoisie. Priest also realizes that there's no real future in dealing coke, and one day he makes a proposal to his partner, Eddie (Carl Lee), to take their $300,000 savings, buy thirty kilos of cocaine, and use their street team to move it out in four months, leaving them a million-dollar profit. This would allow them to exit the business for good. Eddie is wary but willing to go along, but Scatter (Julius Harris), a former dealer whom set Priest up in the cocaine trade, is both unwilling and unable to sell them that much product. As Priest looks for a new source for his big score, one of his street sellers, Fat Freddie (Charles McGregor), is picked up by the police and, under violent interrogation, tells the cops about Priest's underground empire. When the police confront Priest, however, he learns they're less interested in putting him behind bars than in making him a partner. *Superfly* ends with Priest outsmarting the white cops, making his score, and walking off free to begin life without having to deal drugs.

Sweetback began, and *Shaft* and *Superfly* codified, many of the key formal and thematic features that went on to embody the Blaxploitation genre. All three films were set in a gritty urban locale and included specific settings—churches, restaurants, bars—that were home to a working-class African American subculture. The representation of this black urban under-class and their culture—clothes, music, and language—helped to define the Blaxploitation genre. All three films contained black male heroes that fought against a white power system that included corrupt officials or law enforcement or an underworld crime syndicate.

Superfly was a major financial success, eventually earning over $10,000,000 in its theatrical run. Ron O'Neal as Youngblood Priest was a style-maker in the black community. Several of the major factors that made *Shaft* such a success bled into *Superfly*. The first was the title character as style icon. Richard Roundtree, as Shaft, brought turtleneck sweaters and black leather coats into style in 1971. Ron O'Neal had a similar impact. Black men began straightening their hair, and the crucifix/cocaine spoon that *Superfly* used in the film started to be replicated and sold in large urban areas. Second, both *Shaft* and *Superfly* had blistering soundtracks. While the theme from *Shaft* won Isaac Hayes an Academy Award, Curtis Mayfield's score for *Superfly* in some ways eclipsed the film and would go on to be one of the most respected movie soundtracks of the 1970s. Third, *Superfly* had an intriguing political message in which Priest ridicules both the white establishment—in a legal and illegal fashion—and black radical activists.

Superfly also seemed to be the catalyst for a significant backlash against the explosion of black-themed films. Former NAACP official Julius Griffin argued, "*Superfly* glorifies the use of cocaine, casts doubt upon the capability of law enforcement and casts blacks in roles which glorify dope pushing, pimping and grand theft." He continued, "In short, the film makes no pre-tense in being either socially relevant or merely artistically entertaining. It is an insidious film which portrays the black community at its worst" (Culbert 1972, 5). A national debate erupted within the black community in 1972 over so-called Blaxploitation movies. The Kuumba workshop for black artists also joined the fray in a politically concerted way. In June 1972, Kuumba printed a position paper entitled "'Superfly': A Political and Cultural Condemnation."

The divide within the African American community was split along several different lines. One was clearly generational. In Los Angeles, activists formed the Coalition Against Blaxploitation. CAB was formed by local civil rights organizations such as the NAACP, the SCLC, and CORE. Conrad Smith, leader of the Los Angeles branch of CORE, said, "We're prepared to go all the way with this, even to the extent of running people out of the theaters. We're definitely going to see that this thing comes to an end." But as one *Newsweek* reporter claimed, "the group is known to have objections to practically every successful black film made in the past two years" ("Blacks v. Shaft" 1972, 88). This fault line could also be divided between lines of activists who were concerned about African American cinematic imagery and those who simply wanted black faces on the screen. Ron O'Neal, star of *Superfly*, said, "They're saying that they know better than the black people themselves what they should look at, that they're going to be the moral interpreters for the destiny of black people. I'm so tired of handkerchief-head Negroes moralizing on the poor black man" ("Blacks v. Shaft" 1972, 88). The third line could be drawn between those who were active in the new boom of black filmmaking, gaining star recognition and making profits off the films, and those who criticized them for it. The highly charged and divided response to *Superfly* confirms Jacqueline Stewart's claim that black filmgoers were members of "a variously constituted group that can mediate engagements with the text and/or exert pressures on individual viewers to perform in particular ways" (2005, 100). *Superfly* was a cultural phenomenon, though, and studios and independent producers attempted to capitalize on the film's success by creating films that chronicled the exploits of black gangsters.

The Mack (1973) confirmed the potential "danger" of the recent cycle of Blaxploitation films. The film revolves around Goldie, a former drug dealer recently released from prison, who becomes a big-time pimp. Numerous obstacles stand in his way in achieving his "goal," including Pretty Tony (another pimp), corrupt cops, a local crime boss, and his own Black Nationalist brother. The film starred Max Julien as Goldie and featured Richard Pryor. The most infamous scene in the film was the "Player's Ball," which featured actual pimps within the cast. This scene would be a cultural touchstone for the hip-hop generation.

A radically differing construction of black masculinity emerged within the Blaxploitation genre in comparison to previous cinematic renderings of black men. Images of black men in films such as *Sweet Sweetback*, *Superfly*, *The Mack*, or *Three the Hard Way* (1974) contrasted sharply with those in *Judge Priest* (1934), *Cabin in the Sky* (1943), or *Lilies of the Field* (1963). A very specifically limited masculine version of Black Power emerged within the genre. Critics often described it as the "Super Nigga" or "Superspade" formula. Masculine heroes within the genre were often outlaws, such as Youngblood Priest in *Super Fly*, the title character in *Willie Dynamite* (1974), and J. J. in *The Black Godfather* (1974). This "Superspade" type challenged paradigms of whiteness by tenaciously winning in the end.

Black male bodies were often on display within Blaxploitation, a trope that was considered "dangerous" for pre-1970 Hollywood. Many of the male stars of the genre were former or current professional athletes (Jim Kelly, Jim Brown, Fred Williamson), and their bodies were often half-naked both within the film and in its promotional advertising. There was a definite connection between this display of black male flesh and sexual prowess, which capitalized on centuries of racial sexual stereotyping. Keith M. Harris has argued, "the muscular, brute, athletic body was counter to the slim, clothed, middle-class body as the sexual to the asexual" (read Poitier) (Boys, Boyz, Bois, 67). The *New York Times* film critic Clayton Riley was one of the first prominent African Americans to publicly critique this new masculine image. In a 1971 article entitled "Shaft Can Do Everything—I Can Do Nothing" he argued that Blaxploitation films like *Shaft* were dangerous simplistic fantasies in which hypermasculine black men could use violence to triumph over the white man without any consideration of the institutional and social constructs that created such racism. While such films provided African American audiences a means for escape or a type of wish fulfillment, critics often argued about the dangers that such portrayals created, particularly if black male youth attempted to copy such behavior.

In many of the black action films of the genre, black women were depicted as sexualized girlfriends, prostitutes, or working-class tramps, leading to the development of a stereotype of black femininity. Black women's bodies were "on display," and their primary purpose was to illustrate the sexual allure of their protagonist, a recognized player. Early criticism of the roles of African American women in Blaxploitation pictures eventually gave way to strikingly different depictions. Frances Gateward accurately argues that "African American women would emerge as the first female action heroes" (2007, 108). Combining the political rhetoric of Black Nationalism with the attitude that "Black is Beautiful," a series of black action films featured women who fought racism, crime, and patriarchy. They were objects of desire for heterosexual men in the audience and role models for women everywhere. From 1973 to 1974, a series of films challenged these highly sexist depictions. Black female star vehicles began to emerge and significantly broke with the traditional marginal and subordinate role of black women in film.

Pam Grier was undeniably the female star of Blaxploitation, and she is the African American actress most associated with the genre. Grier first rose to prominence in a number of women's prison films (*Women in Cages*, 1971; *The Big Bird Cage*, 1972). These films were often described as sexploitation and focused on the scantily clad prisoners. Blaxploitation films offered a form of role reversal, casting the black body as the normative body of desire. Grier starred in a number of films while under contract to AIP that became classics in the genre. These included *Black Mama, White Mama*; *Coffy*; and *Scream, Blacula, Scream* (all 1973); *Foxy Brown* (1974); and *Sheba, Baby*; *Bucktown*; and *Friday Foster* (all 1975). Grier is important to film history because in many ways she initiated the female action hero, a role largely unknown to Hollywood. She is also unique as an African American actress because she emerged as a star working for a second-tier, independent studio, without the benefit of studio promotional machinery. Other films that featured black women in positions of power and control emerged. *Cleopatra Jones* (1973) epitomized the radically new female personae in Blaxploitation film. The movie concerned a compassionate black heroine who was invested in her community while serving as a US special agent. She replaced the traditional white male action hero with a powerful, assertive, intelligent, savvy black heroine.

Gay and lesbian individuals played a prominent role in Blaxploitation films but almost always in a highly stereotypical or derogatory fashion. The genre developed only a few years after the Stonewall riots of 1969 and the blossoming of the gay rights movement. Three gay "queens" are evident in a scene in *Sweet Sweetback* in which they fail to provide information leading to the title character's capture. In *Blacula,* Bobby and Billy, an interracial gay couple, purchase the Count's coffin and become the vampire's first victims. A policeman investigating their murders refers to the two gay men as "faggots." Joe Wiodarz explains that, "Blaxploitation films are notable for the ways they frequently situate "normative" black male identity amongst a variety of ideological 'others'" (2004, 10). Gay men were highly stereotyped and deemed as less than men, particularly as compared to the highly sexualized, aggressive, masculine black protagonist. Another dichotomy emerged as the heroines of Blaxploitation often fought against white lesbians. Examples included Shelley Winters' character of "Mommy" in *Cleopatra Jones.* Lesbianism was a trait that was marked as indicative of white culture.

Whiteness was often demonized within the Blaxploitation genre. White men were often associated with corruption or vice, be it in their role in organized crime, as the police department, as politicians, or as crooked businessmen. Many films portrayed whiteness as "evil" and further transgressed racial norms by having African American protagonists sexually involved with white women.

While Blaxploitation is often considered a genre of film, the term actually encompasses many different traditional genres, including action films, westerns, dramas, comedies, horror films, and gangster pictures. The action subgenre dominated within the Blaxploitation umbrella. Prominent westerns that often fall within the Blaxploitation label include *Soul Soldier* (1970*), The Legend of Nigger Charley* (1972), and its sequel *The Soul of Nigger Charley* (1973). The horror subgenre of Blaxploitation included *Blacula* (1972), *Ganja and Hess (1973),* and *Abby* (1974). The smash success of Bruce Lee and the martial arts genre in the period from 1973 to 1975 also led to a rash of cheaply made motion pictures that incorporated kung fu into the Blaxploitation genre. These films included *Black Belt Jones* (1974) and *Force Four* (1974). The gangster genre also played a prominent role within the Blaxploitation umbrella in films such as *Hit Man* (1972) and *Black Caesar* (1973).

Films that were lumped into the "Blaxploitation" genre were sometimes serious social critiques of American society. Sam Greenlee's *The Spook Who*

Sat by the Door (1973) was one noticeable example. The film, and the novel upon which it was based, tells the story of Dan Freeman, the first African American man to integrate the all-white Central Intelligence Agency (CIA). Freeman retires from the CIA to launch a revolution against American society. The film accurately reflected the mindset of many African Americans who had become disgruntled with the empty promises of American life.

One element that connected the various subgenres of Blaxploitation film was the genre's emphasis on urban space. Blaxploitation films were almost always centered on urban black spaces. While the Blaxploitation genre was often criticized for being "cartoonish," urban geographic spaces gave an air of both authenticity and realism to the genre. The gritty street location of the Blaxploitation genre was well documented by Paula Massood in *Black City Cinema*. She argues that the urban milieu was central to the articulation of black film culture. Massood claims that Blaxploitation films shared "a temporal immediacy and documentary-like realism produced by cinematic devices such as location shooting, handheld camera, and sync-sound" (2003, 117).

The financial success of early Blaxploitation features such as *Sweet Sweetback, Shaft,* and *Superfly* drove the genre during the early 1970s. Each of these films was produced relatively cheaply, and they paid profits that were often twenty times their original cost. The high water marks for production of black-themed and Blaxploitation films were 1972 and 1973. By early 1973, two black-themed films that were clearly not Blaxploitation features—*Lady Sings the Blues* and *Sounder*—did good box office and won critical acclaim, with both pictures receiving multiple Academy Award nominations. Kung fu films hit the market in 1973, and the dominance of Blaxploitation pictures in the urban community was challenged for the first time. Nonsequel Blaxploitation features flooded the market and it was soon overcrowded. The major film studios discovered, though, that certain films had cross-racial appeal and could bring in a wider contemporary audience. In 1974 *The Exorcist* demonstrated to film producers that black moviegoers could be drawn to films that weren't black themed; it was estimated that one-third of the audience for the classic horror film was African American. Studios continued to produce Blaxploitation features, although the number dropped from the previous year. Through the rest of 1974 and into 1975, African American audiences were drawn to films that were black-themed but not necessarily Blaxploitation features in the traditional sense. *Claudine (1974)*, *Uptown Saturday Night (1974)*, *Cooley High (1975)*, and *Let's Do It Again* (1975) resonated with black audiences and also drew in some white moviegoers. By 1975 the genre of Blaxploitation was fading away at the box office as profits from the films continued to plummet.

The audience for Blaxploitation films often differed significantly from any that had existed in the past. While segregation was often the rule for motion picture theaters, particularly those in the South, theaters for Blaxploitation films in the 1970s were often predominantly African American by choice—white moviegoers simply refused to go to theaters that had majority black audiences and that exhibited Blaxploitation films. Spectatorship in such films has often been described as "participatory"; that is, audiences often interacted with the screen when the film was being shown. bell hooks has argued that for most of the twentieth century, black moviegoers embodied an "oppositional gaze" when watching racist or limiting Hollywood films. In the Blaxploitation genre, filmmakers were taking the political and cultural configurations of Black Power and its rejection of nonviolent protest and commodifying it for a young urban audience. Blaxploitation films allowed black moviegoers to formulate a position of spectatorship that challenged dominant cinematic practices and to do so in a way that was communal.

By the mid-1970s, the Blaxploitation genre had begun to run out of steam. Fewer black-themed and Blaxploitation films were produced as profits began to drop. The market had often become oversaturated with the same type of film, and audiences began staying away from such movies. A contributing factor was the fact that individual theaters that exhibited Blaxploitation films were often contained in downtown areas, and hundreds of these theaters were bulldozed in the name of "urban renewal." Another contributing factor to the genre's demise was the rise of the blockbuster film. Hollywood discovered that films such as *The Godfather* (1972), The *Exorcist* (1973), and finally *Jaws*, in 1975, could have massive crossover appeal and draw in audiences regardless of race or ethnic makeup.

The Blaxploitation genre has had a tremendous cultural impact upon later generations of filmmakers, the musical world, fashion, and literature. Amy Obugo Ongiri has claimed that "the essence of African American culture in the street-savvy urban dweller rather than within the African American folk life of the South celebrated by earlier African American literary and cultural movements" was one of the hallmarks of the Black Arts and Black Power movements and the Blaxploitation genre (2010, 95). Hip-hop has incorporated this motif, as seen in the video for Common's 2005 "The Corner," in Biggie Small's adopting his rap name from a character in *Let's Do It Again* (1975), and in the lyrics of a host of rappers from Tupac Shakur to Snoop Dogg. The Blaxploitation genre was overdetermined enough to lead to a number of spoofs, including Keenan Ivory Wayans's *I'm Gonna Get You Sucka* (1988). Blaxploitation continues to serve as a reference point for many discussions of black cinematic images, particularly those included in rap or hip-hop videos.

References

Bennett, Lerone. 1971. "The Emancipation Orgasm: Sweetback in Wonderland" *Ebony,* September 1971, 106–18.

"Blacks vs. Shaft." 1972. *Newsweek,* August 28, 1972, 88.

Culbert, Michael L. 1972. "New Group Joins 'Super Fly' Fray," *Chicago Daily Defender,* September 7, 1972, 5.

Dunn, Stephanie. 2008. *"Baad Bitches" and Sassy Supermamas: Black Power Action Films.* Champaign: University of Illinois Press.

Gateward, Frances. 2007. "Movies and the Legacies of War and Corruption." In *American Cinema of the 1970's: Themes and Variations,* edited by Lester Friedman, Paula J. Massood, Michael DeAngelis, and Mimi White, 95–115. New Brunswick: Rutgers University Press.

Guerrero, Ed. 1993. *Framing Blackness: The African American Image in Film.* Philadelphia: Temple University Press.

Hamilton, Charles S. 1969. "An Advocate of Black Power Defines It." In *The Rhetoric of Black Power,* edited by Charles L. Scott and Wayne Brockreide. New York: Harper & Row.

Harris, Keith. 2005. Boys, Boyz, Bois: An Ethics of Black Masculinity in Film and Popular Media. New York: Routledge.

Kuumba Workshop. 1972. "'*Superfly*': A Political and Cultural Condemnation." Kuumba Workshop Papers, Box 2, Folder 3. Chicago: Harold Washington Library.

Lawrence, Novotny. 2008. *Blaxploitation Films of the 1970s*. New York: Routledge.

Newton, Huey P. 1971. "He Won't Bleed Me: A Revolutionary Analysis of 'Sweet Sweetback's Baadasssss Song.'" The Black Panther 6, June 19.

Ongiri, Amy Obugo. 2010. *Spectacular Blackness: The Cultural Politics of the Black Power Movement and the Search for a Black Aesthetic*. Charlottesville: University of Virginia Press.

Riley, Clayton. 1972. "Shaft Can Do Everything—I Can Do Nothing," *New York Times*, August 13.

Sieving, Christopher. 2011, *Soul Searching: Black-Themed Cinema from the March on Washington to the Rise of Blaxploitation*. Middletown, CT: Wesleyan University Press.

Sims, Yvonne D. 2006. *Women of Blaxploitation: How the Black Action Film Heroine Changed American Popular Culture*. Jefferson, NC: McFarland and Company.

Stewart, Jacqueline. 2005. *Migrating to the Movies: Cinema and Black Urban Modernity*. Berkeley: University of California Press.

Wiodarz, Joe. 2004. "Beyond the Black Macho: Queer Blaxploitation." *Velvet Light Trap* 53 (Spring): 10.

MILITANT BLAX

Screening Revolution in the Films of Oscar Williams, Christopher St. John, and Ivan Dixon

Jonathan Munby

FRAMING BLACK-ORIENTED CINEMA IN terms of black lives consciousness involves an acknowledgement of the representational violence African American filmmakers necessarily have to engage in any articulation of their difference. For black directors and actors in the era of Blaxploitation cinema, questions of complicity with and resistance to white racist visions of blackness were particularly acute. As novel and exciting as films such as *Shaft* (1971) and *Super Fly* (1972) seemed to be in putting black actors and elements of black experience center screen, the apolitical and macho character of Blaxploitation's action heroes was open to condemnation as counterproductive to any improvement of black representation in mainstream cinema. Indeed, Blaxploitation films were excoriated by many African American critics for supporting rather than dismantling the fictions that buttress the master's house. This having been said, a small number of Blaxploitation films did make a concerted attempt to interrogate and subvert the racist semiotics that determined the conditions of viability for a black-oriented commercial cinema in the 1970s. Importantly, these more militant entries in the Blaxploitation cycle are distinctive for the way they advanced a nihilistic and death-bound understanding of resistance and revolt. In line with Abdul JanMohamed's thinking, these films testified to the way the threat of death (socially, psychologically, and aesthetically) has been constitutive of black subjectivity and political agency.

The first black-oriented film advocating revolution to make it big at the box office was an independent, X-rated, low-budget story of a heterosexual male prostitute who, having attacked two cops he discovers brutalizing a Black Panther suspect, goes on the run. He outwits his law-enforcement pursuers using his sexual prowess in exchange for favors in the South Central Los Angeles ghetto community before escaping over the US-Mexico border. Dedicated to "all the brothers and sisters who have had enough of the Man," *Sweet Sweetback's Baadasssss Song* (1971) provided the blueprint for the superstud image of black empowerment that would proliferate in the Blaxploitation cycle. While its advocacy of empowerment through masculinization made it compulsory viewing for members of the Black Panther party, its graphic political incorrectness clearly had a broader mass appeal among inner-city black audiences.

Made for only around $500,000, it is estimated that the film grossed between $4,000,000 and $10,000,000 in its first year ("Big Rental Films of 1971"; Guerrero 1993, 86). The big return on small investment model was immediately taken up by a film industry in deep financial crisis. *Sweetback's* formal experimentalism and its confrontational theme were significant. Yet the film's reliance on a particularly masculine, even misogynist, notion of empowerment was arguably the film's most important legacy for black-oriented filmmaking. For example, the two most popular black-directed films that followed, *Shaft* and *Super Fly*, subordinated thematic and aesthetic militancy to an apolitical vision of black male independence. Both John Shaft and Youngblood Priest constituted twists on *Sweetback's* sexualized notion of black empowerment.

This cycle of low-budget vehicles featuring black action figures in stories of sex and violence was labeled Blaxploitation—both a term of derision used by those who saw such films as damaging the image of black America and an acknowledgement of the cycle's adoption of an exploitation model of film production. While prurience took priority over the chance to relay a radical political message about racism, Blaxploitation did meet the desire of black audiences for films with black actors as main protagonists who had a chance of still being alive when the end credits rolled.

Given the way the terms of commercial success for black-oriented film developed in the early 1970s, the criteria for defining a militant Blaxploitation film are difficult precisely because a common charge against the cycle is that it was counterproductive to progressive antiracist politics. Contemporaneous commentators in the African American press, for example, tended to produce unproductive polarizations in trying to summarize the problem this cycle of films presented for black advancement. Writing for *Ebony* in 1972, B. J. Mason posed an either/ or question about the value of the "rash of 'black' movies" that drew "both condemnation and praise":

> Do we really have "artistic freedom"—or are our chains simply longer than before?
>
> Ultimately, the black filmgoer will have to settle the issue. He [*sic*] will have to decide if, by supporting the current black films, he is, in fact, assisting in his own degradation, for the merit of a given film lies not in its popularity but in its moral and aesthetic values alone. He will have to decide for himself, whether those values must include the stale rhetoric, meaningless sex and pointless violence seen in today's films, or whether they ought to include black pride, black strength and visions of black liberation. (Mason 1972, 68)

Civic leadership groups such as the NAACP, CORE, and PUSH (People United to Serve Humanity) came together as a coalition campaigning against Blaxploitation. While not *taking* sides in this debate, Mason glosses over the differences between films in favor of a generalized image of the cycle. Symptomatically, this article threw two of the films under scrutiny here, *Top of the Heap* (1972) and *The Spook Who Sat by the Door* (1973), into the same basket as *Shaft* and *Superfly*. In lumping these together, however, Mason undermined the chance to advance a more nuanced discussion of how Blaxploitation proscribed or opened up opportunities for a more militant and independent filmmaking ethos. Rather than being encouraged to seek out those films that constituted distinctive and different contributions to Blaxploitation, filmgoers were left with a choice to accept or reject the cycle in toto.

Significantly, Mason's informing question about the contingent terms of "freedom" (artistically and politically) is precisely one that both *Top of the Heap* and *The Spook Who Sat by the Door* engage as part of the cycle. *Top of the Heap* provides a deterministic vision of a man trapped in irrevocable processes of degradation because of the racist clichés that predominate in the United States. More optimistically and more radically, *Spook* makes a case for playing with the semiotics of degradation (pandering to white racism) in order to ambush the Man. These films generate their political meaning from within the cycle through an overt engagement with Blaxploitation tropes. In this sense, they are necessarily "commercial" and belong to Blaxploitation in a way that the more declaredly "independent" and avant-gardist films of the L.A. Rebellion school (e.g., Charles Burnett's *Killer of Sheep* [1977] and Haile Gerima's *Bush Mama* [1979]), for example, do not. This having been said, as films made by directors and producers trying to minimize any dependence on white financing, *The Final Comedown* (1972), *Top of the Heap*, and *Spook* exist somewhere between the fully independent and the commercial. Moreover, their political meaning is generated precisely by an overt engagement with Blaxploitation tropes.

The Final Comedown—The Nihilistic Logic of a Militant Stand

IN A THINLY VEILED treatment of the Black Panthers, *The Final Comedown* focuses exclusively on a "last stand" confrontation between armed black activists and police. In its attempt to make activism a basis for action cinema, *The Final Comedown* is innovative in two key ways. Formally, the story is structured around a series of flashbacks in the midst of an armed confrontation between black militants and cops. Thematically, the film's uncompromising view of violent insurrection as the only means to black empowerment makes this a rare entry in black-oriented 1970s commercial cinema. The nihilistic understanding of violence promoted in *The Final Comedown* leads to its pyrrhic conclusion. The armed militants are gunned down, hopelessly outnumbered by the white cops. Here it is the act of taking up arms that matters, even if it leads to certain death, to a final comedown where one can be free of white racism only through a defiant exit from life itself.

Johnny Johnson (Billy Dee Williams) is an angry young black militant at odds with the white power structure and the various forms it takes. These are mainly provided as flashback scenes and include his father's servile occupation as a bootblack, his mother's role as a servant to a white family, and the prejudice that stopped him getting a white-collar job despite his outstanding academic record. The film opens with a flashback sequence of memories and images consequent on Johnny being shot and wounded as a part of a militant group's confrontation with the police. Black children are playing touch football. Child Johnny catches the ball only to freeze on seeing something off-frame. Cut to an older Johnny in bed looking at a football. A funky military drumbeat strikes up. The camera pans his room, revealing posters of militant icons Angela Davis and Black Panther leader Huey P. Newton. A rifle rests against the wall, and we hear voices starting to recite the Declaration of Independence. The Declaration becomes an increasingly louder voice-over for a series of shots featuring Johnny's mother going to work and serving food to her white employers, a white loan shark opening his business and exploiting the black neighborhood, a rat disturbing a black girl asleep, and guns being cleaned and assembled by black hands. Finally we see the source of the Declaration's recitation with a shot of a group of armed black militants looking directly at camera. The sound of gunfire accompanies a cut to the image of police standing over a dead black man. Cut back to the militant group. This time Johnny walks into frame and joins them in declaring independence with a revolver in hand. The sequence brings us into the present of the film's action, as the group are now seen exchanging gunfire with police in the maze of a multistoried building. Johnny is shot and wounded. Cut to child Johnny again and we see what made him freeze with football in hand: white police assaulting a black girl. The opening credits follow.

On the way to its fatal denouement, *The Final Comedown* features Johnny's brief affair with a white "dropout" countercultural radical, Rene. He accuses her of hypocrisy in adopting a nonviolent protest philosophy that will allow her later in life to drop back into mainstream white culture. In this way, *The Final Comedown* deliberately raises questions about the relationship between white radicals and the specific needs of African Americans in their struggle against the Man. Moreover, it also inverts the way the image of black militancy had been co-opted by the previous cycle of student protest counterculture films, such as *Zabriskie Point* (1970), *Getting Straight* (1970), and *The Strawberry Statement* (1970). In these films, the image of Black Power is exploited to help authenticate the revolutionary context for the actions of disaffected white protagonists.

This having been said, the film does not totally separate white from black radicals. An aging white man, for example, declares that he, too, is a brother because he is of no use to the system. White and black activists subject black cops to abuse for selling out. At the film's end, nonviolent white supporters of the black militants transform themselves from sympathetic onlookers to participants willing to die alongside their black comrades, going down with their black brothers and sisters in a flurry of police bullets. Everyone dies, including Johnny's mother. This death-bound conclusion represents an ironic and uncompromising understanding of black and white solidarity in the struggle against racism. Johnny proclaims, "If we have to die, then let it be so that the language of the young brothers and sisters coming behind us can be the dialogue of living men."

While *The Final Comedown* flirted with the commercial possibilities of selling militant activism as violent action entertainment, it remained earnest in its representation of the way Panther-like organization was tragically doomed. The film's deterministic notion of armed rebellion constituted a nod in the direction of realism, even as it also tried to keep alive an idea of black political agency against the odds. This particular mediation of revolutionary possibility was afforded by its producers' determination to remain as free as possible from major studio funding. The film had been independently financed by Oscar Williams, Billy Dee Williams, and D'Urville Martin and distributed by Roger Corman's antiauthoritarian low-budget exploitation company, New World Pictures (Koetting 2009, 37). *The Final Comedown*'s independent credentials were augmented by an AFI award of $11,000, Oscar Williams having been an Advanced Film Fellow at AFI from 1970 to 1971 (Crist 1972, 69; *AFI Catalog of Feature Films: The Final Comedown*). In the end, the film was made with a budget of $96,000 and earned $118,000 in its first three weeks in Chicago, according to the *Daily Variety* (May 16, 1972, 9) and *Jet* (42, no. 9, May 25, 1972, 54). However, the first run promise was short-lived. *Variety* figures report dwindling audience interest (Bogle 1988, 81).

The tagline, "The Man Got Down. The Brothers Were Ready," may have attracted an initial wave of black moviegoers, but the fact that "the Brothers were ready to die" may have undermined positive consequent word-of-mouth support for the film. As white Blaxploitation director Larry Cohen recounts over his experience in making *Black Caesar* (1973), African American audiences wanted their heroes to survive for a change:

> [A]t our first preview in Los Angeles audiences were very upset with the fact that the main character was killed at the end. The fact that white gangster films like *Public Enemy* and *Little Caesar* had the main character die at the end didn't matter to black audiences. They wanted their gangster to live. (Howard 2008, 27)

Top of the Heap—An "Alternative" Black Militant Vision

TOP OF THE HEAP told a similarly death-bound tale but this time not from the perspective of a Panther-like militant but from that of a black cop fed up with taking abuse for working for the Man. It also adopted an experimental form of montage in which a series of surreal fantasy-dream sequences interrupt the flow and logic of a more conventional story about a black flatfoot cop and his frustration at being the object of hate in his own community and the victim of racist police employment practices that mean he will never be promoted. As much as the film's writer, producer, director, and star, Christopher St. John, wanted to make a film that departed from exploitation, he was dependent on his previous association with a key Blaxploitation film, *Shaft*, in which he had played the costarring role of a black militant activist, Ben Buford, in order to generate interest in his screenplay. Despite this association, St. John experienced rejections from potential major backers such as MGM, who "complained about the dream sequences" and thought the script "too unconventional" (Clark 1973). Perhaps the screenplay's ironic twist on the line most associated with militant Buford, "I'll say any damn thing I want," was also a source of concern. For in *Top of the Heap*, George Lattimer (St. John), the cop-protagonist, ups the ante by declaring "I can do any goddamn thing I want." Parlaying his Blaxploitation credentials, however, did eventually garner St. John investment from Joe Solomon, president of Fanfare Productions, a small production and distribution company associated with low-budget exploitation biker and road films.

Top of the Heap opens with a scene of protestors fighting construction workers outside a Washington, DC, chemical plant. When the police turn up, we see George Lattimer for the first time as he lifts his police visor to survey the scene, spits, and utters the film's first word, "Bullshit." The credits, "Produced, Written, Directed by and Starring Christopher St. John" appear below his face. We get the first image of the Stars and Stripes in the film. Here it is being fought over by protestors and construction workers in the mud. The flag will reappear several more times in the film as a leitmotif connecting the idiosyncrasies of George's personal problems to the state as a black man serving the Man in a white racist culture. He moves in to stop the fracas only to have a balloon filled with urine smash into his face. The film then cuts to a living room where our now-cleaned-up policeman is watching the same scene on television. His wife appears, complaining about their daughter's sexual proclivities and her husband's lack of concern. A heated argument ensues as he prepares to go to work. We learn that George is uneasy about attending the funeral of his recently deceased mother in Alabama. At work we find out that he has been passed over for promotion, condemned to taking overtime on the patrol car nightshift beat with his white partner, Bobby. This opening sequence frames George's subsequent slipping into various reveries, the first of which features him as an astronaut scheduled for a moon landing.

A wavy dissolve transforms the depressed and seated patrolman into a corridor-striding astronaut in a bright orange space suit. He walks into a brightly lit white meeting room, having signed himself in as "Captain" George Lattimer in a NASA logbook titled "Top of the Heap." The senior ranking in this fantasy scene is clearly counterposed to his real-life subordination. Significantly, in this and all the other dream sequences, George sports more Afro-style hair, sideburns, and a moustache. This more "natural" hirsute look blends in with his aspirations to be quite literally, as an astronaut, somewhere other than here, possessed of adventurous agency. Comparatively, his position as a subordinated subject in reality is marked by forms of sartorial compliance, such as wearing a low-ranking police uniform and being clean-shaven and short-haired.

An abrupt cut sends us back into the present reality of George the police patrolman. He busts two blow-snorting black hustlers, who deem him a race traitor. The epithet "Black pig" is intercut with his wife's earlier accusation "Nigger cop." Cut to George next day preparing to do overtime work at the Air and Space Building guarding War Department officials. He sees young black kids in army uniform playing with the Stars and Stripes until they form an image replicating the iconic Iwo Jima photograph and memorial. His gaze then fixes on one of the museum's rockets, triggering a wavy dissolve to an astronaut descending the ladder of the lunar module and jumping onto the moon's surface. George is joined by fellow astronaut Bobby as they plant the Stars and Stripes. The flag, however, is hanging upside down. The symbolic meaning of the flag flying the wrong way up, as a distress signal, can be read as a comment on a nation in danger and as a protest against the State's failure to live up to its ideals as a democracy. The astronauts are revealed to be on a film studio sound stage when George falls over, unable to support himself because Bobby has removed the flagpole. Bobby claims this won't happen when they do the real thing. George retorts by saying, "Bobby, this is the real thing!"

The play between fantasy and reality is taken up precisely as the problem that George, as a black man in a white racist culture, wrestles with daily. Negotiating stereotypical mass-mediated assumptions about black people is his constant struggle. On the nightshift he tells Bobby he will never take the sergeant's exam again, as there's no chance of promotion. Later, on a bus ride home, he witnesses a black passenger being accused of not paying full fare by the white driver. The passenger invites George to agree that this is symptomatic of a racist culture. George, however, defends the driver from the irate passenger's violent threats. With George's police uniform hidden beneath a white coat, the driver assumes the worst of George and jumps out to call the police. A white cop arrives and subjects George to excessively rough handling before realizing he is beating up a fellow policeman. George contemptuously rejects any apology and goes home to disappear into a dream that reduces his state to something stereotypically elemental. He and his mistress run naked through a jungle until they find watermelons, which they devour with animal-like passion. The revisiting of racist clichés in fantasy is counterposed with the reality of how such clichés continue to control George's life.

The next day he announces to his wife that he will not go to his mother's funeral. He states: "I don't want to go all the way to Alabama to be with a lot of sad people singing and praising the Lord for all the fucking pain." The film cuts to George sitting in the back of a black limo that stops in front of a massive telegram pasted to a brick wall in the middle of the street. The telegram invites George to his hometown in Alabama to celebrate his new-found fame as an astronaut who walked on the moon. As George smashes his way through the telegram and wall we glimpse graffiti: "Fuck Spiro" (referring to Republican politician Spiro Agnew, the then vice president to Richard Nixon); "Free Angela, D.C. Sucks" (referring to the arrest and imprisonment of prominent black radical and communist activist Angela Davis by the FBI in 1970). This militant political context for George's frustrations is underscored when he comes across a table decked in mini Stars and Stripes and a record player that blares out "America the Beautiful." The patriotic hymn does not draw a crowd to celebrate the black astronaut's achievements. George screams out, "Where is everybody? It's me, George Lattimer . . . You invited me here . . . What's the matter with you people? Don't you realize that I've walked on the moon?" He spots a woman in a chair at the end of the street. On discovering that it is his mother, he cries and softly restates that he has walked on the moon. She caresses his face, a drum starts beating, and he pulls her out of the chair. They dance, and she transforms into a young African woman, replete with Afro and dashiki top and skirt. From this scene we are transformed by a wavy dissolve back to George at home as he announces his intention to resign from the force, fed up with the abuse that comes with wearing a police uniform. "I ain't going out there to fight the Man's war no more," he declares.

The dramatization of impossible choices in the real environment is restaged in the consequent fantasy sequence. George is back in his astronaut suit, this time being corralled by police cars in a parking lot. This scene is intercut with one featuring a dashiki-clad George delivering a Black Power–styled speech directly to the camera in front of the Stars and Stripes defaced by a skull and crossbones: "Fathers have died. Mothers have been broken.

Babies have cried. No man can be a slave. No man can be a judge. No man can justify the taking of another man's life." The concatenation of these images, of the black astronaut hunted down by the police and the sloganeering Black Power advocate, services a deterministic narrative trajectory. The national imagination cannot tolerate the idea that an astronaut could be black (the first African American in space was Guion Bluford in 1983). The nation, embodied in the various ironic treatments of the flag, remains indifferent to the consequences of white racism.

Having resolved to flee DC, George outwits chasing patrol cars and ends up standing in front of the Washington Memorial. He walks up to the camera, his black face filling the screen in an extreme close-up, and we cut to a close-up of the white marble head of President Lincoln at the Lincoln Memorial. The camera tracks back to reveal George turning away while we hear a child's voice reciting Lincoln's "Gettysburg Address." Underscoring the visual comparison between black George and white Lincoln, the words "dedicated to the proposition that all men are created equal," naively and innocently enunciated, are juxtaposed ironically with George's predicament.

The film cuts to George back at home, resigned to having to settle for his lot in life. In a melancholy voice he tells Viola that he is "ok and . . . together now" as he leaves for another night shift. George seems reconciled to the banality of a life without dreams, where an African American cannot be top of the heap. As he takes a walk to stretch his legs, however, he finds himself back in Waterville, Alabama, as the film cuts away from reality again. This time he sees himself in a ticker-tape parade riding in the back of an open-top Rolls Royce with his fellow astronauts, taking the plaudits of Richard Nixon waving from a balcony. As the car turns out of shot the film cuts back to George doing his flatfoot beat. The film cuts back to Waterville as the motorcade makes it way up another street. We see the barrel of a rifle part the curtains of an upstairs window. The sniper shoots. The film cuts back to George on his police beat being shot in the head. A series of cuts between astronaut George and cop George falling to their deaths ends on a freeze frame of cop George lying on a heap of trash. The end credits start to the no-exit lyrics of the title song, "Top of the Heap": "Why do we try to make it better/ Tell me what does it get you?/ Why plan it/ it's only life/ and no one gets out alive."

In its own way, then, *Top of the Heap* repeats the determinist logic that underpins *The Final Comedown*. Such a nihilistic view of black possibility might have explained concerns financiers may have had about the film's chances at the box office. The particular differences between St. John and his backer and distributor, Solomon, illustrate further how proscribed the opportunities were for African American filmmakers trying to make more than just money out of the wave of public interest in black-oriented films. St. John would assert that Solomon interfered with the final cut and undermined efforts to market the film as anything other than Blaxploitation. While *Top of the Heap* had been entered into the Twenty-Second Berlin International Film Festival in June 1972, St. John maintained that Solomon rejected an invitation for the film to be screened as part of the Director's Fortnight at the Cannes Film Festival (Clark 1973). Whatever disagreements there may have been between Solomon and St. John, it was clear that producers and distributors had a fixed idea about what a black-oriented film needed to be in order to sell. Indeed, the film's poster underscored the fact that the producer, writer, director, and star of *Top of the Heap* was Christopher St. John, "Whom You Last Saw in *Shaft*." Even having found a willing financier, it remained paramount that *Top of the Heap*'s "arty" credentials were suppressed when it came to publicity and distribution. As St. John put it, "they didn't want it associated with class—they were pushing it as exploitation" (Clark 1973). Yet, while St. John lamented the difficulty in realizing a truly independent film, *Top of the Heap*'s aesthetic and political interest depended precisely on a satirical and an intertextual relation to the clichés and stereotypes that hindered the realization of its protagonist's dreams. Even if St. John felt Solomon had interfered too much, audiences still experienced a film that was hardly "standardized." Solomon's marketing strategy may have sold the film as a Blaxploitation product highlighting the sex and action, but the experimental montage remained intact.

The Spook Who Sat by the Door—Stereotype as Militant Trojan Horse

WHILE ST. JOHN COMPLAINED about the way the industry constantly tried to make black-oriented film service an exploitation agenda that tended to compound rather than challenge racist stereotype, Sam Greenlee deliberate-ly indulged white racist expectations of black Americans as a kind of Trojan horse strategy in bringing down the Man. The writer and coproducer of *The Spook Who Sat by the Door* saw his main protagonist not as a victim of stereotyping but as someone who was literally a "double agent." Arguably, in terms of African American commercial film, *Spook* constitutes the most sustained engagement with racist stereotype as an instrument of political subterfuge. It is also a supreme case study in State oppression, for this film's challenge to the white establishment went too far for the FBI.

The title of the film itself reveals the way such subterfuge is put into operation. "Spook" is both a white racist epithet and a colloquial term for spy. The film's story line concerns the hiring of the first black American intelligence officer by the CIA out of pressure to integrate the organization. In overcoming strenuous and prejudicial physical, psychological, and aca-demic tests, the main protagonist, the teasingly named Dan Freeman, plays up to stereotype as an Uncle Tom out to please the white man. His "spook" performance enables him precisely to join the ranks of the CIA. His phony humility is an act of dissembling that allows him to learn all the tricks of counterintelligence through agency training. He learns "the guiding prin-ciple of an underground guerrilla army," including how to make bombs with the bare minimum of resources and how to build an armed organization that has proper command structures that can survive the killing or capture of its leaders. After five years and having become a trusted servant of CIA senior officers, Freeman announces that he is leaving to take up a position with the Social Services Foundation in Chicago, to "help my people help themselves . . . use what I've learned here."

His words have a double meaning, of course. The foundation is really a front covering his real intentions to help his people help themselves. Freeman uses his CIA training to build a Black Panther–like militant orga-nization out of the existing gangland culture, turning street hoodlums into disciplined revolutionary soldiers capable of using tactics deployed in Alge-ria, Kenya, Korea, and Vietnam. And he teaches his students how to make the most of the white racist gaze: "Remember, a black man with a mop, tray or broom in his hand can go damn near anywhere in this country. And a smiling black man is invisible." Adopting the maxim that white prejudice is your camouflage becomes the film's most dangerous political message. He commands the lighter-skinned blacks to rob a bank because they will be mistaken for being Caucasian and authorities will not be able to connect the heist with a black militant organization. At the same time, having also raided the National Guard's armory, Freeman reassures the militant black group of ex-gangbangers that they will escape detection by the FBI and CIA because "They'll be looking for everyone except us. You see, this took brains and guts, which we don't have, right?" Indeed, when the time comes to activate all the revolutionary cells spread across ten cities, Freeman adopts the ironic moniker "Uncle Tom" as the freedom fighter leader in issuing ultimatums that the police and National Guard, as an army of occupation, leave the black inner city community. Although Freeman appears to be mortally wounded at the film's conclusion, he has put into place an underground army that knows how to revive its command structure and overcome any acephalous condition. In this sense, *Spook* is a movie that both transcends and critiques the way Blaxploitation makes the condition for box-office success that its main protagonists need to be alive at the end of the film. The subordination of individualism to a collective sense of agency constitutes a radicalization of the otherwise undirected and apolitical ambitions of black-oriented films of the 1970s.

The inspiration behind the film came from its writer-producer, Green-lee, and its director, Ivan Dixon. The latter had achieved national popularity through his role as Sergeant Kinchloe on the hit television series *Hogan's Heroes* and had recently made his directorial debut with *Trouble Man* (1972), a Twentieth Century Fox release that recycled typical sex and violence Blax-ploitation conventions, featuring a macho private investigator, Mr. T., who is hired by a syndicate to find out who is interfering with their gambling business. While Dixon also had experience working in an independent film-making context as star of *Nothing But a Man* (1964), he was all too aware of the concessions an African American actor-director had to make in order to make it commercially. He had been active in the civil rights movement and had campaigned against the racist exclusion of blacks from television, stating that "we must have access to it in terms of control—not just 'Give the spooks an hour." We have to be able to choose the material ourselves and see that it's done in a way that befits the black ethos" (Hayward 2008). He made *Trouble Man* precisely as a necessary first step toward realizing a more autonomous production:

> I had to do something to prove I could make a (theatrical) film to go to backers and say, "Now, Twentieth Century Fox gave me a couple of million dollars to do a film for them; maybe you can invest some money in me to do a film that I really want to do. (Moon 1997, 90)

When it came to finding material on which to base a film more befitting African American needs and experience, Greenlee's popular but controversial 1969 novel, *The Spook Who Sat by the Door*, stood out. The book was an imaginative reworking of Greenlee's own experiences as a black operative in the United States Information Agency working at home and overseas. It became compulsory reading for both the FBI and the Black Panthers ("Sam Greenlee Speaks" Part 3, 2011). Given the controversial history of the novel, a film version was bound to attract adverse attention from state authorities. Moreover, the involvement of Panther party members in the film (Illinois Chapter member David Lemieux, for example, played the role of Pretty Willie) lent militant credibility to the project that could only compound its subversive status. A film about successful organized armed black radical uprising that was destined for exhibition in inner-city houses like most other black-oriented films constituted a potential incitement to revolt.

From the outset, then, Dixon and Greenlee were fully aware of the need to counter attempts to censor or politically tame the project. To retain as much control of the film's making and distribution as possible, Dixon and Greenlee sought out black financing. Like St. John, however, they found themselves in need of finishing funds from white-dominated distribution organizations. Only $150,000 short on a film costing $1,000,000, Greenlee found his quest to glean the remaining finance from black investors blocked by civil rights activist and PUSH campaign leader Jesse Jackson, who deemed the film's message to be counterproductive to the interests of the race ("Sam Greenlee Speaks" Part 4, 2011).

In turning to major studios for finishing funds and a distribution contract, Greenlee and Dixon adopted a strategy similar to that used by St. John in attracting such interest to *Top of the Heap*. The film's editor, Michael Kahn (who had worked with Dixon on *Trouble Man*), cut together a promotional print from rushes featuring violence and sex, avoiding any reference to militant ideology. This was presented to United Artists, who fell for the ruse that this was the latest Blaxploitation picture (*Infiltrating Hollywood 1972*; Nichols 2004). In the process, the filmmakers replicated the political philosophy of dissembling at the heart of *Spook* itself. When United Artists saw the final cut, they expressed deep reservations about fulfilling their contract to distribute the film (Nichols 2004). Dixon and Greenlee successfully countered arguments that the film might incite a race riot by insisting United Artists honor its contract. While the studio was ultimately interested in recovering its investment, behind the scenes it had been put under pressure by the FBI not to distribute the film. And, as Christine Acham and Clifford Ward's documentary, *Infiltrating Hollywood: The Rise and Fall of The Spook Who Sat by the Door* (2010), reveals, this instance of FBI interference was part of a more general policy of discouragement. Dixon's widow, Berlie, for example, recounts how her husband had traveled to Nigeria and was on the verge of securing a $400,000 investment from the national bank, when this offer was suddenly withdrawn. Apparently the bank executives had been "visited" by white American agents.

At the very beginning of the project they had been refused permission to film in Chicago by Mayor Richard J. Daley, a politician who was never hesitant about mobilizing public fears about rioting and who had a track record of suppressing protest cultures with maximum force. By contrast, the neighboring city of Gary, Indiana, with its first African American mayor, Richard Hatcher, in office, was very welcoming. Greenlee and Dixon were given permission to location shoot in the city and were even offered the use of a police helicopter to do an overhead shot. Symptomatic of the film's espousal of guerrilla practice, the film crew covertly shot some footage in Chicago (of the "L" on the South Side, for example) in order to help locate the screen action in that city. By the time of the film's release, then, Greenlee and Dixon were relatively inured to the systematic attempt to suppress the film's production. They now had to deal with interference in its consumption.

According to Greenlee, not only had the FBI attempted to stop United Artists from distributing the film, their agents had also harassed exhibitors (such as the manager of the McVicker's Theater in the Chicago Loop), demanding that they withdraw *Spook* from their screening schedules (*Infiltrating Hollywood*). Despite such attempts at censure, the film enjoyed a successful first run. Released over the Labor Day weekend in 1973, *Variety* reported that the film had done a "Wow 62G in Loop Opening" (at the Woods Theatre in Chicago). This figure compared very favorably to the "sizzling" $65,000 for *Enter the Dragon* and the "dull $10,000" for *Electra Glide in Blue* (as reported in *Variety*, September 5, 1973, 14). It would do well in its second week, as well, clearing a "brawny" $50,000 (see *Variety*, September 12, 1973, 17).

The film's promising initial returns were accompanied by reviews, especially in the African American press, that drew attention to its difference from the bulk of black-oriented films of the period. *The New Pittsburgh Courier*, for example, praised the film for being

> an interesting alternative to the run of the mill ghetto jungle dramas we've been offered recently. . . . After six months of watching carbon copy "revenge" action films, a Black movie with a definite guiding rationale behind it is welcome . . . this time around the action is directed against the U.S. government which has long been deaf to the needs of Black people. (Mims 1973)

Other newspapers expressed concern about the incendiary potential of the film. *The Chicago Defender* asked if it might "touch off race warfare," describing *Spook* as "a primer for oppressed minorities who believe that waging bloody guerrilla warfare is the only path to freedom" (Thomas 1973). Yet this encouraging box office record and critical attention did not lead to prolonged general release. In February 1974, after a run of just five months, United Artists, having recovered their investment and made a small profit, acquiesced to FBI demands that the film be withdrawn from exhibition. At a time when the film industry was in economic crisis and Blaxploitation was offering a means to recover, this was an unusual decision, clearly indicative of the FBI's pressure.

The film could have disappeared forever but for Dixon and Greenlee's adroit maneuvering to buy back its distribution rights and secretion of a pristine print in an undisclosed vault. The movie's cult reputation would be sustained for many years through bootleg prints and videos, again something symptomatic of the film's guerrilla ethos and much appreciated by Greenlee ("Sam Greenlee Speaks" Part 3, 2011). In early 2004, the film was restored and released on DVD by Obsidian Home Entertainment, which was established "to revive black films of particular interest" (Nichols 2004). With its rebirth in DVD form came renewed interest in the backstory of the film's making and distribution problems.

One could conclude that the only province for overtly political filmmaking on race and racism in the 1970s would have to be "indie." Members of the "L.A. Rebellion," for example, took their stance in working precisely against what they perceived to be the shortfalls in Blaxploitation. Equally, the filmmakers most associated with the few militant commercial black-oriented film productions also tended to dissociate themselves from the bulk of Blaxploitation. Yet this seems too simplistic a separation—one that leads to overly generalized critical attacks on the rest of the cycle's complicity with counterproductive representations of the race. Clearly films such as *The Final Comedown*, *Top of the Heap*, and *Spook* were perceived as belonging to the cycle. And we can see how their significance depends on a complex relationship to putatively standard examples of Blaxploitation. Militancy is not simply erased from the picture in the cases of many of the more celebrated examples of the cycle. As *Shaft*, *The Mack* (1973), and *Cleopatra Jones* (1973) demonstrate, Black Power activists can be more than incidental to the plot. Indeed, their dramatic presence constitutes a troubling reminder of a more general absence or suppression of militant political messages in commercial black-oriented films. Given the trouble *Spook* experienced, perhaps this was the only way the more seditious elements of 1970s African American culture could be screened.

Works Cited

AFI Catalog of Feature Films: The Final Comedown, http://www.afi.com/members/catalog/DetailView.aspx?s=&Movie=54504.
"Big Rental Films of 1971." 1972. *Variety*, January 5, 1972, 9.

Bogle, Donald. 1988. *Blacks in American Films and Television*. New York: Simon and Schuster.

Clark, Paul S. 1973. "Talented Black Actor Pays High Price for Success." *Los Angeles Times*, November 19, 1973, D18.

Crist, Judith. 1972. "Movie." *New York Magazine*, June 19, 1972, 69.

Guerrero, Ed. 1993. *Framing Blackness: The African American Image in Film*. Philadelphia, PA: Temple University Press.

Hayward, Anthony. 2008. "Ivan Dixon: Kinchloe in 'Hogan's Heroes.'" *The Independent*, May 16, 2008. http://www.independent.co.uk/news/obituaries/ivan-dixon-kinchloe-in-hogans-heroes-829237.html.

Howard, Josiah. 2008. *Blaxploitation Cinema: The Essential Reference Guide*. Godalming: FAB Press.

Koetting, Christopher T. 2009. *Mind Warp! The Fantastic True Story of Roger Corman's New World Pictures*. Hailsham: Hemlock Books.

Mason, B. J. 1972. "The New Films: Culture or Con Game?" *Ebony* 28, no. 2 (December): 60–62, 64, 66, 68.

Mims, Greg. 1973. "'Spook': Thought Provoking, Relevant Drama." *New Pittsburgh Courier* 17, no. 3 (November 1973).

Moon, Spencer. 1997. *Reel Black Talk: A Source Book of 50 American Filmmakers*. Westport, CT: Greenwood Press.

Nichols, Peter M. 2004. "New DVDs: A Story of Black Insurrection Too Strong for 1973." *New York Times*, January 20, 2004. http://www.nytimes.com/2004/01/20/movies/new-dvd-s-a-story-of-black-insurrection-too-strong-for-1973.html.

"Sam Greenlee Speaks." 2011. Part 3. Swahilitv, May 2011. http://www.youtube.com/watch?v=NiqeYd-RZIs.

"Sam Greenlee Speaks." 2011. Part 4. Swahilitv, May 2011. http://www.youtube.com/watch?v=7ZBcxMt8IkU.

Thomas, Leroy. 1973. "Will 'Spook' Touch Off Race Warfare?" *Chicago Defender* 2, no. 18 (August 1973).

African American Film Noir

Dan Flory

African American film noir has a history that parallels as well as inter-twines with both the classic Hollywood cycle, roughly from 1941 to 1959, and with the more contemporary era of neo-noir that began in the 1960s. African American film noir also arguably reaches beyond the standard pa-rameters of the genre. As historian of black film Thomas Cripps has noted, "[I]t could be said that with the release of *Dark Manhattan* in 1937, race movies had anticipated postwar *film noir*, perhaps because the actuality of black life echoed the dark street scenes of the genre" (2003, 19). During the classic noir–era, African American directors produced occasional noir films, such as *The Girl in Room 20* and *Dirty Gertie from Harlem USA* (both 1946), as Cripps notes (1993, 148). At times, Hollywood, too, directly con-fronted problems facing African Americans through film noir, as in *No Way Out* (1950) and *Odds Against Tomorrow* (1959). Moreover, it is plausible to argue that these Hollywood films qualify as African American film noirs, particularly in light of Tommy Lott's discussion of black film as a politically oppositional practice that concerns itself with issues that "define the politi-cal struggle of black people" and "aim to foster change" (T. Lott 1999, 151).

In general, film noir has possessed the capacity to be critical cinema, since it cohered as a genre during the 1940s; unlike most Hollywood genres, it could easily be turned to critical analysis of the societal institutions it depicted. In the classic noir period, this capacity was typically directed toward problems of class, as in *Raw Deal* (1948), or gender, as in *The Damned Don't Cry* (1950), but it was also sometimes aimed at anti-ethnic or antiblack prejudice, as in *Crossfire* (1947), *Call Northside 777* (1948), *Border Incident*

(1948), *The Lawless* (1950), *Touch of Evil* (1958), *The Crimson Kimono* (1959), *Odds Against Tomorrow*, and *No Way Out*. Yet in a very real sense, during the years immediately following World War II, neither Hollywood nor mainstream America were yet ready to fully confront antiblack racism in the way that they could face forms of anti-ethnic prejudice, such as that exhibited against Jewish- and other hyphenated Americans. In spite of occasional if noteworthy outliers, a full-blown development of African American film noir would have to wait for five decades after the genre's inception before filmmakers produced a series of films that thoroughly explored antiblack racism in significant numbers, nuance, and range.

However, Charles Scruggs (2011) has advanced a remarkable consideration regarding mainstream Hollywood's noir treatment of African Americans by making a case for *Out of the Past* (1947) being, in part, a veiled fugitive slave narrative, with the detective played by Robert Mitchum metaphorically hunting "runaway" Kathie Moffat (Jane Greer) to bring her back to her "master," Whit Sterling (Kirk Douglas). Scruggs points out that this film's original title, that of its source novel, and its release title in Great Britain—*Build My Gallows High*—was explicitly taken from an African American poem that inspired Geoffrey Homes, the novel's author as well as the movie's screenwriter (Scruggs 2011, 111n4). It is further worth noting that the source novel explicitly raises the issue of anti-Irish prejudice (Homes [1946] 1988, 135). Additionally, other "white" film noirs of the classic era containing noteworthy if secondary subplots involving African Americans and the political struggles they faced include *Body and Soul* (1947) and *The Breaking Point* (1950). The Humphrey Bogart vehicle *Knock on Any Door* (1949), based on a novel of the same name by African American writer Willard Motley, obliquely confronts issues of race in the way that it, like its literary source, deals with anti-ethnic prejudice, poverty, and disadvantage (Motley [1947] 2001). The film itself is furthermore unusually evenhanded for its era in depicting its main African American character as deserving full civil rights and moral consideration, as it is regarding its other racialized characters, including its Italian-American protagonist. Some critics have further argued that mainstream film noir itself often manifests a "racial unconscious" such that the genre's white characters are "blackened" through shadow, chiaroscuro, or other forms of stylistic allusion to invoke a meta-phorical racial dimension. Eric Lott argues that the male protagonists of such films as *Double Indemnity* (1944), *A Double Life* (1946), and *Kiss Me Deadly* (1955) are illustrative examples of this metaphorical racial blackening, while E. Ann Kaplan points to the female leads in *Cat People* (1942) and *The Lady from Shanghai* (1948) (E. Lott 1997, 546–53; Kaplan 1998, 186–98).

It is safe to say, then, that classic versions of African American film noir exist, even if the range and scope of membership in this category remain in dispute. African American film noir from the classical era thus deserves to be recognized not only as a subgenre in its own right but also as a film form that manifests itself in central examples of Hollywood-produced noir. Arguably, it furthermore amounts to a classification that ranges significantly beyond many more orthodox conceptions of the genre. For these and other reasons, African American film noir represents not merely an additional group of films that supplement this familiar Hollywood genre but also a challenge to its boundaries as they are typically understood. Moreover, as will become evident in the following text, African American film noir's full power and sophistication emerged in the 1990s, after social advances as well as marketing opportunities coalesced to create unprecedented openings for African American filmmakers. To make the range of these matters clearer, in the remainder of this chapter I will outline additional precursors to African American film noir's full development, its flowering in the period from 1991 to 1995, and its ongoing influence and legacy in the twenty-first century.

Early African American Neo-noir

As WILLIAM COVEY NOTES (2003, 59), African American film noir is on dis-play during the Blaxploitation era, alongside Hollywood neo-noirs like *Klute* (1971) and *Chinatown* (1974). Detective narratives such as *Shaft* (1971) and *Black Eye* (1974), crime capers like *Across 110th Street*, *Cool Breeze*, and *Super-fly* (all 1972), and explorations of the black underworld like *Sweet Sweetback's Baadasssss Song* (1971) borrow significantly from the noir canon as they con-front problems of antiblack racism. Of the last film, Cripps notes that "Sweet-back's transformation experience [from political innocent to race-conscious hero] would have been implausible but for borrowings from the genre of *film noir*. Van Peebles, a lifelong moviegoer, saw how to use that genre's darkened streets, glistening half-lights, bumbling and villainous cops. Even the raspy sound . . . contributes to the urban streetscape" (1978, 135–36). Tommy Lott further points to this film's use of noirish social realism to enhance its storytelling and thematic impact (1997, 300n27). There is also a case to be made for some of Pam Grier's early vehicles concerning tales of women negotiating underworlds of oppression, racism, and revenge being African American film noirs, notably *Coffy* (1973) and *Foxy Brown* (1974). The former, in particular, fits well into the contours of the subgenre, with its at times moody noir lighting and downbeat ending involving betrayal by her boyfriend and the heroine's subsequent disillusionment. Certain Fred Williamson vehicles, such as *Hell Up in Harlem* (1973), in addition to the above-mentioned *Black Eye*, deserve mention here as well for their blend of noir themes and techniques with explorations of antiblack racism (Silver et al. 2010, 396–97).

Kaplan is probably right to note that one reason this kind of intersection between race and noir went virtually unnoticed by scholars in the 1970s and for decades after is that doing so would have raised uncomfortable considerations that white film scholars did not want to ponder: namely, the racial implications of calling a group of relatively mainstream American movies from the 1940s and after by the terms "black film" or "black cinema," which would have confronted Anglophone critics with matters they preferred to ignore or forget (Kaplan 1998, 183). "Black film" and "black cinema" are, of course, the most straightforward translations of the French term "*film noir*," and the second of these English terms was actually employed in an early introduction of the genre in Britain and America (Higham and Greenberg 1968, e.g., 19, 36). But the racial implications that many French critics explicitly noted were obscured when the French expression won the terminological battle and was carried over into discussions of the genre in English, even if it was also partly due to the fact that, as James Naremore notes, "the term sounded more artistic in French" (2008, 13). More recently, the term "film noir" has been de-italicized on account of its widespread use both in scholarly and lay contexts, further obscuring its racial implications.

Of course, most Blaxploitation-era films constitute problematic means for exploring issues of antiblack sentiments because they do so in ways that often seem ham-handed, unconvincing, or contrived. Even when they employ classic noir or neo-noir tropes, some critics might argue, these films remain poor examples of the genre because they seem aesthetically inept or unpersuasive. On the other hand, those flaws (even if they are accurate) do not disqualify them from being members of this category. As Tommy Lott has noted, by appealing to more "mainstream" tastes through noir conventions, they become "politically ambiguous" and generate "ambivalence" in the viewer (1997, 288, 294). It is worth noting that ambivalence and ambiguity have been definitive traits of film noir reaching all the way back to early French studies such as Borde and Chaumeton's pioneering work ([1955] 2002, 7–13). Ironically, then, such viewer affects tend to verify some Blaxploitation-era films' membership in African American film noir by virtue of reaffirming their effectiveness in applying the genre's conventions to racial difficulties experienced by black people and aimed at fostering change. It thus seems reasonable to conclude that at least some Blaxploitation-era films, such as those mentioned above, should be counted as African American noirs because the stories, themes, and techniques used, as well as the feelings they generate, assure their place in the category. In addition, they anticipate the subgenre's more full-blown development roughly a decade and a half later.

Also preceding black noir's fuller development, and to an extent paving its way, were "independent" works such as Julie Dash's *Illusions* (1982) and Wendell Harris Jr.'s *Chameleon Street* (1989). The former work, a thirty-four-minute short, explores how an African American femme fatale who can pass for white might be able to use her deception to the advantage of black people (T. Lott 2012, 152–53); while the latter, a full-length feature, is an astonishing expression of black rage against racial limitations. By turns dark, bizarre, and humorous, *Chameleon Street* chronicles the life of an African American con man who is motivated by the frustrating restrictions of race to impersonate, by turns, a reporter, a surgeon, a student, and a lawyer. Harris's film won the Grand Jury prize at the 1990 Sundance Film Festival but barely received commercial distribution. Yet its combination of black rage and noir thematics make it a noteworthy example of how film noir conventions may be employed to effectively portray the difficulties facing African American men during the latter half of the twentieth century. Jacquie Jones and Manthia Diawara lump *Chameleon Street* together with other African American neo-noirs that were released in its wake (Jones 1991, 33; Diawara 1993, 263), but the film deserves recognition as a work that slightly anticipates the cycle that subsequently emerged.

African American Film Noir's Heyday

NOIR BY NOIRS (TO use Diawara's apt phrase) discernibly coheres as a film cycle during what Ed Guerrero (1993) describes as the New "Black Film Wave" that began in the late 1980s. With a Hollywood need for "gritty urban dramas" (Rhines 1996, 89–90), coupled with the rise in popularity of rap and hip-hop (Watkins 1998, 77ff.), there arose unique possibilities for African American filmmakers to control how their stories were told in ways not generally available since the demise of race movies around 1950. As a result, there appeared a spate of black noir films, including *A Rage in Harlem* (1991), *New Jack City* (1991), *Boyz n the Hood* (1991), *Straight Out of Brooklyn* (1991), and *Juice* (1992). The early part of this cycle frequently centered around at-risk teenagers and the circumstances, lifestyles, and music that defined them. As Diawara notes (1993), these works typically express a sense of black rage at the restrictions and limitations imposed on young African American men. The uses of film noir style and themes in these works help to make contemporary black life and culture visible as well as understandable, especially for mainstream audiences. Most prominently, such visibility is achieved in these films by means of combining their narratives symbiotically with rap and hip-hop music, and exploiting both artistic forms' capacities to influence consumers to identify with lawbreakers (Diawara 1993, 263, 272–73).

Of course, not all viewers are sanguine about this cycle's early development: Jones (1991) dubbed these works "the new ghetto aesthetic," which she criticized for all too often reiterating rather than subverting existing Hollywood stereotypes concerning black people; and Mark Anthony Neal somewhat disparagingly refers to them as "ghettocentric *noir*" (2002, 188). While Jones also admits that this genre holds out possibilities for political transformation and acknowledgment of American culture's plurality, she argues that many of these films (mainly, those backed with studio money or with slightly larger budgets) instead conform to standard Hollywood protocols by reinforcing caricatures of African American men and women. I have argued elsewhere (Flory 2008, 153–68) that Jones's assessment is overly pessimistic regarding this type of youth-oriented film, although I admit that she correctly analyzes many problems in a number of its early instantiations. But more to the point, like Paula Massood I argue that *Menace II Society* (1993) and *Clockers* (1995), films admittedly released a few years after Jones published her broadside, fulfill the possibilities she held out mainly for "independent" films that could be produced below the radar of Hollywood, and provided greater promise to escape its stereotypical imagery (Flory 2008, 124–52, 168–84; Massood 2003, 143–205).

Both *Menace II Society* and *Clockers* alluringly depict drug dealing and criminality so that audiences may readily understand why some African American youth would see them as viable life choices, as well as why what Cornel West (1993, 11–20) has termed "black nihilism" might appear to be a reasonable outlook on life. At the same time, these films do not shy away from portraying the ugly and often fatal consequences of such life choices; in fact, like many of their Hollywood predecessors, these films' narratives place such outcomes front and center. *Menace II Society* and *Clockers* also share a continuity with "black experience" novels of ghetto life written by authors such as Robert Beck (aka Iceberg Slim) and Donald Goines, as American popular culture scholar Jonathan Munby notes (2011, 149–74; see also Reid 1993, 152)—a trait additionally shared by a significant portion of rap and hip-hop. These different literary, musical, and cinematic traditions moreover share roots in the "bad man" tradition of African American folklore, a connection noted by both Tommy Lott (1997, 290–91) and Munby. These films furthermore share a good deal in common with Blaxploitation-era movies (Massood 2003, 145–46), an element cinematically encoded into the protagonist's flashback to his childhood in *Menace II Society* (Munby 2011, 163–64).

Suffused with violence and a kind of fatalistic determinism, told by means of an extended flashback narrated by its dead protagonist's reflective voiceover, and taking place frequently at night, *Menace II Society* wears its noir credentials on its sleeve. Additionally taking advantage of its relatively low-budget origins by means of adopting a gritty documentary-noir cinematic style, the film deftly presents the story of how a child might grow up to become first a casual lawbreaker, then a drug dealer, and ultimately a murderer. The narrative trajectory for its protagonist, Caine (Tyrin Turner), is one of taking him from being a relative innocent (a guilty bystander of armed robbery and murder) to becoming a hardened criminal himself. His descent into lawbreaking provides a sort of textbook case for how children might become "criminals out of desperate conditions," as one of its co-creators, Allen Hughes, explains (Hughes 1994). By turns sympathetic and reprehensible, Caine becomes humanized by virtue of such traits as his loving attachment to his grandparents as well as to his friend and romantic interest Ronnie (Jada Pinkett). His resistance to more brutal forms of criminality (even if it is often overcome) also illustrates a core of moral value that allows many viewers to remain attached to him, even as he declines further into gangster life. The film's noirish ending, reminiscent of classics such as *Sunset Boulevard* and *D.O.A.* (both 1950), thus comes as a jolt that plays on the critical sympathetic understanding that the film has carefully built up for this character and that aims to thrust the viewer into a mood of reflection regarding why the sorts of horrific conditions that produce such individuals exist, and what might be done to address them.

Clockers, on the other hand, aims to affect those falling into such doomed forms of existence by focusing more squarely on the moment-to-moment desperation of black youth trapped by the misery-laden conditions. Opening with a montage of reproduced crime scene photos graphically depicting half-grown teens who have died from gunshot wounds, the film quickly moves to a group of black youth arguing over whether being a hardcore rapper requires committing actual violence. Several members point out that the alleged "authenticity" of such gangster rap appeals to them because it reflects the bleak negativity they feel surrounds them. These characters' attitudes mirror the hardship, lack of opportunity, and disadvantage that they see as their lot in life. Assigned to desolate urban spaces and seemingly condemned to live out their brief existences there, these youth have reacted by taking on a sense of "life without meaning, hope, and love," to use West's characterization of black nihilism (1993, 14–15). Because they have been told so often by the dominant culture and its media that they are lesser human beings and therefore much more inclined to be violent, sexually predatory, and immoral, they have succumbed to this drumbeat of characterization and internalized its imagery. Thus they enthusiastically embrace this image's artistic expression in the form of hard-core gangsta rap, as it seems perfectly attuned to what they have been encouraged to think about what it is to be a young, urban, and impoverished African American male. Without sufficient positive affirmation regarding who and what they are, and what they might be capable of attaining, they have instead reverted to embracing damning stereotypes of themselves that incorporate most, if not all, of white America's worst fears about them—thus becoming "America's nightmare," to use the term employed in *Menace II Society*. In this way *Clockers* constitutes an analysis of one form of self-destructive behavior in the black community that plays itself out in the actions of many young African American men.

Director Spike Lee's film focuses primarily on Strike (Mekhi Phifer), leader of a crew of young, round-the-clock drug dealers who ply their trade from the flagpole court of their housing project. The film goes out of its way to depict the oppressive sense of surveillance that overlies Strike's life, from his bristly, resentful crew, to the cops, both straight and bent, and ultimately to his drug-supplier boss, Rodney (Delroy Lindo), who cruises the projects like an overseer and tells Strike time and again that he knows everything, as if he were some omniscient deity. Hemmed in at virtually every turn, this confused teen finds solace in a toy train set he keeps in his apartment and a budding friendship with a younger boy, Tyrone (Pee Wee Love). Plagued by a raging ulcer that manifests a growing anxiety over his chosen profession, Strike is by turns charming and offensive, vulnerable and alienating, which keeps viewers off-balance and ambivalent toward him, yet overall helps to construct this character as sympathetic and to an extent empathetic, even as those feelings are also mixed with a deeply critical perspective of his choices and actions. Not surprisingly, the stated aim of *Clockers*, as Lee himself has pointed out, is not only to depict the bleak, noirish circumstances of its characters' lives but to demystify gangster life itself—drain it of its seeming glamour and show that it is a "dead end" (Fuchs 2002, 171). The film means to accomplish this goal by having Strike himself come to grasp the mistakenness of his chosen path and where it is leading, and consciously turn away from it. Thus the critical sympathetic and empathetic understanding that viewers have forged with Strike means to encourage them to achieve similar insights—and, by virtue of his escape, offer them hope that something better might be possible.

It should come as no surprise that, as black noir films of the early 1990s by and large proved to be profitable, movie producers backed similar projects, resulting in a relatively robust cycle of modest to mid-budget African American film noirs. In addition to *Menace II Society* and *Clockers*, other noteworthy examples from the first half of the decade include *Deep Cover* (1992), *One False Move* (1992), *The Glass Shield* (1995), and *Dead Presidents* (1995). These films are marked by a degree of sophistication and subtlety regarding antiblack racism that is at times as startling as it is insightful to experience. Using techniques and themes sharpened by decades of refinement in nonblack films and employed with a subtle dexterity and grace by African American filmmakers, these works make visible troubling aspects of the state of the race in America during the final decade of the twentieth century. By taking advantage of film noir's subversive possibilities (see Flory 2008, 23–27), black filmmakers were able to fashion many of their movies into a critical cinema that aspired to at least some of the goals of imperfect "Third Cinema," the international movement that arose mostly from underdeveloped nations during the 1960s and 1970s, the relevance of which to black film has been outlined by Tommy Lott (1997) and Clyde Taylor (1998, esp. 254–73). In particular, black noir films from the first half of the 1990s made broadly accessible to African American audiences and newly attracted crossover white audiences elements of black life that had been hitherto seldom seem on movie and TV screens. Problems of black subordination as well as the deleterious effects of white privilege are made available to anyone willing to cinematically explore the black underworld. In these ways, African American film noir developed into a form of critical cinema capable of trenchantly portraying antiblack racism for mass audiences.

Of course, no discussion of African American film noir's development during the first half of the 1990s would be complete without reference to

Devil in a Blue Dress (1995). Here, unlike most other films in the 1991–95 black noir cycle, we are presented with a "retro-noir" focused squarely on historical black life: *Devil in a Blue Dress* is set in the classic period of film noir and aims to make visible the black life-world during that era. Its opening line of dialogue, "It was summer 1948 and I needed money," introduces not only the protagonist, Ezekiel "Easy" Rawlins (Denzel Washington), but also the period, as well as a tone of desperation that pervaded much of post–World War II America, especially for African Americans coming out of the war experience and possessing a heightened sense of civil rights. The film directs our attention to a world seldom if ever depicted in film noir's classical period: the rich and vibrant African American culture of postwar Los Angeles. We are given luxuriant senses of Central Avenue and the respectable, working-class neighborhood of Watts, seventeen years before it became synonymous with the urban uprising that exemplified similar disturbances across the United States in the 1960s. By contrast, the Santa Monica pier and Hollywood Hills, as spaces reserved for whites, are shown to be places of danger, violence, and crime for Easy. Naremore notes that this strategy "defamiliarizes the entire city" for us as viewers, particularly as it was depicted in noirs of the classic era (2008, 250).

Like Franklin's earlier film *One False Move*, *Devil in a Blue Dress* exploits the figure of the femme fatale to revise the stock "tragic mulatta" character type. Justus Nieland argues that both of Franklin's works highlight the racial unfairness that their female leads experience in order to show that their supposed lethalness is attributable not to presumed "evil" natures but to circumstances that are profoundly unjust (1999, 68–75). The disruptive and sometimes criminal actions of Lila Walker (Cynda Williams) in *One False Move* and Daphne Monet (Jennifer Beals) in *Devil in a Blue Dress* are not due to greed, selfishness, or some other wicked motivation but rather a desperation to fit in and live a decent human life relatively unencumbered by race. *Devil in a Blue Dress* is further distinguished by the fact that its protagonist, unlike many other noir characters, wants to live a law-abiding and comparatively ordinary existence, but is sucked into criminality against his will because presumptions about being an African American male distort the views of whites with whom he must interact. He is seen as "uppity" by his white factory boss, as a criminal by the police, and as a resident in good standing of the underworld by white gangsters and politicians alike. He has little choice but to accede to the pressures of their imposed perceptions and play the role that they have forced on him. He calls on his old friend Mouse (Don Cheadle), someone who has maniacally embraced criminality and made it his own, for help. With Mouse's murderous assistance, Easy is able to extricate himself from circumstances that would otherwise have doomed him. Also an instance of "noir doubling," whereby characters are paired in psychological counterpoint (Guerrero 1996, 40), Mouse and Easy function to highlight each other's actions. In particular, Mouse's psychotic behavior works to foreground Easy's attempts to resist evil and maintain a fuller sense of humanity. Complimented by a rhythm-and-blues soundtrack from race records of the era and marketed as a "black *Chinatown*" (Naremore 2008, 249), *Devil in a Blue Dress* offers a template "for a fully developed black cinema," according to Guerrero, by illustrating how filmmakers may "struggle against, represent, and mediate the fundamental condition of black people in America" (1998, 329, 351).

African American Film Noir's Ongoing Legacy and Influence

UNFORTUNATELY, THE YEARS 1991 to 1995 constitute a "bubble" in terms of both African American film noir's popularity and its success. Whether as a result of having saturated the market, of recoil on the part of white America to black reactions regarding the O. J. Simpson trial, as Guerrero argues (1996, 41; 1998, 349), or of reactions to the Million Man March, this form of cinema noticeably declined after the release of *Devil in a Blue Dress* and its lack of box office success. A number of productions subsequently had cable television premieres or went straight to video rather than having movie theater releases, reflecting this downgrade in production cost support. Still, even as production, in terms of both numbers and budget, slacked off in the latter half of the 1990s, compelling examples of African American film noir continued to be released. Notable titles from the second half of the decade include *Eve's Bayou* (1997), *I'm 'Bout It* (1997), *Always Outnumbered, Always Outgunned* (1998), *Summer of Sam* (1999), and *Bamboozled* (2000). These last two titles, both from Spike Lee, constitute an interesting contrast in the sense that, while *Summer of Sam* is a fascinating exploration of white ethnicity and the ways in which the early punk movement rejected the signifiers and markers of success for whiteness, *Bamboozled* is a blistering exploration of American blackness and its complicity with blackface minstrelsy. I would argue that both of these films remain underappreciated, and agree with Guerrero that "*Bamboozled* stands as Lee's most accomplished, disturbing, satirically sharp and politically relevant feature since *Do the Right Thing* (1989)" (2012, 114), but would add that it does so partly by means of film noir techniques and thematics. For instance, in order to convey the film's political satire, Lee noirishly narrates his story using a dead man's voice and employs tilted camera angles to indicate the off-balance nature of his characters. *Summer of Sam*, on the other hand, critically examines events surrounding the 1977 Son of Sam murders through the eyes and experiences of a group of young Italian-Americans. At times this film directly quotes from Jules Dassin's noir masterpiece *The Naked City* (1948) and offers us fascinating narrative figures that generate the same ambivalence and ambiguity that have so often been a hallmark of film noir characterization. *Always Outnumbered, Always Outgunned* and *I'm 'Bout It*, by contrast, did not receive theatrical releases, but nonetheless deserve careful attention (see Flory 2008, 244–53; T. Lott 2012, 156). *Eve's Bayou*, on the other hand, constitutes an example of African American film noir that applies itself to problems facing black women. Writer and director Kasi Lemmons uses conventions of female Gothic melodrama that edge their way into film noir to fashion a gripping tale of mystery, danger, and ambivalent redemption.

African American film noir has continued into the new millennium in the form of such works as *Training Day* (2001), *Stranger Inside* (2001), *Out of Time* (2003), *Never Die Alone* (2004), *Get Rich or Die Tryin'* (2005), *Faster* (2011), *LUV* (2012), *Fruitvale Station* (2013), and *Moonlight* (2016), in addition to numerous straight-to-video releases in the mold of *I'm 'Bout It*. Black noir has also substantively influenced international productions focusing on race such as *City of God* (Brazil, 2002), *Dirty Pretty Things* (Great Britain, 2002), *Hotel Rwanda* (USA/UK/Italy/South Africa, 2004), *Catch a Fire* (France/UK/South Africa/USA, 2006), and *Gangster's Paradise* (South Africa, 2009), as well as more mainstream Hollywood fare like *Crash* (2005), *Traitor* (2008), and

Straight Outta Compton (2015), and TV series like *The Wire* (2002–8), *Power* (2014–), and *Empire* (2015–).

In addition to challenging the boundaries and conception of film noir itself, among African American film noir's most distinctive traits is its capacity to humanize what would otherwise be regarded as criminalistic characters for mainstream, predominantly white audiences, often through developing empathy and a sense of identification with black youth or men (and less often, women). Typically foregrounded by such efforts are intersections of race, class, and hopelessness—what West refers to as "black nihilism" (West 1993)—and challenges issued to audience members to think reflectively about the political struggles facing African Americans in real-life situations that are mirrored in these fictional worlds. This subgenre's importance historically, sociopolitically, and cinematically thus involves its lucid depiction of conditions of great concern to African Americans and others as they advance deeper into the twenty-first century.

Some might argue that film noir is fundamentally nihilistic and offers little in the way of hope or prospects for the future. But I would argue that this perspective shows a misunderstanding of what nihilism is. If anything, film noir, and especially African American film noir, shows that nihilism can be not only negative and destructive—nihilism's usual meaning—but also positive and constructive. As philosopher Jacqueline Scott (2006) has argued, this positive side of nihilism can be applied to race in ways that could help us to find our way out of difficulties posed by antiblack racism (see also Flory 2008, e.g., 173–84). In showing and giving us occasion to understand the soul-destroying grounds for black nihilism, many of these films provoke us to reconceptualize race's role in the societal institutions that shape our lives. The best of these films give us a basis for hope of fostering change as well as reasons to be critical of the state of race in America. In this way African American film noir has an ongoing role to play in not only exposing the ugly underside of race but also its eventual dissolution.

Works Cited

Borde, Raymond, and Etienne Chaumeton. [1955] 2002. *A Panorama of American Film Noir, 1941–1953.* Translated by Paul Hammond. San Francisco: City Lights Books.

Covey, William. 2003. "The Genre Don't Know Where It Came From: African American Neo-Noir Since the 1960s." *Journal of Film and Video* 55, no. 2–3: 59–72.

Cripps, Thomas. 1978. *Black Film as Genre*. Bloomington: Indiana University Press.

———. 1993. *Making Movies Black: The Hollywood Message Movie from World War II to the Civil Rights Era*. New York: Oxford University Press.

———. 2003. "Introduction to 1929–1940: Hollywood Beckons." In *Instructor's Guide to African Americans in Cinema: The First Half Century*, edited by Phyllis R. Klotman. Urbana: University of Illinois Press. CD-ROM.

Diawara, Manthia. 1993. "*Noir* by *Noirs*: Toward a New Realism in Black Cinema." In *Shades of Noir*, edited by Joan Copjec, 261–78. London: Verso.

Flory, Dan. 2008. *Philosophy, Black Film,* Film Noir. University Park: Penn State University Press.

Fuchs, Cynthia, ed. 2002. *Spike Lee: Interviews*. Jackson: University of Mississippi Press.

Guerrero, Ed. 1993. *Framing Blackness: The African American Image in Film*. Philadelphia: Temple University Press.

———. 1996. Review of *Devil in a Blue Dress*. *Cineaste* 22, no. 1: 38–41.

———. 1998. "A Circus of Dreams and Lies: The Black Film Wave at Middle Age." In *The New American Cinema*, edited by Jon Lewis, 328–52. Durham: Duke University Press.

———. 2012. "*Bamboozled*: In the Mirror of Abjection." In *Contemporary Black American Cinema: Race, Gender, and Sexuality at the Movies*, edited by Mia Mask, 109–27. New York: Routledge.

Higham, Charles, and Joel Greenberg. 1968. *Hollywood in the Forties*. New York: A. S. Barnes.

Homes, Geoffrey. (1946) 1988. *Build My Gallows High*. London: Simon and Schuster.

Hughes, Allen. 1994. Interview. In *The Hughes Brothers Talk About "Menace II Society*. Supplement on *Menace II Society* DVD, directed by Albert and Allen Hughes, 1993. New Line Home Video, 1997.

Jones, Jacquie. 1991. "The New Ghetto Aesthetic." *Wide Angle* 13, no. 3–4: 32–43.

Kaplan, E. Ann. 1998. "The 'Dark Continent' of Film Noir: Race, Displacement and Metaphor in Tourneur's *Cat People* (1942) and Welles' *The Lady from Shanghai* (1948)." In *Women and Film Noir*, edited by E. Ann Kaplan, 183–201. New Edition. London: BFI Publishing.

Lott, Eric. 1997. "The Whiteness of Film Noir." *American Literary History* 9: 542–66.

Lott, Tommy L. 1997. "Aesthetic and Politics in Contemporary Black Film Theory." In *Film Theory and Philosophy*, edited by Richard Allen and Murray Smith, 282–302. Oxford: Clarendon Press.

———. 1999. "A No-theory Theory of Contemporary Black Cinema." In *The Invention of Race: Black Culture and the Politics of Representation*, 139–151. London: Blackwell.

———. 2012. "Film Noir, Realism, and the Ghettocentric Film." *Film and Philosophy* 16: 148–161.

Motley, Willard. (1947) 2001. *Knock on Any Door*. DeKalb: Northern Illinois University Press.

Munby, Jonathan. 2011. *Under a Bad Sign: Criminal Self-Representation in African American Popular Culture*. Chicago: University of Chicago Press.

Naremore, James. 2008. *More Than Night: Film Noir in Its Contexts*. Second Edition. Berkeley: University of California Press.

Neal, Mark Anthony. 2002. *Soul Babies: Black Popular Culture and the Post-Soul Aesthetic*. New York: Routledge.

Nieland, Justus J. 1999. "Race-ing *Noir* and Re-placing History: The Tragic Mulatta and Memory in *One False Move* and *Devil in a Blue Dress*." *Velvet Light Trap* 43: 63–77.

Reid, Mark A. 1993. "The Black Gangster Film." *Journal of Social Philosophy* 24: 143–54.

Rhines, Jesse Algernon. 1996. *Black Film/White Money*. New Brunswick: Rutgers University Press.

Scott, Jacqueline. 2006. "'The Price of the Ticket': A Genealogy and Revaluation of Race." In *Critical Affinities: Nietzsche and African American Thought*, edited by Jacqueline Scott and A. Todd Franklin, 149–74. Albany: SUNY Press.

Scruggs, Charles. 2011. "Out of the Black Past: The Image of the Fugitive Slave in Jacques Tourneur's *Out of the Past*." *African American Review* 44: 97–113.

Silver, Alain, Elizabeth Ward, James Ursini, and Robert Porfirio, eds. 2010. *Film Noir: The Encyclopedia*. New York: Overlook Duckworth.

Taylor, Clyde. 1998. *The Mask of Art: Breaking the Aesthetic Contract—Film and Literature*. Bloomington: Indiana University Press.

Watkins, S. Craig. 1998. *Representing: Hip-hop Culture and the Production of Black Cinema*. Chicago: University of Chicago Press.

West, Cornel. 1993. "Black Nihilism in America." In *Race Matters*. Boston: Beacon Press.

III

POSTNEGRITUDE BLACK FILM

PASTICHE AND RACE

7

"WHO'S THAT NIGGA ON THAT NAG?"

Django Unchained and the Return of the Blaxploitation Hero

Melba Joyce Boyd

WHEN SAMUEL L. JACKSON's character, Stephen, exclaims "Who's that nigga on that nag?" in *Django Unchained* (2012), it captures the outrageous timbre of Quentin Tarantino's film and the bravado with which the writer and director presents the historical and cultural experience of slavery in a spaghetti Western set in the antebellum South in 1858. Tarantino is a problematic director for many critics, and his controversial aesthete occupies a particularly ambiguous reception with American theatergoers. *Django Unchained* is no exception, and perhaps instigates even more debates because this film attacks slavery and critiques various aspects of the "peculiar institution" in provocative ways and language that is reminiscent of the 1975 Blaxploitation flick *Mandingo* (1975), a favorite of Tarantino's.

 Django Unchained provides cultural and historical insight, "signifies" on blackface stereotypes, and chastises Hollywood cinema's misrepresentation of slavery. The film's tragic dimensions convey the horrors of slavery; consequently, the revenge executed against those guilty of profiting from it and enforcing abuse that sustains it, can be exhilarating for the audience and possibly cathartic for African Americans who experience a vicarious sense of satisfaction through the main character's heroic actions. In sync with the Black Power movement, the Blaxploitation hero is always a macho character who never backs down and is often in pursuit of revenge for some serious racial transgression, a theme applauded by 1970s audiences. Tarantino further complicates and intensifies this cinematic genre by incorporating excessive violence that is sometimes juxtaposed with humor for comic relief.

Similarly, Tarantino insists that the audience deal with racism in the raw. In his review of *Django Unchained*, David Denby (2013) stated: "How much of this n-wording is faithful reporting of the way people talked in 1858, or necessary dramatic emphasis, and how much of it is there to titillate and razz the audience" (Lyman 2013)? In response to his query, the word was pervasive and commonplace in 1858. The "N-word" may be disturbing to contemporary ears, especially when a black character exclaims in mixed company, "Who's that nigga on that nag?" Although the word is fraught with deep and complex contradictions that have not been adequately addressed or resolved, "nigga" is still spoken in the vernacular. The word, like the ideas associated with it, persists because racist conditions persist.[1] Regardless of how uncomfortable the word feels, its use in *Django Unchained* is historically accurate and aesthetically honest.[2]

This discussion of *Django Unchained* considers the myriad complexities of the film, including historical details, cinematic fantasies, transtemporal, contradictory characterizations, and multiple thematic intersections. It also considers how the film engages and entertains African American audiences, and why that interaction is uniquely linked to the cultural memory of slavery and an unresolved sense of injustice and anger. In this regard, the discussion recognizes Tarantino's transcultural identification with African Americans, as exemplified in the film's perspective, its black hero, and the thematic projections in a work that received five Academy Award nominations for 2012, including Best Screenplay.

Spaghetti Westerns, Django Flicks, and Black Cowboys

TARANTINO'S UNPRECEDENTED, POSTMODERN CONFIGURATION of genres combines a broad range of thematic and structural elements to comprise *Django Unchained*, which has tributaries in *Viva Django* (1968)[3] and *Django* (1966). Written and directed by Fernando Baldi, *Viva Django* is a spaghetti Western with a typical plot wherein a wealthy and greedy landowner attempts to get rid of the other ranchers so he can take over their land. He hires Django, a gunfighter, to kill off his competition, but Django flips the script by enlisting the would-be victims to join his gang in order to get revenge because the villain is responsible for the death of his wife. In the Japanese *Sukiyaki Western Django* (2008), written and directed by Takashi Mike, Quentin Tarantino actually appears as Piringo, one of the gunfighters. Tarantino incorporates the revenge theme and extensive gunfight scenes from these previous *Django* flicks, except his Django is black.

Films that feature black cowboys are rare, though some earlier "race" films from the 1930s and 1940s, such as *The Bronze Buckaroo* (1939), were modeled after mainstream westerns and were shown primarily in theatres in black urban communities, or on off-nights in segregated, white theatres. As Bogle (1973) cites, these films were produced for black audiences and primarily contain a black cast. It is important to note the historical presence of black Westerns that featured African American characters. This ethnic film genre receives minimal consideration in mainstream film studies culture.

Herbert Jefferies starred in *Harlem on the Prairie* in 1937 as a singing cowboy, Bob Blakely, and then in *The Bronze Buckaroo*, directed by Richard C. Kahn and released in 1939. Jefferies faded into obscurity, but he was finally honored with a 1996 Golden Boot Award for his contributions to cowboy films. In *Sergeant Rutledge* (1960), released at the height of the civil rights movement, Woody Strode plays a Buffalo Soldier falsely accused of raping a white woman. This drama about race in a major motion picture received considerable attention. Sydney Poitier's character in *Buck and the Preacher* (1972) actually faces the contradictions of his past as a Buffalo Soldier. He avenges an attack on a black wagon train in his debut as a film director. The production quality and the pedigree of the actors (Harry Belafonte and Ruby Dee costar) resulted in a classic piece of cinema grounded in historical accuracy with a progressive political perspective. During a negotiation with a Native American nation, Buck is reminded of his military past as a US soldier during the Indian Wars. However, the wagon train is given safe passage across Indian Territory, and Native American warriors even provide cover for Buck and Preacher, who are escaping a white posse. Mario Van Peebles's *Posse* (1993) revisits the characterization of Buffalo Soldiers, who seek justice after a racist attack.

Whereas these previous films illuminate African American cowboys in American history, and in some instances use the West as a setting for resistance against white oppression, other Westerns exemplify black/white friendships. Lou Gossett and James Garner partner in *The Skin Game* (1973) to hustle slave traders, and Danny Glover costars in Lawrence Kasdan's *Silverado* (1985) and partners with three white friends to defeat the greedy rancher responsible for killing his father and stealing their land. These integrated films are forerunners to the black/white team of Django Freeman (Jamie Foxx) and Dr. King Schultz (Christoph Waltz) in *Django Unchained*.

Variations of Violence for Thematic Purpose

IN *DJANGO UNCHAINED*, VARIATIONS of violence appear in particular patterns in order to facilitate action or to articulate meaning. Tarantino films are associated with excessive violence, but at the same time, a closer look at execution reveals purpose. The inclusion of Mandingo wrestling as a critical aspect of the plot provides another context to emphasize the violent exploitation of the black body for its sheer masculinity, which was an essential aspect of slavery. Its historical accuracy or lack thereof is irrelevant. The owners of these wrestlers, and in particular, Calvin Candie (Leonardo DiCaprio), are exposed for their obscene thirst for violence as entertainment and their power over these strong men, which gives the slave masters a false sense of superiority. The Mandingo wrestlers are controlled by the threat of death as they engage in fights to the death. Conversely, if they are victorious, they are rewarded with sex and alcohol.

The inclusion of Mandingo wrestlers alludes to the film *Mandingo*, which, unlike most other 1970s Blaxploitation flicks, was a full-scale Hollywood production directed by Richard Fleischer and produced by Dino Delaurentis. Based on a novel and a play with the same title, the film included interracial sex, which was considered controversial at the time; and with a few exceptions, the film was condemned as cliché and stereotypical. The combination of sex and violence moves the script, as the slave Mede (Ken Norton) trains to fight other slaves and becomes sexually entangled with the wife of his master, who is likewise engaged in a sexual liaison with a lovely slave girl (Brenda Sykes).

Despite the film's dubious critical reception, it was very popular with black audiences, primarily because, unlike most mainstream films that portray slavery as an unequal but benign institution, *Mandingo* includes strong, handsome, black men who are not bowing and scraping. Mede's character is supposed to be Mandingo, which is a corruption of Mandinka, the name of a West African people.[4] An indication of Tarantino's awareness of the term appears in a line of dialogue of *Jackie Brown* (1997) when Odell (Samuel L. Jackson) inquires about the muscular Winston (Tommy "Tiny" Lister): "Who's that big, Mandingo-looking nigga you got up there on that picture with you?"

Just as in the film *Mandingo*, sex is presented as a critical component of the slave experience in *Django Unchained*, and in the latter, sex appears as a complement to the wrestling matches. Candie's beautiful slave mistress, Sheba (Nicole Galicia), whose biblical name is symbolically ironic, exudes sexuality and obvious familiarity with Candie. She attends the wrestling matches and sits at the dinner table. While the Mandingo wrestlers fight to the death, the white men drink, laugh, and mix sexual seduction with physical destruction. Django surmises that Broomhilda (Kerry Washington) is probably a "comfort girl," and this probability is confirmed at the Candieland Plantation, when it is suggested that she likes being "boned" by the Mandingo wrestlers. These sexual arrangements are not consensual; therefore it is rape, another crime of violence.[5]

A similarity between the two slave masters in the film is their sexual intimacy with slave women, and Big Daddy (Don Johnson) breeds these "ponies." Tarantino frames Big Daddy on the balcony with his house servants and his biracial offspring. While most of the slaves struggle in the cotton fields, attractive black women casually relax because they are to be sold for their physical beauty and sex appeal. To get access to Big Daddy's plantation, Schultz expresses interest in buying one of his "beautiful nigger gals." This mixture of sex and violence is characteristic of slavery, as well as a dominant feature of American cinema, but in this context there is a political critique.

Tarantino and Violence

DESPITE SOME DIFFERENCES, THERE are parallels in presentations of violence between Tarantino's *Kill Bill* (2003) and *Django Unchained*. In *Kill Bill*, dark red blood contrasts against a white background (snow) as the tempo slows and causes the audience to concentrate on the moment of death. Similar slower-paced scenes occur during the assassinations of the slave masters, Big Daddy and Calvin Candie. Large-scale shoot-outs and dynamite explosions constitute excitement throughout these films, but the more measured and deliberate acts of assassination transfer stronger symbolic and thematic emphasis.

When Django kills two Brittle brothers, who are overseers on Big Daddy's Carrucan plantation, their deaths are humiliating and agonizing. Flashbacks of John Brittle whipping Broomhilda appear intermittently as Django approaches Brittle,[6] who has pages from the Bible pinned to his shirt and is quoting Scripture as he snaps his whip, as he prepares to punish the young slave girl, Jodie, "for breaking eggs."[7] After Django kills John Brittle with a bullet through a page from the Old Testament, he stands there in shock as blood drips down the print. Before Django kills Roger Brittle, he whips him mercilessly. Dr. King Schultz kills Ellis, the third Brittle, attempting escape on horseback through the cotton fields. As the impact of the bullet is heard, Ellis falls off his horse and blood splatters across the white cotton blossoms, symbolism that underscores slavery as a deadly, evil industry.

Because killing white men dispels the illusion of white invincibility, Big Daddy recruits a hooded gang of white men to murder Schultz and to lynch Django. A flashback interrupts the attack. Their white hoods foreshadow the Ku Klux Klan, and the scene mocks D. W. Griffith's *Birth of a Nation*. The seriousness of this posse as an immediate threat is circumvented by the comedic conversation about their dysfunctional disguises. Their incompetence is further accentuated when the hooded thugs are blown to Smithereens. Big Daddy's death, however, is paced to the slow-motion gallop of his white horse, as a single shot is heard and he falls off the horse and off camera. A medium shot of the horse's white neck reveals a large smearing of dark blood. As in the death scene of the villain in *Kill Bill I*, juxtaposing red blood against a white object, such as the cotton blossoms or a white horse, emphasizes revenge as bloody justice.

Unlike the climactic death of Big Daddy, which occurs after all the shooting and the explosion, the death of the slave master Calvin Candie initiates a gunfight. Schultz realizes his carefully measured decision to kill Candie will certainly result in his own death and other dire consequences, a fact that is reflected in his apology to Django just before pulling the trigger. The bullet passes through a white carnation pinned to the left lapel of Candie's jacket. Dark blood oozes out the center, slowly discoloring the white flower. Shock and disbelief appear on Candie's face. Everyone is momentarily stunned until Stephen's scream breaks the silence.

The shoot-out that ensues is like a scene from *Kill Bill*, hectic and fast-paced. Schultz is immediately killed, and Django responds by shooting his assailants. Blood gushes everywhere, spray-painting the white walls and doorways red as bullets rip through bodies. One pathetic character yells in pain and disbelief, and the audience experiences an incredulous, horrific response to the excessive, effusion of blood. Django is forced to surrender and escapes death by castration, but is sold to the LeQuint Dickey Mining Company. This foreshadows another form of slavery after abolition, whereby black men are unjustly accused and convicted of crimes they have not committed in order to supply free labor for the mines, which is documented in Sam Pollard's film, *Slavery by Another Name* (2012).

Django escapes this fate after another shoot-out, and blows up Tarantino's character, carrying a saddlebag full of dynamite. This cameo appearance is Tarantino's signature and underlines the fantasy aspect of the violence.

Django returns to Candieland to avenge Dr. Schultz's death, to destroy the Big House, and to free his wife. In a surprise attack, he kills the gunmen and the masked gunwoman (who is symbolic of Tarantino's thematic disruption of gender identity). After the burial of Candie, Miss Laura, Candie's main henchmen, and the house slaves enter the Big House to find Django dressed in Calvin Candie's expensive, burgundy suit and posed above the foyer with a gun pointed at them. As "master" of the situation, Django casually announces his purpose. He shoots Billy Cash (Walter Goggins) in his crotch because this gunman, who switches throughout the film like a gay queen, was sexually excited about castrating Django.

He tells all the black people to leave, "except you Stephen," and to "tell Miss Laura good-bye." When Django shoots Miss Laura, the impact literally lifts her off her feet and hurls her backward and offscreen. As a stereotypical slave mistress, she is not a sympathetic character, so this cartoonish exit evokes laughter in the audience. What follows is the execution of the rest of the white people in the foyer.

After the shooting, Stephen discards his cane and his fake limp and walks toward Django, saying, "I counted 6 bullets." To wit, Django replies, "I count two guns." In a scene that shifts the tempo of the mise-en-scène, Django shoots Stephen in both knees, forcing him into a submissive pose and trapping him inside of the Big House. As Django walks slowly toward his wife, waiting for him on horseback, Stephen screams "Candieland is forever!" and then the Big House explodes in the background.

Violence and Historical Reality

IN CONTRAST TO OUTRAGEOUS shoot-out scenes created for fantasy or assassinations designed for metaphorical or thematic statement, the violence reflected in the portrayal of the slave experience in the film is historically grounded. The inclusion of various forms of torture and torment of slaves exceeds most other cinematic presentations of slavery. Moreover, the manner of presentation is as aggressive and intrusive as the methods of punishment. Beginning with the opening scene, the contrast between white and black, or master and slave, is established. White men riding horses wear warm coats while pulling shoeless, shirtless slaves in tattered pants with only rough blankets to cover their torsos in winter weather. A close-up shot focuses on the chains around their ankles. The disparity in this scene illustrates the cruelty of chattel slavery and establishes the racial context of the film.

In another scene in Greenville, Mississippi, and the site for slave auctions, iron bridles or masks appear on slaves being led through town in chains. Others are constrained by iron collars with long hook extensions that make escape nearly impossible. Bridles or masks were used to punish a slave for something he or she might have said, or in some cases to prevent them from poisoning themselves in an attempt to end their miserable existence.[8] When Django is captured after the shoot-out in the Candieland Big House and hung upside down in the barn, an iron mask restricts him from speaking as Billy Cash, framed between Django's legs, stares and toys with Django's genitals as he prepares to castrate him. The inversion of Django's body symbolizes the sexual perversion in this gruesome form of execution, which is also an act of emasculation.

Whippings were the most common method of control, and the whipping scenes in the film are effective because they are relayed through close-up shots of the victim's face, screaming in sync with the crack of the whip. The scars shown on Django's back and the backs of the other slaves in the opening scene are subsequently associated with whippings in subsequent flashbacks. But it is Broomhilda's face that evokes the horror of the actual experience, a fact that is confirmed later when Candie exposes her scars and jokes about it at the dinner table. In a flashback, Django pleads with John Brittle to let him take her lashes, saying he is the cause of their attempted escape. Likewise, a close-up shot of the branding of Broomhilda's cheek with the "r" for runaway is terrifying to view; as the hot iron smokes and sizzles, the audience recoils. The disfiguring of the beautiful Broomhilda (Kerry Washington) is to some extent a more horrific image than the branding of a man because she is small in stature and the perpetrator is a large, overbearing white man.

Django winces and places his hand over his gun when Stephen tells Calvin Candie that Broomhilda is locked inside the hotbox for trying to escape again. "How long has she been in there?" Calvin inquires. "Most the day," Stephen responds. The camera cuts to the dry grass in the field, but the hotbox, an iron solitary confinement cell that was developed at Yuma Prison (Tarantino 2012), cannot be seen until she is taken out because it is below ground level. Broomhilda is completely naked, and when Billy Cash throws a bucket of water over her, the sound of the water sizzling on hot metal is heard. Tossed inside a wheelbarrow, she is carted away like a sack of flour. One can only imagine the range and severity of suffering that results from being locked inside this box. Moreover, if Candie had not ordered her release, her punishment, as decreed by Stephen, was to be a week.

The most disturbing scene in the film is the killing of a Mandingo wrestler by bloodhounds. Though the dramatic tension heightens, the dismemberment of the man is unanticipated. Like the whipping scenes, the dog attack is implied through quick, cryptic, jagged shots and the sounds of growling dogs and the man's chilling screams, juxtaposed with longer close-ups of the facial reactions of Schultz, who is horrified, and Candie, who

Bounty hunter Dr. King Schultz (Christoph Waltz) and Django (Jamie Foxx), a former slave whom Dr. Shultz freed and who assists in his vengeance against slave owners, overseers, and house Negroes in *Django Unchained.*

is exhilarated. The killing of this Mandingo wrestler reoccurs as flashback images in Schultz's thoughts shortly before he assassinates Candie.

Dynamic Symmetry and Characterization

INTERACTION BETWEEN CHARACTERS DETERMINES the dynamic symmetry that facilitates meaning relative to plot and theme. Dr. Schultz is a bounty hunter, another spaghetti Western aspect of the film. About his profession, he explains: "Like slavery, it is a cash for flesh business." Of course, the key difference is that a bounty hunter delivers a corpse and gets paid, but a slave's body is only valuable alive. The intersection of the two businesses brings Schultz and Django together, and as the two lead characters, their relationship is the most significant in the film.

Schultz purchases Django because he needs him to identify the Brittle brothers, and then apologizes for engaging in the slave trade. He enters into an agreement with Django that assures his freedom and payment upon the completion of the mission. Schultz's method of collection is to execute the wanted men, not to take them alive. There is no due process. "They are very bad men," he says. Django willingly participates because he knows just how evil the Brittle brothers are, and this pursuit also serves his own vendetta.

The dynamic symmetry between Django and Schultz is symbiotic. They are an unlikely pair due to differences in race and national origin. However, these differences are superficial and inconsequential because of similar inter-

Big Daddy (Don Johnson) welcomes Dr. Schultz.

ests, talents and a German fairy tale. Their partnership evolves into friendship, and to convey this camaraderie and racial equality, they are often framed in two shots on the same level, riding side by side in panoramic long shots. At the same time, Schultz maintains his European style, wearing fur coats and narrow-brim hats, while Django exchanges his flamboyant valet outfit of royal blue velvet for a slick cowboy outfit with a leather jacket, hat, and boots.

Django's change in costume represents his transformation into a dangerous gunslinger. As he assumes his free identity, he begins to respond to the word "nigger" differently. In the earlier scenes, he does not flinch when the word is used in reference to him because he is a slave, but after he becomes Django Freeman, he responds by insulting the speaker. He calls Billy Cash "white boy" and Stephen "snowball." His attitude says as much as his words. Django's identity is a wonderful articulation of difference and defiance. He repeatedly says, "the D is silent," a declaration of independence and individuality as well as a pronouncement of his literacy. Schultz teaches him the trade of bounty hunting and to read. Since it was forbidden to teach slaves to read, literacy is another aspect of freedom. Django is consistently introduced as a free man, and the translation of that status completes his identity—Django Freeman. Big Daddy correlates Django's "free" status as on par with that of a poor white man, a person with no status or real power, and refers to Schultz as "a nigger lover," which from his cultural perspective is an insult. However, Tarantino presents the relationship between Django and Schultz as one of respect and genuine friendship.

Considering the antislavery movement and other progressive, socialist movements in nineteenth-century Germany, Schultz's political consciousness is historically grounded. Although he is a nonpracticing dentist, he is an educated man whose English vocabulary exceeds the comprehension of most Americans he encounters. In fact, many of the lower-class white characters are illiterate and ignorant, which correlates with their bigotry and an illusion of superiority relative to black slaves. In a similar regard, the film identifies how class and race divisions benefit the ruling class.

When Schultz pledges to go with Django to Mississippi (which appears in huge, upper-case letters on the screen to emphasize the significance of the setting) to help free his wife, the relationship moves to another level. After all, Schultz says, "As a German, I cannot ignore meeting a real live Siegfried." A symbolic parallel is drawn between Django's enslaved wife and the unjust imprisonment of Broomhilda in the German fairy tale. Django is the hero of the black Broomhilda von Schaft, whose identity is enhanced by the fact that she can speak German.

The dynamic symmetry between Django and Broomhilda is mediated by love, but the absence of nude lovemaking scenes differentiates their connection from the sexualized slave experience, where others control the body. Their love is elevated to another level, representing far more than physical attraction—the spirit of freedom. Indeed, the scars on their backs and the "r" on their cheeks seal a transcendent bond. Despite the possibility that his wife is used as a "pleasure girl" for the Mandingo wrestlers, her enslaved situation does not diminish Django's love. Tarantino excluded a love scene in the script that turns into a brutal rape of the couple by the overseers, which would have further intensified and sexualized the violence (Tarantino 2012). The audience is reminded of Django's devotion and undying love for Broomhilda when she appears in his daydreams dressed in a yellow satin dress, strolling nearby in a field, smiling at him. Their connection is so strong that Stephen detects it and surmises the true purpose of Schultz's engagement with Candie—to purchase Broomhilda.

When Django arrives in Candieland, he assumes the role of a slave trader. As a free black man, he operates outside the rules of social fiction that govern racial interactions. He talks back to all the white men, includ-

House Negro Stephen (Samuel L. Jackson) suspects that Broomhilda von Schaft (Kerry Washington) had a previous relationship with Django.

ing Candie, who accepts Django's defiant attitude because he wants to do business with Schultz. Stephen is far more disturbed by this disruption of the racial hierarchy, and demands to know, "Who's that nigga on that nag?" His response echoes the amazement of white people in Daughtry, Texas, and likewise when Big Daddy insists that "niggers are not allowed to ride horses on my plantation." Riding a horse, as reflected in the opening scene, is indicative of status and racial staging.

In his review, film critic Peter Bradshaw (2013) explains: "Tarantino shoves everything like this under your nose. Only he and Jackson could possibly have gotten away with that Stephen character: it is genuinely gasp-inducing. Like the word "nigger," this character is a cultural irritation to whites and a hated figure to blacks." Samuel L. Jackson's compelling portrayal of a provocative, diabolical character he called "the most hated black character in cinema history" should also be considered with all his layers and thematic implications. The dynamic symmetry of this pair is the opposite of the Django and Schultz duo, which is one of respect and equality. However, beyond the obvious ass kissing, the power dynamics and codependency between Stephen and Calvin Candie operate outside and inside the library, where we first see Stephen signing checks in Candie's name. Stephen's literacy is indicative of his access to information and power. He even gives orders to the overseers and the white workers.

Despite his disgruntled complaining, Stephen knows not to disrupt protocol in public. Close scrutiny of the interactions and contradictions between Stephen and Candie resolves an understanding about humanity and disputes claims about the simplicity of the film. For example, after Candie returns to Candieland, Stephen explains how much he has missed him, but also cleverly signifies on his master by saying, "I missed you like a rock in my shoe." Although Candie explains to Stephen that Django "is another cheeky bastard, just like you," Stephen is outraged because Django is going to be a guest in the Big House. Although Stephen acquiesces to his master's instructions, he loudly exclaims: "Yo Daddy is turning over in his grave!" Django upsets the racial hierarchy, an order that Stephen straddles and supervises in Candieland. Just like the arrangement of the dinner table that is meticulously set by house slaves, the order of things must be strictly maintained if Stephen is to preserve his power and influence.

While Stephen's balding image appears to be abstracted from a box of Uncle Ben's Rice, which desexualizes his masculinity, his limp and his cane are likewise suggestive of the African trickster god, Legba. This devious intellect is portrayed during the dinner scene, by framing Stephen behind and near Candie's left ear, indicating his psychological influence as an advisor. A statue of two naked wrestlers with their posteriors framed slightly above and behind the right side of Candie's head appears in the background, suggestive of the intimacy between the two men and of the fact that Candie is an ass. Stephen echoes Candie's words, affirming his master's opinions and observations. However, he interrupts the sale of Broomhilda, insisting that Candie meet with him in the kitchen to discuss dessert. "White cake" assumes racial symbolic significance that defines the dinner course and reverses the discourse.

Stephen is like a fly, buzzing in the background, observing whatever escapes his master's gaze, but his sense of superiority is reflected in his posture when they confer in the library. While lounging and sipping bourbon, Stephen explains to Candie that Schultz and Django are "playing him for a fool." Stephen's paradoxical identity becomes even more intriguing during his conversation with Django after his capture, and Stephen reveals his self-image and inflated sense of superiority: "You would think white folks ain't ever had an original idea." Stephen manipulates his "superiors" through subversive persuasion. Candie benefits and profits from Stephen's council behind closed doors; but conversely, Stephen's subservient devotion to Candie confirms his master's belief in African civility, which is dramatically demonstrated in the dinner scene.[9] Because his power and his mentality are an extension of the slavery, Stephen's character has to be destroyed with the explosion of the Big House. In what will later be identified as "Stockholm Syndrome,"[10] his pathology evolves in response to extreme, violent, and immoral circumstances into a willingness to do anything in order to survive in this environment.

Multigenres in Imagery and Sound

THERE ARE THIRTY-EIGHT PIECES of music on the *Django Unchained* sound track, twenty-four of which are included on the album/CD release. Ennio Morricone, who worked on previous Tarantino films and spaghetti Westerns, composed original songs and incorporated some of his other compositions for the film.[11] However, Lyman (2013) cites "the prolific Italian composer and conductor who has written some of the most recognizable musical scores in cinematic history, says he will never again work with director Quentin Tarantino because he places music in his films without coherence."

Morricone's caustic response to Tarantino's musical arrangement of the soundtrack could be related to his incomprehension of the film's eclectic construct. As the executive music producer, Tarantino included country and western, African American folk, rhythm and blues, as well as classical and contemporary rap, including one that features Jamie Foxx singing. This arrangement interfaces with the film's multigenre, cross-cultural, trans-historical configuration and engages the tempo and thematic shifts in the film; hence, different genres complement or enhance the purpose of a scene, the perspective of a character, or the energy of the action.

For example, "I Got a Name," a contemplative country song by Jim Croce, is heard as Django rides through the countryside, while the rap "100 Black Coffins," an edgy, aggressive rap by Rick Ross, represents Django's political reality as a black person and expresses his attitude about life and death. The thematic inclusion of "The Payback" by James Brown and Tupac and "Too Old to Die Young" by Brother Dege appeals to the younger generation, thereby connecting a contemporary audience to the historical experience

Django and Broomhilda reunite after they have settled their past brutal treatment.

of the film. "Who Did That To You" by John Legend has cross-generational appeal, while Richie Havens combines a classic blues piece, "Sometimes I Feel Like a Motherless Child," with "Freedom," a folk song from the civil rights era.

An example of Tarantino's eclectic incorporation of song occurs during an insidious moment in the film when Miss Laura plays Beethoven's "Ode to Joy" on the harp after her brother's death threats and disgusting display of racism at the dinner table, including the sale of a human being for $12,000.[12] Her oblivious insensitivity while playing this classical German composition offends and infuriates Schultz. Tarantino's musical selections are not incoherent; they are axiomatic to the identities of the characters, their actions, multifarious thematic intersections, and audience reception. Moreover, African American culture hinges on and is most often represented through musical expression, and Tarantino's musical choices indicate a keen sense of cultural awareness of this sector of his audience.

Conclusion

DJANGO'S CHARACTER IS NOT an anomaly. Many ex-slaves ignited insurrections and participated in acts of rebellion. Some fugitives participated in the freeing of other slaves, such as in Nat Turner's Rebellion, while others joined John Brown's military activities against slavers in Kansas and in the Raid on Harper's Ferry in 1859. One might envision Django Freeman joining up with John Brown after leaving Mississippi. However, heroic characterizations of nineteenth-century black men rarely appear in mainstream culture, while the "master's narrative" has been effectively enshrined in films like *Birth of a Nation* (1914) and *Gone with the Wind* (1939). And, more importantly, the unfortunate corruption of John Brown as a historical figure in *Santa Fe Trail* (1940) portrays blacks as pathetic, submissive slaves forced by Brown to flee for freedom. While the 2012 production *Lincoln* does a commendable job of presenting legislative politics, it ignores the role African American activists, such as Frederick Douglass, played in myriad facets of achieving the Thirteenth Amendment.

The violence executed against slaves in *Django Unchained* conveys the inhumanity and cruel practices of slavery, while, like a Blaxploitation flick or a spaghetti Western, the shoot-out scenes represent the bloody cost to end it, and the execution of the slave masters emphasizes revenge on those responsible for the evil. About *Django Unchained* Peter Bradshaw (2013) concludes in his review that:

> Slavery is a subject on which modern Hollywood is traditionally nervous, a reticence amounting almost to a conspiracy of silence—except, of course, in the explicit context of abolition. As far as Hollywood is concerned, the day-to-day existence of unabolished slavery has been what welfare reformists called the live rail: don't touch it. It takes a film unencumbered with liberal good taste to try. Lars von Trier's *Manderlay* was one, and here is another. (Bradshaw, 19)

Tarantino stated in an interview with Cathy Hughes on TV One, "I'm making films for the future" (Hughes 2012). If there are any questions about what this writer and director created in *Django Unchained*, this pronouncement answers them. The younger generation and certainly subsequent ones process and experience culture differently than many of Tarantino's critics. The multicultural, postmodern, multigenre construct of the film deliberately contradicts any conventional perception of this cinematic experience. It is an attempt to illuminate the gravity of slavery and to purposefully disrupt a linear reading of history. And, in lieu of the fact that most Americans are ignorant of the severity of slavery and its racist legacy, Tarantino's aesthetics just might be one way to communicate and even transform America's oblivious conscience and consciousness.

Notes

1. In his review of *Django Unchained*, David Denby (2013) remarks: "Tarantino uses the n-word—a hundred and ten times, apparently—in a way that whites normally can't use it. The word is all over hip-hop and street talk, of course, but the taboo against it is the most powerful of all taboos in journalism and public discourse."

2. If one considers any novel written by white authors during the antebellum period, slaves are referred to and called "niggers" in the dialogue. Most recently, literary censorship of Mark Twain's *Huckleberry Finn* deleted "Nigger" from the book, including in the name of one of the main characters, Nigger Jim. Twain did not name him this because he agreed with the term, as Jim is the noblest character in the book. In fact, the expression only appears in the dialogue, and not in Twain's narrative.

3. Terrance Hill, Horst Frank, and George Eastman star in *Viva Django*.

4. "Mandingo" became a term in the black vernacular for a particular male archetype of the big, strong buck with sexual prowess.

5. The argument that a slaveholder would never destroy his property because it would not be profitable is not a sound syllogism in this context. There is profit in the sport of death as the owners wage bets, and the thrill of the final kill contributes to the gruesome satisfaction of the winner. Moreover, only very wealthy slave owners could indulge in the sport, and the whimsical disposal of "property" is yet another display of wealth. Such demonstrations are as ancient as the Roman Empire, when the emperor and the spectators could determine the ultimate fate of a gladiator slave.

6. In the script, Tarantino refers to these as spaghetti Western flashbacks.

7. Published in 1851, *Bible's Defense of Slavery* by Josiah Priest was a widely circulated book that used religion to justify slavery and to oppose abolitionists.

8. Ironically, this form of punishment or constraint was developed in Scotland sometime in the sixteenth century as a way to silence women who spoke out or against their circumstances (Edwards 2011). There are obvious parallels between the concept of the ownership of a servant and the ownership of a wife

in patriarchal societies where men determine and adjudicate laws and punishment.

9. Published in 1851, *Bible's Defense of Slavery* by Josiah Priest was a widely circulated book that used religion to justify slavery and to oppose abolitionists.

10. "Stockholm Syndrome" is the psychological tendency of a hostage to bond with, identify with, or sympathize with his or her captor.

11. Morricone is known for his music in Sergio Leone's spaghetti Westerns *The Good, the Bad and the Ugly* and *A Fist Full of Dollars*.

12. "Ode to Joy" is the theme of Bethoven's Ninth Symphony.

References

Bogle, Donald. 1973. *Toms, Coons, Mulattoes, Mammies and Bucks: An Interpretative History of Blacks in Films*. New York: Viking Press.

Bradshaw, Peter. 2013. "Quentin Tarantino makes a dizzy return to form with a horribly funny slavery western—and Samuel L. Jackson is extraordinary as the ultimate Uncle Tom." *Guardian* (online edition), January 17, 2013. https://www.theguardian.com/film/2013/jan/17/django-unchained-review

Denby, David. 2013. "'Django Unchained': Put-On, Revenge, and the Aesthetics of Trash

New Yorker (online edition), January 22, 2013. https://www.newyorker.com/culture/culture-desk/django-unchained-put-on-revenge-and-the-aesthetics-of-trash

Edwards, Ron. 2011. "Slave Tortures: The Mask, Scold's Bridle, or Brank," US Slave, usslave.blogspot.com, September 23, 2011. http://usslave.blogspot.com/2011/09/slave-tortures-mask-scolds-bridle-or.html

Hughes, Cathy. 2012. "Interview with Quentin Tarantino, Jamie Foxx, Kerry Washington, and Samuel L. Jackson." TV One, December 15, 2012.

Lyman, Eric J. 2013. "The 84-Year-Old Conductor, Who Has Worked with the "Django Unchained" Director on Four Films, Says He Uses Music "without Coherence." *Hollywood Reporter* (online magazine), March 15, 2013. https://www.hollywoodreporter.com/news/italian-composer-morricone-slams-tarantino-428954

Priest, Josiah. 1851. *Bible's Defense of Slavery*.

Tarantino, Quentin. 2012. *Django Unchained*. Best Original Screenplay. The Weinstein Company.

8

BARRY JENKINS'S
MEDICINE FOR MELANCHOLY

Race, Individualism, and Denisian Influence

Mark D. Cunningham

IN BARRY JENKINS'S FILM *Medicine for Melancholy* (2008), a love story blossoms between Micah (Wyatt Cenac), the "number two aquarium guy in the whole Bay Area," and Jo' (Tracey Heggins), a woman who designs T-shirts celebrating women filmmakers. Over the course of a one-night stand against the background of an increasingly gentrified San Francisco, these young lovers get to know one another while engaging in a series of conversations about race and societal constructs and experiencing the joy and reflecting on the frustrations that can be found in the city in which they dwell. What unfolds before the audience is a story featuring young twenty-something black people that is vastly different from the broad urban and romantic comedies and crime/hood dramas usually offered.

In fact, outside of its leads, nothing about Jenkins's film is decidedly what many, if asked, might consider or identify as "black." For example, the soundtrack eschews the obligatory hip-hop fare and instead features obscure alternative/indie type songs from equally obscure alternative/indie type artists and bands like The Changes, White Denim, and The Octopus Project. The lead characters trades hip-hop gear, Nikes, and Jordans for statement tees, Vans, and clothing made by Rebel 8, a San Francisco–based streetwear company with "deep roots in skateboard, graffiti, and tattoo culture," as their website describes. Bicycles replace "whips" with expensive chrome rims, while museums, alternative clubs, carousels, and co-op style grocers are the entertainment and places of choice for these young black folks.

Yet, despite the "white" framework, at the heart of the film are characters that have definite opinions about what it really means to be black in a city that does not truly consider them active and viable participants. In this essay, I want to explore both sides of the coin as it pertains to this couple. Micah sees himself as black first and a man second and this greatly affects how he sees himself as a San Franciscan and in the world in general. It is clear that he is doing all he possibly can to maintain some connection to his blackness, yet his personal interests seem to find him in situations where he is the only black, and this is troubling for him. Conversely, Joanne defies any racially specific descriptors and instead embraces an ideology that preferences individualism. This puts them at odds throughout the film, particularly as it pertains to interracial dating (Joanne's boyfriend is white and so is Micah's ex-girlfriend), and I will explore the basis for these viewpoints and why both characters might be correct in their assessment of what it means to be black in San Francisco, an area that is giving way to the upper and upper middle class at the expense of its less financially secure (and, most often, as a result, ethnic) denizens. I believe the events in Jenkins's film create a dialogue that includes the following questions: When a person of color moves in "successful" or "alternative" circles, do we have to ask where the other people of color (in this case black) are? Do we partner up simply based on race? Finally, in the case of the black hipsters of the sort that populate this film, where do we find people of color with similar interests?

However, first, I will discuss Jenkins's inspiration for the foundation of the narrative and the cinematic composition of *Medicine for Melancholy*: French filmmaker Claire Denis. While the fledgling writer and director has made it clear that he is in no way suggesting any parallel in their filmic abilities (Ekanayake 2008), Denis's work has definitely influenced the way he has visualized this modern Romeo and Juliet of sorts, simultaneously brought together and distanced by their warring ideas of blackness and self-identification.

"That Real Thang": The Next Claire Denis or the First Barry Jenkins

As POINTED OUT IN numerous periodicals and the portion of the blogosphere devoted to film appreciation, *Medicine for Melancholy*'s two-character focus clearly owes a debt of gratitude to Jean-Luc Godard's classic *Breathless* (1960) and Richard Linklater's companion pieces *Before Sunrise* (1995) and *Before Sunset* (2004) because of its similarities to these films' two-character focus and narrative emphasis on a particular geographic region. But despite the obviousness of these comparisons, the source of Barry Jenkins's inspiration were the films of Claire Denis, particularly her 2002 film *Vendredi Soir* (*Friday Night*). Of Denis's films, Jenkins, when asked whose work he could sit through for a twenty-four-hour marathon, expresses his admiration this way, "[Her films] most closely approach the cinematic representation of real life. There's a place for escapism, we all need it time to time. But sometimes you just need that real thang, and Ms. Denis is all about bringing that real . . . thang" (Obenson 2011).

Bringing the "real thang," as Jenkins puts it, is certainly considered a beacon of Denis films by other scholars and critics as well. Martine Beugnet emphasizes that a succinct understanding of the complexity of human emotions, especially those belonging to individuals on the periphery of the mainstream, marks her storytelling. Beugnet explains that Denis "focuses on ordinary people" and "disconnected souls" in "tales of foreignness—a foreignness that is simultaneously physical and mental, geographical and existential. In its narrative, stylistic and aesthetic aspects, her filmmaking strives to find the cinematic form best suited to evoke the often unspoken feeling of exile and sense of the want that besets contemporary individual consciousness" (Beugnet 2004, 2–3). Judith Mayne provides further support of Jenkins's "real thang" perception of Denisian narratives, qualifying that her "cinema is a cinema fully engaged with a complex world" (Mayne 2005, 2). In an extension of this insight, Mayne observes, in Denis's films, "the small detail, the brief moment of connection, is never taken for granted. Upon such moments are built a fascination with human interaction and cinematic vision. Claire Denis' films teach you how to be attentive to these moments . . . [they] are about watching, bearing witness, and making contact" (xi).

Micah (Wyatt Cenac) and Jo' (Tracey Heggins) remain far apart even though they are seated in the same taxi in *Medicine for Melancholy.*

More specific to Jenkins's vision for *Medicine for Melancholy*, Denis's film *Vendredi Soir* is a significant example of Denis's predilection for chronicling the human condition and creating viable spaces cinematically for such to be explored. Based on the novel of the same name by Emmanuèle Bernheim (and also coauthor of the screenplay with Denis), the film tells the story of Laure (Valérie Lemercier), a woman who, as the film opens, is sifting through and boxing the articles of the life she currently knows as she prepares to build a new life and home with her boyfriend, François. As she travels to dinner with friends, Laure is ensnared in horrible traffic resulting from a recent public transportation strike in Paris and, encouraged by a radio disc jockey, offers a ride to stranger Jean (Vincent Lindon). Seemingly innocuous conversation and pleasantries bring about a one-night stand that is distinguished as much by introspection and curiosity as it is by attraction and sexuality.

Denis approaches this narrative with a minimalist style. The burden of the story is placed on the shoulders of these two characters, with very little of the Parisian background to support them. In fact, the Paris Denis presents us here is not the romanticized version one might imagine from previous films or books, but instead the City of Light appears cluttered, dark, and muted.

After a party and night of first-time sex, a walk sheds light on the differences between Micah and Jo'.

This is the Paris where those aforesaid disconnected souls Beugnet discussed in her assessment of Denis's work dwell and engage in self-discovery. The entire premise for the film is what French film critic Serge Kaganski called a "sum of narrative, formal and technical challenges" (Beugnet 2004, 184). But, instead of "being limited by these apparent hindrances, Denis appears to thrive on them, the minimal framework allowing her to pursue her exploration of uncharted territories in search of an enigmatic chemistry . . . and continue work on the dissolution of the récit (narrative)" (184).

As mentioned prior, *Medicine for Melancholy*, like *Vendredi Soir*, is a minimalist-style narrative that concentrates on two characters embarking on a one-night stand against the backdrop of a major metropolis. Yet, unlike in that film, Jenkins presents the audience with a San Francisco that is vibrant, picturesque, and wholly romantic. Still, while the backdrop is more splendorous in this film, thematically Jenkins mines much of the same territory as Denis. He, too, is interested in understanding the nuances of and interactions between humanity and specifically how such is affected in marginalized communities. He, too, explores the inner psyche of people whose stories are often overlooked or undervalued. He, too, is about "bringing that real thang."

Because Denis grew up in multiple African countries and, as a result, has been treated to different perspectives regarding race, Mayne writes that, "Denis's films are fully immersed in a world shaped and defined by the aftermath of colonization and decolonization . . . [and] her cinema reflects a world where people live through the complex legacies of colonialism" (Mayne 2005, xi). Knowing this and given that Jenkins distinctly investigates countering arguments on the issue of race, it is interesting that *Vendredi Soir* is so influential to the framework of *Medicine for Melancholy*. With its two white protagonists, *Vendredi Soir* represents one of the few films made by Claire Denis that does not prominently feature someone of color or from a marginalized community.[1] So, while Jenkins may have turned to this film for composition, it can be assumed that he turned to other films in Denis's oeuvre for the leitmotif of his narrative.

Yet, despite the striking similarities between these two films, *Medicine for Melancholy* is not some frame-by-frame copycat of or a cinematic metaphor for *Vendredi Soir*. While the influence is unmistakable (he even incorporates the same instrumental by Dickon Hinchliffe [then of the English band The Tindersticks] Denis uses to underscore the moment when the relationship between Laure and Jean shifts to something more substantial to do the same for Micah and Jo'), Jenkins has express reasons for the choices he makes as a filmmaker. Initially, he sought to extend on Denis's framework and depict what happens the morning *after* a one-night stand, revealing, "My reasoning was that, at my age (then 23), the characters would be much more naïve and seek to forge a continuing emotional relationship rather than leave the experience unto itself" (Ekanayake 2008). Realizing his deficits in maturity personally and professionally, Jenkins tabled the idea until he recognized a shift in his thought process after his own personal experiences in San Francisco, which included his first interracial relationship, its subsequent deterioration, and his realization that a city he had grown to have affection for merited criticism for not making its beauty and urbanity available to everyone because of its exclusionary and gentrifying practices, produced a certain pain and disillusionment that needed to be assuaged and investigated. He explains, "Melding those experiences to the frame inspired by Ms. Denis' film, I thought there was enough to proceed with the premise. It just didn't seem worthwhile without them" (Ekanayake 2008).

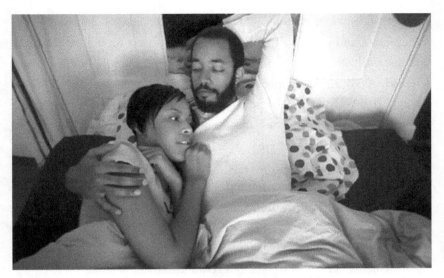

Micah and Jo' make an attempt at salvaging an impossible romance in *Medicine for Melancholy.*

Artistically, *Medicine for Melancholy* represents an unconventional style of telling black stories that extends beyond just trading the usual fare for one more in the black hipster vein. In every sense of the definition of minimalism, which scholar Edward Strickland, in his history on the subject, describes as "a style distinguished by severity of means, clarity of form, and simplicity of structure and texture" (Strickland 1993, 4), Jenkins does not allow ornate camera angles and editing and overly expository dialogue to diffuse what he wants to discuss filmically with audiences about alternative definitions of blackness and what it means to be cast aside geographically because your socioeconomic status is wanting. As with Denis, there is room in Jenkins's film for the audience to question or draw their own conclusions about the topics conveyed. One can argue that this is much needed in the realm of black film: a narrative that leaves enough unanswered or unexplored so as to encourage the audience to engage in an honest or fruitful discussion about the still-taboo subject of race.

One of Us Clinging On to One of Them

IN THINKING ABOUT THE matter of race in *Medicine for Melancholy*, Barry Jenkins says of his film, "I think both characters represent different answers

I have to the same question, which I can't even articulate. . . . I guess if you're a filmmaker, and you have two different points of view on the same subject, you just put them into two different characters and have them duke it out" (Resnick 2008). As mentioned earlier in this chapter, the verbal and ethical fisticuffs boil down to Micah strongly identifying with being black and all the inconsistencies and narrowness that accompany it, while Jo' is less interested in simply reducing herself to just race. Interestingly, the film's contemplation on the subject brings forth a postracial America slant, something that has been increasingly deliberated since Barack Obama, who, during his campaign, often eschewed direct discussions on race in favor of themes more universal and class based, was first elected president of the United States in 2008. Moreover, when blogger Sujewa Ekanayake referred to *Medicine for Melancholy* as "the Barack Obama of indie films," Jenkins responded that the film

> isn't a race based film, nor is it an anthropological study of black hipsters. The issues of race are present because they drive the character, Micah, and in so much as he's a character we come upon in a moment of intellectual crisis, whatever notes on race that can be gleamed from the film are chaotic and shifting, not at all a thesis statement. . . . What human being on this planet hasn't at some point struggled to come to terms with their identity? It's in this way the film reaches some notion of the universal experience. (Ekanayake 2008)

Indeed, Jenkins's rejoinder to such a proposed moniker smacks of the individualist spirit that imbues Jo', and in this recent climate, that is not surprising. Some younger generations of blacks, despite continued examples of racism, discrimination, and other cultural injustices and disparities, have moved away from the dialect and traditions of the civil rights movement and into an arguably more progressive position that trades the group for the personal, which, from some perspectives, is done at a price. As David H. Ikard and Martell Lee Teasley express, "For this new generation of blacks, racism is experienced more abstractly—like having a 'kick me' sign taped to one's back and being the butt of a mean joke that no one is willing to acknowledge. In a paradoxical and perhaps ironic way, the absence of visible and blatant markers of oppression becomes itself a menacing obstacle" (Ikard and Teasley 2012, 8). Still, whatever discrepancies one could point to that arise from either a postracial or a more nationalist outlook, Jenkins is solid and somewhat polemical in his narrative evaluation of race relations and the tension they inspire in a budding relationship.

That said, the biggest instigator of the contention mentioned above is Micah himself. It is clear, watching the film, that he is conflicted about his place as a black man in San Francisco and in the world overall. From a stereotypical outlook, he is a walking contradiction. His conversation is peppered with activist language about the redevelopment of his native city, which I will discuss later in this chapter, and about the unevenness of interracial relationships, a subject he knows about firsthand, as Jo' learns looking through the pictures on his Myspace page, but his visage is that of a skateboarder. And though they could be qualified as hipsters themselves, Micah arguably does not project the kind of blackness his fellow skateboard aficionados rapper Lil' Wayne and musician Pharrell Williams employ, which, admittedly, no doubt is the result of the genre of music in which they largely operate artistically. However, self-acceptance and struggles with self-identity are tremendous factors here, and because he is in a quandary himself about these issue, he tries to project that onto Jo'.

Still, their conversations on the subject are benign in the beginning. After a wrongly listed address on Jo's driver's license has him spending a great portion of the afternoon going door to door in the effort to return her wallet, Micah eventually finds her and an awkward conversation develops about the very nice, if conspicuously spare, house she lives in. When the subject of mortgages and rents comes up and Jo' reveals that her boyfriend foots the bill, Micah suddenly broaches race.

MICAH: Is he white?

JO': Does it matter?

MICAH: Yes and no.

JO': What if I told you he is white and we met in a volunteer program in Bay View? Would that matter?

MICAH: Yes and no.

JO': Okay, I see . . . you're one of those people.

Micah and Jo' take a bike ride, thinking it might help.

MICAH: Those people?

JO': Yes, *those* people . . . that think that Black History Month is in February because it is the shortest month of the year.

MICAH: It is.

JO': Black History Month is in February because Carter G. Woodson wanted Negro History Week to coincide with the births of Frederick Douglass and Lincoln—both in the same week in February.

While we are unsure of their personal philosophies about race specifically at this point, the foundation for opposition is established. It can be ascertained that Micah has some problem with interracial relationships because of his noncommittal answer about whether or not the race of Jo's boyfriend matters, which she concludes is a flaw in his then seemingly nationalist perspective. Therefore, Micah's misinformation about a basic fact in black history compromises that perspective somewhat and gives Jo's individualist position if not heft then maybe validity. But, if any real debate were going to occur at that instant, Micah dispels it with one of those aforementioned charming moments, which, this time, is in the guise of a goofy rendition of the theme song from *Mister Roger's Neighborhood*.

Jo' eventually lets her guard down with Micah and accepts his offer of company while she runs an errand for her boyfriend. Later, they decide to go to a museum, and the conversation indirectly returns to race, as Micah shoots down Jo's suggestion of going to the San Francisco Museum of Modern Art and takes her, instead, to the Museum of the African Diaspora. Once there, Jenkins, in this silent sequence, provides the characters and the audience with a moment of meditation about what they are witnessing. Like Micah and Jo', we follow them up staircases where the walls are lined with black faces from different time periods and parts of the globe and different skin tones and shapes. We go with them into a room with the name of poet Maya Angelou printed on the door and hear samples of musical sounds of African origin. With the characters, we are faced with the picture of the *Door of No Return* from the slavery museum and memorial on Gorée Island in Senegal. As they "walk through it," Micah, Jo', and the audience are encased in darkness and consumed by a robust reading of excerpts from Olaudah Equiano's recollection of the horrors of the Middle Passage. After, Jenkins focuses on Micah and Jo' in a contemplative state, thinking about what they have seen and heard. It is one of the film's most poignant and powerful moments, but it also reflects the one instance in the film where both characters are on the same page as it pertains to the discussion of race. Interestingly, in this key moment in the film, they do not talk at all, as this, and the pensiveness etched on their faces, is the evidence of their solidarity and sympathy.

Unfortunately, this cohesiveness soon comes unraveled, as a succession of increasingly tender moments between them are interrupted by yet another dialogue about race, once again initiated by Micah.

MICAH: Hey, you ever think about how black folks are only seven percent of this city?

JO': You have a real issue with race, you know that?

MICAH: Obviously, but I'm serious . . . you ever think about how we're only seven percent of this city?

JO': You're not seven percent, you're Micah.

MICAH: You know what I mean. Like, if black folks is seven percent of this city, and then, you take whatever one or two percent considers itself like punk or indie or folk or, you know, just not what you see on BET. You ever realize just how few of us there really are?

JO': Mmm, no.

MICAH: I mean, check it, you might go to a show and for like every three hundred people, there's probably one black person. They damn near guaranteed to have their arm around somebody white. I'm just sayin' . . . all right, check it, how do you define yourself?

JO': Excuse me?

MICAH: Like, how do you define yourself? If you had to describe, you know, your idea of how you see the world, like how would you do it in one word?

JO': That makes no sense. People aren't that simple. How can you define yourself in one word?

MICAH: Easy. Me, I'm a black man. That's how I see the world. That's how the world sees me. But if I have to choose one, I'm black before I'm a man. So, therefore, I-am-black.

JO': I don't see it that way.

MICAH: Why not?

JO': (pause) That's your problem. You feel you *have* to define everybody. You limit them to the point where they're just a definition and not people.

MICAH: How you figure?

JO': You just said it. You went from "I am Micah" to "I am black."

MICAH: I'm not?

JO': Yes, but you're everything else, too.

MICAH: That's not how society sees it.

JO': Well, who gives a shit about what society thinks?

Perhaps, Micah's need to define others comes from his confusion about how to define himself. Conveying an assessment of the character in a review of the film in the *Village Voice*, Barry Jenkins paraphrases:

> (Ernest Hardy) said that the complexity, the conundrum for the character Micah, is that in trying to define a more dynamic definition of what it means to be black, he has to gravitate to these things that he feels are more stereotypically white—like

being in the indie scene—that will make him a more dynamic African-American. But instead he can't help but feel that it's pulling him away from being black. ("Q+A: *Medicine for Melancholy*'s Barry Jenkins" 2009)

But, clearly, the indie thing is who he is. At the end of the aforesaid conversation, when Jo' mentions she no longer wants to talk about the subject and would like to go dancing instead, he inquires about the kind of club she wants to go to by presenting the choice, "White folks or black folks?" Out of exasperation with his relentless musings about race, she does not answer, but, instinctively, he chooses to take her to dance with "the white folks." What's more, his evaluation of the racial makeup of the indie scene is verified because he and Jo' are, in fact, the only black people in the club. Jenkins shows them dancing, enjoying themselves freely and without boundary, and no distinction is made by any of the club's white patrons or, for that matter, Micah, about racial dynamics. However, Micah is trading one form of marginalization for another. As he informs us, as a black man, he is already doomed to the periphery, however, the same can be said about his involvement with the indie movement. In a culture that prides itself on difference and detachment from the mainstream, Micah is still just as marginalized because, as he also reminds us, the number of blacks on the scene is scarce, to be sure. As Jenkins explains, "(Micah's) a guy with feet in what he sees as two worlds, but he can't be comfortable in either because he's always afraid that having a foot in one will negate his authenticity in the other. It's a total mind job" (Ekanayake 2008). Therefore, it can be argued that Micah is ill at ease no matter where he tries to fit in.

Conversely, Jo' is a lot more comfortable with her identity than Micah. However, she is more concerned with the actual direction of her life. As she tells Micah at the beginning of the film when he asks what she does for a living, "I'm figuring it out." She reveals that she makes T-shirts with the names of unheralded female filmmakers like Alice Guy-Blaché and Barbara Loden emblazoned on them, which she does for a reason beyond that of just making money. This is a luxury that Micah does not have (his small studio apartment and frequent comments to her about paying rent or a mortgage attest to this), but one Jo' can afford, we assume, because of the generosity of her museum curator boyfriend. Yet, while Jo' does not lean heavily on race as a factor to shape who she is as an individual, it can be assumed that gender does play a significant part in how she identifies herself. Yes, the shirts do speak to her being a cineaste, but the fact that she chooses to use these shirts as a form of feminist activism is noteworthy and adds dimension to her character. Jenkins does not expressly say that she is a feminist, but using the shirts as proof, Jo's alleged feminism could make it very difficult for her to be in a position where she is not paying her own way and, in fact, relying solely on the financial assistance of a man. On the other hand, as a black woman and in relation to Micah's standpoint, why Guy-Blaché and Loden and not Kathleen Collins or Julie Dash? Does not identifying oneself chiefly by race mean ignoring its existence altogether? And does Jo' consider blackness and feminism singularly or separately? In this way, Jo underlines the polyphonic nature of one's identity and, thereby, encourages discussions of identity or self-perception as a polyvocal and nonfixed subjectivity. Jenkins does not qualify these as concerns in the film, but he feasibly does not do so because, as discussed earlier here, Jenkins himself is still on the path to formulating the right questions about race and individuality. He chooses not to give the audience an easy set of circumstances or a pat solution here, and because he does not, he again is Denisian in his choice to narratively reflect life as it actually functions.

If a relationship *could* form between Micah and Jo', that likelihood is damaged in one of the last scenes in the film. After a fun night of dancing and uninhibitedness, an unexpected phone call from Jo's boyfriend brings forth a drunken diatribe from Micah about every issue involving identity and race that seems to weigh on him.

> Who is that? Is it any surprise? Is it, is it any surprise that folks of color in the scene date outside the race . . . I mean think about it, like everything, think about it, everything about being indie is all tied to not being black. Like everything is all tied to not being black. Like friends who are indie—white. Bands who are indie—well, you got TV On The Radio, but the rest of them are white . . . No, it's not okay, it's not. Like *everything*. People call it interracial dating, but there's nothing interracial about it.

> 9 out of 10 times it's, it's, it's somebody of color hanging on to a
> white person. Like you never, you never see . . . you never see a
> fucking black girl and an Asian dude. You never see an Indian
> guy and a Latino girl. It's always one of us clinging on to one of
> them. I mean look at you. Why the fuck you gotta date some
> white dude?

As reflected earlier, the inability to come to terms with his place as a black
man in the indie scene causes Micah a great deal of consternation, but I find
the hypocrisy in which he invalidates interracial dating to be particularly
striking. Specifically, during Jo's impromptu investigation of his Myspace
page, we see a strip of pictures ripped down the middle of Micah and his
assumedly white girlfriend (she could be of another ethnicity, but she is not
black) and written atop them are the words "I Want My Fuckin' Heart Sewn
Back Together." This, along with the Micah's admission that he took a bicycle
he bought for his ex-girlfriend back when Jo' asked about its presence in his
apartment, suggests this was a less than amicable and even painful breakup.
But, given his history, why the vitriol about interracial relationships? It could
be as simple as things just did not work out, but his level of disdain suggests
more occurred. I theorize that the "dynamic blackness" mentioned in the
Ernest Hardy review of the film did not accomplish what Micah thought
it might; that no matter how much he embraced all things less likely to be
assigned as black, ultimately, he believes there is no real overcoming of the
limitations often accorded to this racial group. Micah takes all this personally, as if to wonder why he is even bothering through the example that is
his life to impart that this so-called antithesis to blackness still qualifies as
blackness.

Nonetheless, Jo' does *not* let Micah get away with this outburst, and
she lashes out herself, having grown frustrated and tired of his continual
expressions of bitterness about race.

> Why are you doing this? What do you want from me? You
> think just because I'm black and you're black that we should
> just be together? We're just one, right? We fucked, and I didn't
> even know you. I've been spending the last 24 hours cheating

on my boyfriend and you think because I'm black and you're black that we should be together?! So fucking crazy!

In Jo', Micah is aware that he has the best of both the worlds he is trying to merge, hence his dread that he might be losing her to a white man. However, his despondence about his internal struggles overwhelms any possibilities for romance of any significant depth. So, because of this polarization, the relationship will not work. Though definitely not as idealized, their journey ends in Jenkins's version of Humphrey Bogart saying good-bye to Ingrid Bergman on a foggy tarmac. After a kiss in his front doorway, cloaked in shadows and framed by a sliver of light from the hall, Micah pleads with Jo' to spend one more night with him, assuring her that she "can go back to her life tomorrow." And she does, as, in the last scene, Jenkins rotates his camera around the setting of their last moments together. Micah is sleeping on the couch as morning invades his small apartment, the gurgling noises from his fish tank serving as an ambience. The camera peeks outside to the fire escape, and through the metal slats we see Jo', on her bicycle and looking upward to what was and what might have been, riding away from what surely could be described as a bit of a fairy tale and toward reality.

I Love This City, I Hate This City

IF THE SUBJECT OF race and individualism causes Micah apprehension and irritation, the whitewashing of San Francisco does very little to alleviate his anxiety. In fact, much of the problem he has with being one of the few blacks on the indie scene is directly correlated to the class structure and economics of the city. When his frequent criticisms inspire Jo' to question whether he even likes it there, Micah responds, "No, I love this city. I hate this city, but I love this city. I mean the hills, the fog, any man who can find a street corner's got himself a view. San Francisco's beautiful and it's got nothing to do with privilege. It's got nothing to do with beatniks or hippies or yuppies. It just is. You shouldn't have to be upper middle class to be a part of that."

Because he is a native San Franciscan, it is understandable how the practice of gentrification in the city could be a bitter pill for Micah to swallow. He has witnessed firsthand how the area was abruptly made less palatable for people who economically did not fit this new, reconstructed image of

From a San Francisco hilltop Micah and Jo' contemplate a possible lasting romance through compromise.

San Francisco. He has also heard every excuse possible to suggest that the forced ousting of many citizens to neighboring cities or suburbs was not intentional and was for the overall good of San Francisco. Prominently hung on the wall of his apartment is a framed poster with a quote by architect Leonard S. Mosias, a representative for the San Francisco Redevelopment Agency, dated July 1962, explaining that, in the effort to remedy stifling and overcrowded conditions and rapidly deteriorating and aging residential areas in certain regions of the city, there would be a push for rehabilitation. In the center of that quote is the word "lies" in red. When Jo' asks what the necessity is of having something on your wall that is difficult to forget because you can see it for yourself every day, Micah explains that the very exile his parents experienced in the Lower Haight area of San Francisco, an area then resplendent with black people and white artists, is currently being recreated in the Mission Bay area. As Micah laments, despite the indifference and obliviousness of many citizens, the poster is mostly a reminder that "poor folks still got it hard." That said, in Jenkins's mind, "The whole film is kind of a snapshot of the city . . . [a]nd I felt it would be a shame not to make that point [about gentrification], because it's pretty much the biggest kind of political socioeconomic aspect of . . . modern San Francisco—the housing crisis. Depending on where you fall in the class line, you're at the center of the crisis" (Resnick 2008).

And many of those who fall in the center of that crisis are the city's black citizens. As well noted in the film, San Francisco is 7 percent black and, according to Micah, not much is being done to increase those numbers. It is an opinion Jenkins shares with his protagonist, and therefore he wanted to create a method by which to symbolize that and his character's emotional state about their environment on screen. The choice was made to cinematographically employ a schematic where, as in San Francisco, color is largely absent. According to the Jenkins,

> As far as the color, we (he and his director of photography, James Laxton) decided really early that we wanted to reflect the title *Medicine for Melancholy*. We wanted that melancholy reflected in the actual image. We knew we were going to de-saturate the color palates. We super saturated in production, and de-saturated in post to kind of protect their skin tones. There's certain places in the movie where the characters just react with one another and all these issues with race, and at those moments, it's the most color. Karina Longworth of Spout.com wrote . . . the film is 93% saturated and it's reflective of San Francisco's 7% African-American. If you look at our color files, the film is 93% saturated. We didn't do that intentionally. We really tried to reflect what was the emotional connection with the characters. ("Independent Film Week—'Medicine for Melancholy'—Sept. 15, 2008," 2008)

Like their opinions about race, the emotional state of the characters regarding San Francisco finds them at opposite ends of the spectrum again. Jo' is not as invested in the gentrification of the city because she is a transplant. Micah, on the other hand, is very invested, but to a tremendous fault. For all of his awareness about the area and his understanding of what the poster on his wall then meant and presently means to the city's inhabitants, his conversation about the redevelopment and privileged class of San Francisco is greatly rooted in race. Yet, as Jenkins points out, there are huge parts of the equation Micah is not considering.

> I think the biggest thing in the movie is he doesn't realize his role in the whole cycle of it. The apartment he's living in is an

apartment that some minority family probably once stayed in when the rent was $500 bucks but now he pays $1,250 for this tiny studio. I think we're all part of this horrific puzzle or change that's going on in San Francisco. There's a sequence where the characters are just walking and talking—or walking and not talking . . . through this thing you call the Moscone Center, this huge convention center underground. But before that place was the Moscone Center, there were all these huge tenement buildings, where all these old senior citizens lives . . . And that whole area got razed. They built MOMA, and the Museum of African Diaspora, which the two characters go to. . . . They built the St. Regis Hotel where rooms are $500 a night and they built Yerba Buena Gardens, where that fountain is, and they built that little bridge and the carousel. And beneath it all, are these huge cavernous convention centers where they actually make money to keep businesses coming to the city. And I feel like the two characters, as they're walking, they never once realize the history they are walking over, they never really get it, they never really see the role they are playing in just enjoying these new beautiful places, they never really are witnessing or aware of the history they are walking over. And I think that's what San Francisco really is, it's this place where they just pave over all these different levels of history. . . . ("Q+A: *Medicine for Melancholy's* Barry Jenkins" 2009)

However, Micah's narrow perception of redevelopment concerns in San Francisco is broadened when he returns from a trip to the market with Jo'. As they walk home, they come across a storefront with a group of people, all white, discussing rent control and gentrification in the city and how housing options for the poor are quickly decreasing. While not exactly focused on race, those in assembly here have the same concerns as Micah. They, too, worry about losing the culture and unique characteristics that shape San Francisco. Certainly, Micah needs to look at the renovation of San Francisco in a more even context, but Jenkins does something interesting here. Standing in the doorway listening, Micah and Jo' never join in the meeting, nor are they asked to. The implication here is that black people in San Francisco, even in common struggle with the mainstream, still remain outside the discussion and ultimately the solution. Listening to the conversation, you could surmise that those in the discussion group, indeed, also feel like a marginalized community as a result of class, but for Micah, in particular, the dilemma is twofold. Like not being able to see the proverbial forest for the trees, class is less important to him because race seems to incorporate that and so much more. After they leave the discussion, we see Micah and Jo' overlooking San Francisco, the majesty of the dome of City Hall a lighted blur in the distance, and like at the museum, they are silently in tandem, mulling over the possibility of a San Francisco devoid of all the things they and so many others take for granted.

Despite the push for displacement because of race, economics, or whatever other issues may be involved, for Micah, San Francisco is home. On the surface, a workable solution might be to live amongst the denizens of Oakland, whose black population is considerable in comparison, but this will not work for him because Oakland "is posited as everything Micah's trying to rise above. Not deny, mind you. But he's looking for a place where he can follow his interests and acknowledge his own complexity." To reiterate Micah's earlier declaration, race and class should not be the determining factor in deciding who gets the chance to do that in San Francisco. Ideally, there should be more black people in the area for Micah to connect with, but since that is hardly the case, what he must learn to do is not turn away the ones there who *are* trying to connect with him and help him achieve that strong sense of self-identification he covets.

Notes

1. For films by Claire Denis that explore the themes of colonialism and post-colonialism, consider *Chocolat* (1988), *Beau Travail* (1999), *35 Shots of Rum* (2008), and *White Material* (2009).

References

Beugnet, Martine. 2004. *Claire Denis*. Manchester: Manchester University Press.

Ekanayake, Sujewa. 2008. "The Perception of the American Experience Is a Global Community With Real Fiscal Consequences the World Over; Barry

Jenkins Interview." *DIY Filmmaker Sujewa*. March 19, 2008. https://diy
filmmaker.blogspot.com/2008/03/perception-of-american-experience-is
.html

Fields, Rob. 2009. "'Medicine for Melancholy': Down, But Caught Out, in San
Francisco." Huffington Post. October 27, 2009. http://www.huffingtonpost
.com/rob-fields/medicine-for-melancholy-d_b_334850.html?view.

Ikard, David H., and Martell Lee Teasley. 2012. Nation of Cowards: Black
Activism in Barack Obama's Post-Racial America. Bloomington: Indiana
University Press.

"Independent Film Week—'Medicine for Melancholy'—Sept. 15, 2008." 2008.
The Film Panel Notetaker. September 16, 2008. http://thefilmpanelnote
taker.com/labels/Barry%Jenkins.html. accessed September 16, 2008

Mayne, Judith. 2005. *Claire Denis*. Urbana: University of Illinois Press.

Obenson, Tambay A. 2011. "10 Questions with Barry Jenkins," Shadow and
Act. November 2, 2011. http://blogs.indiewire.com/shadowandact/10_
questions_with_barry_jenkins.

"Q+A: Medicine For Melancholy's Barry Jenkins." 2009. The Fader. February
26, 2009. http://www.thefader.com/2009/02/06/q-a-medicine-for-
melancholy-s-barry-jenkins/.

Resnick, Sophia. 2008. "Frisco Bay Blues: 'Medicine for Melancholy.'" *Austin
Chronicle*, March 7, 2008. http://www.austinchronicle.com/screens/
2008-03-07/599786/.

Strickland, Edward. 1993. *Minimalism: Origins*. Bloomington: Indiana University Press.

IV
BLACK CINEMATIC WOMANIST PRAXIS

9

BLACK FEMALE AGENCY IN HAILE GERIMA'S *BUSH MAMA* AND *SANKOFA*

Patricia Hilliard-Nunn

YOU African Spirits!
Spirit of the Dead rise up!
Lingering Spirits of the Dead
Rise up and possess your bird of passage."
(Gerima Sankofa 1993)

A "BIRD OF PASSAGE," evoked eloquently in Haile Gerima's poetry at the beginning and end of the film *Sankofa* (1993), recalls the Sankofa bird. "Sankofa" is an Akan word that means "go back and fetch it" (Willis 1998), and the Sankofa bird, its head turned backward, is a symbol for remembrance. Through this poem, Gerima implies that there is a sleeping spiritual giant among African descended peoples. It also suggests that by rising up and possessing their "bird of passage," or historical knowledge of their political, social, and cultural realities, black people may be transformed and gain physical and mental liberation in the service of their own humanity in oppressive societies. For over forty-five years, Gerima's films have delineated assaults on black lives via colonization, enslavement, police brutality, politics, and economic exploitation. A black critical consciousness illuminating the humanity and agency of characters that are spiritually renewed—empowered by connecting with their African past—is a centerpiece of Gerima films. Moreover, in Gerima's telling of his stories, he centrally incorporates black women characters that are themselves transformed into agents of resistance able to resurrect their own power.

Black women and girls are agentic forces in Gerima's carefully crafted sociopolitical landscapes, which are inhabited by resistant characters who teach, nurture, transform, rebel, and unabashedly declare and demonstrate their humanity. This is rare in American cinema, mainstream or independent, where black resistance is virtually nonexistent despite the historical reality of enslavement, Jim-Crow oppression, and European cultural and political hegemony. Gerima's films feature black women in key roles and present historical narratives that privilege the consciousness and voices of black characters and traditional African culture.

The agency of the black female protagonists Dorothy in *Bush Mama* (1979) and Mona/Shola in *Sankofa* will be explored through a textual analysis of Gerima's construction of their lives in an "inner-city ghetto" and on a plantation of enslaved laborers, respectively. Although the black female protagonists in both films exist in different temporal and spatial realities, their means of transformation and exerting agency literally and figuratively strike at the core of white supremacy. Mark Reid has used a womanist, postnegritude lens to examine the same films and what he calls "Gerima's womanist film aesthetic of black female empowerment . . ." (2005, 109). This chapter emphasizes Gerima's establishment of contexts and the path to transformation that precipitates and necessitates the violent agency of two black women characters.

Agency, in this chapter, is the self-conscious act of resistance to and rebellion against oppression. The actions of the female protagonists, as agents, are explored to assess how Gerima constructs the contexts and inspiration for their agency. Agency requires that the character act, speak, or behave in a self-determining manner. Mental agency or "consciousness" precedes and inspires direct actions that may change conditions. Toward this end, I agree with Kathryn Abrams, who points out that "Agency must operate within and in relation to . . . socialization" (1999, 18).

Bush Mama, Gerima's master's thesis film made at the University of California Los Angeles, is about Dorothy, a pregnant black woman on public welfare who negotiates political and social realities in her economically depressed Los Angeles community. Her community, as it is presented through Gerima's lens, takes on the features of a prison. When her boyfriend, a Vietnam veteran, is unjustly incarcerated, Dorothy struggles to make a life for her daughter while contemplating the many contradictions in American culture, not the least of which is the state-sponsored oppression of blacks by the police and the welfare system. When her challenges culminate in a police officer attempting to rape her daughter, Dorothy beats him to death.

The life of Mona/Shola, in *Sankofa*, plays out in a different kind of prison as she negotiates her reality as an enslaved laborer during the nineteenth century. The story begins with a photo shoot at the Cape Coast dungeon, a dungeon on the West African coast, featuring a modern-day fashion model, Mona. Mona is posing seductively for a white photographer, who asks her provocatively to, "Give me more sex, Mona. More sex." Mona is then magically transported to the past, where she is kidnapped and branded in a dungeon before being shipped to the Lafayette plantation somewhere in the New World. Once on the plantation, she becomes Shola, a house slave who witnesses and is the victim of regular mental, physical, and sexual violence at the hands of the slave master and overseers. Shola's ordeal reaches a climax when she slashes one of her rapists to death.

The experience of Celia, a nineteen-year-old enslaved black woman who was hanged for killing her slave owner, has similarities to the journeys of Gerima's fictional Dorothy and Shola. On June 23, 1855, a pregnant Celia, tired of being raped by her slave owner, Robert Newsome, beat him to death and burned his body in a fireplace (Linder 2011). Celia was jailed, tried, convicted, and later hanged after the judge prohibited the jury from being instructed that Celia killed the slave owner in self-defense after repeated rapes (Linder). The judge determined that an enslaved black woman could not claim self-defense because she was considered property. The spirit of Celia and her rebellious agency that protects her own honor is mirrored in the protagonists Dorothy and Shola.

Black women who, regardless of their nationality and socioeconomic status, are metaphoric "whipping girls" in a world where mass-mediated representations deny black humanity and reinforce white cultural hegemony. As black women's vocal and physical rebellion remains virtually nonexistent in media, spectators who view uplifting film narratives may hold expectations that social wrongs will be corrected. These filmgoers may experience dissonance.

After 120 years of filmmaking, the Hollywood industrial model dominates, and global representations of black women as simple, overly sexualized, and angry helpmates to white women or white and black men remain (Bogle 2003). Contented slaves, loyal maids, and pathological "welfare mothers" have imbued mainstream narratives and delivered contextless and politically sanitized stories since the early days of film. Despite limited improvements, most film representations reify degrading images of black women and decontextualize or ignore the lingering challenges of white supremacy, patriarchy, and cultural hegemony. Fortunately, Gerima is a part of a small, but critical, number of filmmakers who resist these practices and have expanded the depth and breadth of black female film representations.

Gerima's work reflects his grounding in the social, political, and cultural histories of people around the globe. He is a screenwriter, director, and producer who has earned the label "Jegna," a defender of history and culture. The term "Jegna" comes from Ethiopia, but the concept extends throughout the African cultural sphere. Jegna's have an interest in community survival and are astute observers of the social, political, and cultural dynamics that communities must negotiate. Jegnas are a unifying force, communicating stories imbued with lessons that may be passed on for generations.

Gerima's films radiate the themes of history, politics, oppression, resistance, and liberation. His grounding in literature, film movements, jazz, blues, cultural symbolism, and human relations is synthesized precisely to humanize black lives through characters, female and male, and contextualize their journey. Gerima's work includes narrative, documentary, and experimental and may be described as artistic, didactic, and political. He incorporates unapologetic descriptions of geopolitical power relations that address not only the imposition of white supremacy on the psychological and material conditions of black people but also the intraracial and self-sabotaging practices that often hinder or prevent black liberation.

Gerima was born and raised in Gonder, Ethiopia, and is a key figure among black UCLA film school graduates who emerged during the 1970s, challenging and expanding ways of representing black people (Taylor 1988). Gerima has produced and distributed critically acclaimed films while teaching film in the Department of Radio, Television, and Film at Howard University. He and his wife, Shrikiana Gerima, own the Sankofa Video Books and Cafe, from which they run several production entities, including Mypheduh Films.

Since making *Child of Resistance* (1973), Gerima has privileged the image of black women and given his black female characters a voice. He commonly does this by employing the first-person narrative technique used by other independent black directors (Yearwood 2000). He has used lingering close-ups, extreme close-ups, and long takes to direct the spectator's gaze to the faces of black women. Gerima's extreme close-up shots on the eyes complement complex first-person narrations and expose their internal monologues. In *Child of Resistance*, the camera focuses on the face of the incarcerated Angela Davis character as she sits in her cell. Barbara O, who also later played Dorothy in *Bush Mama*, plays the Angela Davis character. The first-person narrative is also used in *Sankofa* to expose the psychology of Shola.

Gerima meticulously addresses the injustices inflicted and the varied responses of oppressed communities. He emphasizes consciousness raising and transformation that leads to liberation from oppression (Phaff 1988). It is important to know that while black women play key roles in his films, he communicates a message that extends beyond gender. Gerima suggests that his focus is employing characters that carry an extended family message. He said, "I don't see one gender as privileged in the struggle for liberation. I look at a system that victimizes us all" (Safford, Trippllet, and Gerima 1983, 64). Gerima's characters represent different ages and stages of wisdom and humanity. Wisdom is found in teenage girls like Angie, Dorothy's neighbor in *Bush Mama*, and in elders like Grandma, in *Ashes and Embers* (1982). These women exist in complex communities, where they observe, teach, learn, and demonstrate consciousness and purpose, often serving as role models for others in the narrative.

Dorothy and Shola are on journeys that provide rare cinematic glimpses of black women who demonstrate agency by exacting justice in response to oppression. In them, viewers witness the challenges, influences, and transformations that spark their agential actions. Their voices are privileged via camera images and voice-overs that offer unique perspectives on how they process and resist white supremacy and its partner, patriarchy.

The male and female characters in Gerima's films are complex, heterogeneous personalities engaged in collective and individual struggles. While set in distinct times and places, Dorothy and Shola could be contemporary women negotiating ways to secure or maintain mental and physical liberation. The supporting male characters, T.C., Dorothy's boyfriend in *Bush Mama*, and Shango, Shola's boyfriend in *Sankofa*, are important guides, but the growth and ultimate acts of agential rebellion of the women are not solely dependent on them.

Dorothy and Shola live in unhealthy environments that they, at first, appear powerless to control. Dorothy's reality centers on her survival as an unemployed pregnant woman trying to raise her daughter in an "imprisoned" community. This means negotiating in an unhealthy, violent environment plagued by poverty and state occupation, where police shootings are common. As the story unfolds, Dorothy attempts to cope with her challenges.

Like Dorothy, Shola is on a journey to understand and make sense of her environment. Shola is a house slave on a plantation who has been socialized to provide unpaid labor, to resist African culture, and to endure sexual and mental violence at the hands of her owner. Despite constant rapes, Shola has been socialized not to resist. The rebirth of Mona as Shola the enslaved woman initiates her opportunity for resocialization and the correction of the mental slavery that causes her to view the brutality of her owner and the plantation priest, Father Rafael, as normal. Shola considers the practices of the African-oriented people, who meet to hold religious ceremonies in the hills and plot for freedom, abnormal and frightening before she gains consciousness about what the maroon meetings are about. Resocialization, then, is a prerequisite to her gaining African/black consciousness and feeling empowered enough to resist her condition. Shola could symbolize unconscious blacks or others from any historical period who have been socialized to find comfort in antiblack oppressive practices and institutions.

Dorothy, like Shola is on a journey to growth and rebirth. Her imprisonment in an impoverished community under the occupation and control of police and an oppressive government welfare system is evident, but she initially appears passive and defeatist in dealing with it. Dorothy is introduced at the beginning of the film strutting down a neighborhood street in what becomes a recurring image. At first, she appears to be on a distinct mission. She is dressed, purse in hand, wig affixed, and is traveling forward to what appears to be a clear destiny. As the story unfolds and the challenges that she faces are revealed, the strut looks more like a weary stroll. Dorothy's appearance and demeanor begin to mirror the images of the run-down community that she inhabits. She eventually steps out of her shoes, symbolizing that all pretentions are off, foreshadowing that a transformation, good or bad, may be on the horizon.

The filmic landscapes in Gerima's work offer textured perspectives of the humanity of black people. They highlight their oppression and the nuances of their journey to freedom. Gerima's narratives connect the past and present, which is a core principle of *Sankofa*. Gerima directs the gaze of viewers to topics and spaces that people have been conditioned to ignore. Despite the lived experiences of Harriet Tubman, Fannie Lou Hammer, and others, fictional and reality-based films addressing slavery and challenges in economically depressed communities tend to present white characters as socially conscious saviors, as the brains, and as the more visible players while black characters, whether based on real people or not, remain in the background (i.e., *Django Unchained* [2012], *Jefferson in Paris* [1995], *Freedom Writers* [2007], *The Blind Side* [2009], *Dangerous Minds* [1996], *Mandingo* [1975], *Amistad* [1997]).

Basic narrative conflicts underpin Gerima's dramas, but his construction and placement of the forces of evil, good, and irony break from mainstream representations. Gerima labels the inhumane environment of the inner city as the "bush." Dorothy, then, is a "mama," who, like other mothers, confronts the challenges presented in 1970s Watts, a section of Los Angeles, California, with a predominantly poor, black population. Watts is known for the 1960s riots that occurred when residents resisted police brutality. Dorothy's landscape includes small businesses, storefronts with displays of European-styled wigs, regular police shootings of black men, mothers on the verge of suicide, the mentally ill, and the impoverished. Gerima's analysis of the space is presented primarily in images and didactic song lyrics that address US political corruption, the prison industrial complex, police brutality, and so on.

Dorothy's apartment is a primary landscape of her socialization in *Bush Mama*. This is where she nurtures her child, spends time with T.C. before he is incarcerated, and engages with her neighbors and where the welfare representative invades her space. Viewers first gaze at Dorothy's eyes in extreme close-up shots as her voice-overs expose the way that she processes the unpredictable, out of balance nature of her community. From the vantage point of her window, Dorothy's frame from which to view and contemplate the challenges in her community, she daydreams, bears witness, and, when appropriate, intervenes, as she did to stop a mother threatening to jump off a building while holding her baby.

The raw abuse that black people endure at government agencies is rarely presented in film. From the paternalistic interrogation of Dorothy by the welfare worker who has the liberty to enter her living quarters and urge her to get an abortion, to the humiliating questions about who she allows in her living space, Gerima exposes part of the nightmare that some poor black women endure at the hands of the government. This image of Dorothy being victimized by the welfare system, as opposed to exploiting the system, is counterpoint to mainstream representations of black women in the news, let alone in films. Bridgette Baldwin has addressed the historical linking of the black woman's image to the discourse about welfare, particularly as it relates to who is not worthy of compensation (2010). Gerima allows viewers to hear the abuse with Dorothy as he sets the context for the evolution of her consciousness-raising.

Over thirty-five years before Michelle Alexander outlined the systematic incarceration of black men in *The New Jim Crow: Mass Incarceration in the Age of Colorblindness* (2010), Gerima addressed the realities of the prison industrial complex in *Bush Mama*. Through letters to Dorothy, presented as voice-overs, T.C. describes and critiques prison life and shares his analysis of the politics of race and class in the United States. Viewers see successive medium close-up images of the faces of black men behind prison bars as they hear a song with lyrics about "the system" sending "another brother to jail." T.C. draws a correlation between prisons and plantations during slavery as he explains that the prison guard's father and grandfather were prison guards also. Thus, Gerima extends the temporal bounds to connect the contemporary police/prison control of black people with the control of enslaved people in the past.

Despite the collective psychic trauma resulting from the systematic mental and physical brutality that grips people in Dorothy's community, Gerima demonstrates their resilience, dignity, and humanity. He directs the gaze of viewers at the faces of characters rarely depicted and constructs spaces where they engage in discourse about their condition. Dorothy is not an all-knowing, idealized character, but she challenges and engages those in her environment by giving and receiving knowledge. Like real black people, Dorothy and other *Bush Mama* characters contemplate, question, and debate issues related to their lives, communities, and nation. Restaurants, bars, apartments, bus stops, a prison, a welfare office, and an abortion clinic are spaces where people live, learn, and sometimes articulate readings of their own condition. When Dorothy contemplates getting an abortion, she is able to discuss her dilemma with bar and restaurant owner Simmi, who feeds her, listens, and gives advice. Simmi's restaurant is a space where Dorothy is given both food to eat and food for thought. Simmi shares her thoughts about the challenges that black people face and emphasizes the need for "calculation." She educates Dorothy and prepares her for her transformation.

Mental and physical violence also embody the spaces in *Sankofa*. The plantation is a place for rape, punishments, beatings, and other forms of subjugation. Sugarcane fields, plantation quarters, and maroon gatherings in the hills provide the landscape for Shola's socialization process. Gerima is purposely ambiguous about the exact location of the slave plantation. He has noted that the plantation may be interpreted to be in the United States, Jamaica, or any other place where enslaved Africans were forced to labor. For him, the lesson of *Sankofa* is as important in Jamaica as it is in Brazil or the United States.

"The ground is holy ground. Blood was spilled here," declares the Griot at the Cape Coast Dungeon in *Sankofa*. In that instant, Gerima assigns meaning to the space from which Mona will depart for her journey. He defines the dungeon, the place where enslaved Africans were actually held before being shipped throughout the African Diaspora, as sacred. This definition of the dungeon as "holy ground," where "blood was spilled," sets the tone for how Mona and film spectators imagine that space. The dungeons represent the last place that Africans were solidly connected to their cultural traditions, and despite its brutal history, it is a symbolic space from which to launch a narrative related to memory. The Griot shouts, "Go back to your past" at Mona. Mona explores the dungeon on her own and, like a seed, wanders down a passageway and into a holding area that is suddenly filled with African captives. Slave catchers surround her as she shouts, "Let me out of here. I'm not no African," a sentiment shared today by some descendants of enslaved Africans. Despite her pleas, Mona is stripped naked and branded before being transported to the past. Mona is transformed into Shola, a house slave, to begin her journey to consciousness.

Images of the dungeon are intercut in other places during the film. After Kunta, an enslaved pregnant woman, runs away from the plantation and is recaptured with her accomplices, she is strung up and whipped to death—a scene that may have influenced a similar whipping scene of an enslaved black woman in *12 Years a Slave* (2013) over twenty years later. As other enslaved laborers watch and provide protection, Nunu, a warrior-like African-born enslaved woman, grabs a machete and rushes to cut Kunta's unborn baby from her belly. Once the baby is out, and is heard crying, an image of Mona being branded in the dungeon is repeated. Thus, Mona/Shola is identified with the baby, beginning a journey in a tragic space under tragic circumstances.

At the end of the film, Shola/Mona, having been transformed, is transported back to the future and into the dungeon. From there, Shola/Mona emerges from the long symbolic birth canal, or source, and into the light, reborn as a new and conscious Mona. The Cape Coast dungeon, in this narrative, is the space of symbolic death and rebirth, based on the premise that to be transformed, parts of your old self must die so that the new self may thrive.

Film critics have noted Gerima's focus on character transformation (Pfaff 1988). Dorothy and Shola narrate their transformative journeys via voice-overs. Neither woman initially understands all of the dynamics of the oppressive environment she lives in, but both are searching while engaged in a process of constant becoming that is dependent on socialization. This is shown in several ways, including their interaction with teachers, their introduction to and acceptance of African culture, and the styling of hair. Spectators are privileged to watch the demystification process that leads to the consciousness raising and later, conscious acts and agency. Gerima introduces a variety of "teachers" who help to socialize and support his protagonists. Dorothy and Shola are challenged, but they are a part of complex communities of people that have many different things to offer.

Dorothy's consciousness is raised through varied interactions. T.C.'s letters from prison expose her to the horrors of prison life and provide his analysis of some political issues. As the film progresses, Dorothy demonstrates more of her own consciousness. In a letter to T.C., she refers to the needs of "people like me," seemingly calling attention to how best to approach and share with black people locked in a system of poverty. She says, "Talk the same talk, but easy, T.C.," seemingly suggesting that a lack of patience or a more militant tone might turn people off.

Dorothy is also inspired and taught by Angie, a precocious teenage neighbor who exposes her and her daughter to information about black history and community activism, sharing her experiences from demonstrations that she has attended. Angie gives Dorothy a picture of an African woman holding a baby, carrying a gun, and wearing braids, saying, "She got a baby. She got a gun. She must be something." Dorothy listens intently and gazes at the image that becomes central to her transformation.

Shola's main teachers are Nunu and Shango, other enslaved laborers who are instrumental in her transformation. Nunu is a first-generation African who is independent and leads a secret society of maroons. Shola's admiration of Nunu as an example of strength is shown when she says, "Nunu, she wasn't taking nothing" in reference to Nunu's no-nonsense attitude toward others. Nunu's resistance is significant for Shola, who is regularly raped by the slave owner. Shola lacks the courage to resist her rapists, but she is empowered by hearing tales about Nunu's bravery, including one that describes how she killed a man by looking at him. She says, "Whenever the master's abusing me and treating me bad, let me be like Nunu. Just give me a little of the power that she got in the center of my eyes. Killing an overseer just by staring at him." Nunu is a role model for Shola who demonstrates the possibilities of self-determination. She becomes a primary teacher and surrogate mother for Shola.

Shango is another guide for Shola. His grounding in the Yoruba religion and Shola's Christian-centered socialization make them an odd couple. House slaves were forbidden to mix with rebellious field slaves, but the two somehow find a space to connect. Still, Shola is uncomfortable with Shango's rebelliousness. When Shango is punished for participating in a mini uprising, Shola asks, "Why don't you just act right? It don't take that much." Shango responds by asking her why she won't act like him and, presumably, other rebellious slaves. Exasperated, Shola says, "Why don't you make sense?" While Shola cares for Shango, she remains mentally enslaved and concerned about her individual well-being. Shola is negatively impacted by slavery, but she does not see herself as a potential agent to destroy it. Discussions about rebellion, African rituals, and running away do not make sense to Shola.

Shola loves Shango and she both fears and respects his role as a priest of Ifa. She doesn't mind asking Shango to create an herbal love potion for her friend, but when he allows her to attend a sacred initiation ceremony in the hills, she admits, "I couldn't get myself to be initiated. I guess it was just the years of the church in me. I was happy to be there anyway." Still, Shola's "teacher" had allowed her to see enough of the ceremony for her to get "possessed" enough to flee the plantation. After being recaptured, she is stripped, beaten, and forced to denounce the practices of the Africans. Shango nurses her and once she heals, she has progressed to another stage of consciousness of her new status as a field slave.

The murder of Nunu by her son, Joe, propels Shola to the final stage of transformation and positions her for rebellious agency. This process is sealed when Shango officially baptizes her into the secret society, a ritual that she finally has the courage to complete.

Teachers influence and guide Dorothy and Shola through informal rite-of-passage processes. Gerima's curriculum requires both to be exposed to African history and culture to gain clarity about their condition. Thus, both

Dorothy and Mona/Shola literally respond to the words of the *Sankofa* poem, "Spirit of the dead rise up and possess your bird of passage." They go "back to fetch it" to embrace their ancestral knowledge and act, in different ways, to restore order. The acceptance of African culture and African cultural elements is transformative for both Dorothy and Shola. In *Bush Mama*, T.C. says, "I want to go to Africa." Dorothy replies, "I don't know about that, T.C. I don't know." T.C. says that he has wanted to go for a long time. Gerima uses T.C. to pique Dorothy's curiosity about Africa. This begins her socialization about Africa and may have contributed to her openness to the teachings of her neighbor, Angie.

After Mona is grabbed by her kidnappers, she screams, "I am not an African. I'm Mona. I'm an American. Don't you recognize me? I'm not an African. I'm Mona, I'm an American." Gerima then symbolically sends her back to her past. Commenting on this scene, Gerima said,

"I wanted to go straight to the jugular vein. I felt identity crisis is a major settling point to really work out our own dramatic stories and sometimes we dismiss it. Restlessness provides a major entry to the person's life, and so her denial—-her whole idea of 'I'm not African'—is something that needs to go into that collective memory to come back reprocessed, to a point where she accepts that she is African and wouldn't debate it" (Turner and Kamdibe 2008, 976).

Africa, for Gerima, is not a romanticized space but rather a piece of the human story that cannot be ignored. Gerima understands the pathological hate and fear of the black African past. He said,

> Africa is still very censored. I think Blacks have always paid a penalty for discussing or thinking about Africa. At a certain time in this country, people have been lynched for playing the drum. Speaking the African language has been punished. And I think from Denmark Vesey's uprising till now, the whole identification that Africans have with Africa should never threaten any-body. Why is society always running for cover when Africans in this country want to make linkage with Africa? (Woolford and Gerima 1994, 100)

Gerima attacks contemporary resistance to African cosmology in scenes depicting Shola's dissonance about the secret society that Nunu and Shango belong to. The priest, Father Rafael, teaches Shola not to socialize with the "heathen Africans" as he calls them. Shola also knows that since she is not a part of the secret society she is not fully accepted by those who are. She says, "They didn't trust us . . . They'd sneak off when the others were dancing and cuttin' the fool." Once Shola is exposed, things change. Her worst beating from the overseer comes after she is discovered meeting with the secret society. Her master and Father Rafael tie her up and beat her to "exorcise" her African consciousness, not because they care about Shola's soul but because she has rejected their teachings and embraced African identification.

Gerima employs the use of African rhythms to punctuate select points in the narratives. It is important that the character Sankofa, played by the master drummer Kofi Ghanaba, provide the drum rhythms at the beginning and end of *Sankofa*. Jegnas and drummers work together. Drummers may be timekeepers who punctuate the message of Griots/Jegnas. Gerima uses African drum rhythms to mark key transformational moments in the consciousness of both Dorothy and Shola. As Dorothy enters the abortion clinic, classical European music is heard, but the sound of African drums fades in as she leaves the abortion clinic resolved to keep her baby, perhaps reflective of the new challenge ahead of her. Drum rhythms punctuate the scene where Dorothy reflectively gazes at the poster of the African woman given to her by Angie. The drums are heard when Shola is baptized by Shango. Dressed in a white wrap and wearing a white gele (i.e., a scarf) on her head, she allows Shango to baptize her in a river as rhythmic drums and singing are heard. *Sankofa* closes, in part, with a Ghanaba solo. He is covered in ash and white paint, and his rhythms heighten the climax when the ancestors have taken their place outside the dungeon.

Hair and hair styling have had multiple meanings throughout history. Gerima uses hairstyling to help denote Dorothy and Shola's psychological transformation. Viewers of *Bush Mama* are first introduced to Dorothy as she struts down the street wearing what we later learn is a wig. As Dorothy's consciousness is raised, she removes her wig. One day she as she daydreams about one of T.C.'s letters, she suddenly sits up, looks at the poster of the African woman freedom fighter that Angie gave her, and studies the braids in the woman's hair. She is then shown in bed thinking before cleaning her apartment as though she is preparing for something. A medium close-up reveals that her hair is braided, mirroring the braids of the African woman in the picture. The braided hair and the cleaning of her apartment signify her gradual transformation to consciousness. The braided hair is also evident at the very end of the film after Dorothy beats the police officer to death. After that scene, Dorothy is moved to tell T.C. about her new style. She says, "You remember you used to ask why I always wear a wig. . . . All day and all night while I eat and I sleep. . . . T.C., the wig is off my head. The wig is off my head. I never saw what was under it. I just saw on top. The glitter. The wig. The wig is off my head, T.C."

Shola's hair transformation is subtler but no less symbolic than Dorothy's. Her head-wrap was typical of what many enslaved women wore. Her hair is uncovered as Nunu, her spiritual mother, braids it while sharing her story about being raped and impregnated in a slave ship when she was a girl. The ritual of getting her hair braided while sitting at the feet of an older woman who communicates vital history is transformative for Shola. In another scene, Shola is given a red scarf, a symbol of the secret society, which she is afraid to wear. Shola's cornrowed style becomes evident in a scene where the priest points to them and suggests that they show that she has been spending time with what he calls "the heathen Africans." As punishment, the slave owner cuts a braid off of her head. Gerima said, "The fact that she started hanging out with Nunu, who braids her, is a symbol of going towards the rebellion world" (Turner and Kamdibe 2008, 976).

By the end of *Bush Mama* and *Sankofa*, Gerima has set the context for Dorothy's and Shola's transformative agency. The agency is shown through their resistant stance to their oppression. During slavery, black women adopted multiple forms of resistance in order to survive. They broke tools, faked sickness, maimed themselves, and engaged in other acts that helped them to resist their condition. Women dehumanized via welfare and other institutions have resisted in a variety of ways as well. Karen McCormack has outlined some of the discursive strategies that poor women have used to describe their experiences and structure their own identities despite negative external labeling because of their low-income status (2005). These women often attacked for their economic status identified mothering as their priority. McCormack says that by "constituting themselves as good mothers these women are best able to separate themselves from the putative 'welfare mother'" (8). This reinforces their identity in spite of the negative propaganda.

While Dorothy initially avoids physically resisting the psychological oppression she faces, she often daydreams about smashing a bottle over the head of the welfare worker who continuously suggests that she is a deviant mother. On the outside, Dorothy has a blank expression, but Gerima exposes her internal monologue of silent resistance. Dorothy's final transformation results when a white police officer attempts to rape her daughter. The attack on her child by the would-be rapist provokes her violent attack. The scene is slowly disclosed as Gerima employs a nonlinear approach. He also incorporates a montage that forces viewers to piece together what has transpired. One image shows Dorothy in a jail cell and struggling to push herself out of a pool of blood on the floor, having spontaneously, we later learn, aborted her baby because of a brutal police beating. During this montage, a male voice-over is heard saying, "He laid his life on the line for you and your lousy drunken whores. He came to arrest you for doing and all the crap you been doing a rotten job and for taking care of your little whore daughter." The montage includes the image of Dorothy struggling to move as a male voice-over says, "Do you understand, do you understand," and, "Do you understand. Do you agree?" In case the spectator does not understand, Gerima takes viewers to the scene of LuAnne's attempted rape, where he reveals the incident that precipitated Dorothy's violent agency after she enters her apartment and finds a police officer standing over LuAnne. Dorothy beats the policeman in an up and down motion, over and over, ultimately protecting her daughter. After the beating, she rises up, hair braided, and stares straight ahead. Behind her, the poster of the African woman freedom fighter is shown, connecting the two women's realities. Gerima raises the horrors of pedophilia and rape that force Dorothy to take that last step to transformative agency, to save her child from an officer of the state who has exerted psychic abuse against her.

For Dorothy and Shola, the rebellious agency results in their violent exaction of justice, which is similar to what happened with the real Celia, who killed her slave owner/rapist in 1855. While they each use violence that appears choreographed to represent a release of pent up fury, neither attack seems gratuitous or excessive. Gerima has taken the characters through a process of socialization and consciousness, raising that spark's rebellious agency. As Abrams says ". . . numerous, variable factors [that] intersect in a particular time and place may determine their capabilities for self-direction in that context. This intersection not only bears on, but may, indeed, help them to form their own trajectory of self-assertion" (Abrams 1999, 12). The killings in each film are eerily similar, as Dorothy repeatedly raises and lowers an umbrella and Shola repeatedly raises and lowers a machete. Both instances, created in Gerima films made more than seventeen years apart, are rare but revolutionary moments, in that they depict black women protagonists exerting agency as a result of realistic issues.

Through voice-over, Dorothy and Shola tell their side and express the goals and desires obtained through their violent acts. The closing montage of *Sankofa* helps Shola connect her past with the present. She emerges from the dungeon having surrendered old patterns of thinking and acting. Dorothy also changes and tells T.C. about how the police beat the baby out of her and adds,

> I thought that I was born to be poor and be pushed about and stepped on. I don't want LuAnne thinking like that. I can see now that my problem was a place that I was born into. A place with laws that protect the people who got money. It's evil and wrong.
>
> I have to get to know myself, to read and to study so we can change it.

Gerima's lens deconstructs Hollywood narratives where only white women and girls are raped. It takes time, however, before Shola and Dorothy engage in rebellious agency. Early in the film, Shola tells Shango, "As far as I'm concerned, killing's wrong no matter what they've done to me." Though she is continuously raped, she is unable to resist.

The rapes of Shola and the attempted rape of Dorothy's daughter, Luanne, are not fetishized. In *Sankofa*, rape is presented as the violent act that it is. Of the rape scene, Gerima said,

> . . . If I indulged in graphically filming the rape scene, I would be going against my purpose. I think I did not shoot that scene I shot graphically. I shot it to show that white men's relationship to black women was like an outright treatment of an animal. It's not this love story. I wanted to show that he rapes her the way he would rape a cow or an animal. He was not having a human relationship with this African woman. (Woolford and Gerima 1994, 95)

Shola describes her transformation after Shango gives her a wooden Sankofa bird, saying, ". . . after he put that bird on my neck, I became a rebel." She explains that she didn't mind being sent to work in the fields. Her transformation progresses to completion when the rapist/overseer approaches her as she is chopping sugarcane. Shola strikes him repeatedly, up and down with a machete, in a scene that mirrors Dorothy's beating of the police officer. Gerima spares viewers the blood and gore but allows Shola to exact justice before she runs away with the other rebels. This is her liberation day.

Gerima appears less interested in promoting a return to a utopian African reality than in demonstrating some of the ways that history informs how people have engaged and continue to engage with one another. Though Dorothy and Shola are fictional characters, their experiences memorialize the humanity and agency of real black around the world—women like Celia, whose suffering resulted in violent agency. Gerima humanizes them and exposes socializing influences such as political clarity and historical understanding that the characters gain on their journey. These fill the landscapes that spark the coming to consciousness and provide glimpses of the influences that ultimately inspire their rebellious agency.

A Sankofa bird symbol may be represented by a bird with its head turned backward and holding an egg in its mouth. The egg in the bird's mouth represents rebirth. Thus, looking backward is ultimately connected to renewal and moving forward. *Sankofa*'s climactic closing montage features images of the sun, an aerial image tracking toward the ancient Ramses and Nefertiti statue in Abu Simbel, Kemet (Egypt), and the Sankofa bird as Shola/Mona remerges from the Cape Coast dungeon, reborn and the welcomed to the ancestral realm by Nunu. Shola knew that the consequences of her rebellious act and that resistance might lead to her transition to the world of the ancestors. Dorothy's transformation to a higher state of consciousness enables her rebellious act of protecting her daughter despite the consequences. The two films demonstrate the agency of the two black women, in particular, and of African-descended people in general. The reclamation of memory and the raising of black consciousness to aid and win liberation is a consistent theme in the work of Gerima. Both Dorothy and Shola are empowered as human beings when they know and claim their history.

References

Abrams, Kathryn. 1999. "From Autonomy to Agency: Feminist Perspectives on Self-Direction." *William and Mary Law Review* 40(3): 805–46.

Alexander, Michelle. 2010. *The New Jim Crow: Mass Incarceration in the Age of Colorblindness*. New York: The New Press.

Amistad. 1997. Directed by Steven Spielberg.

Ashes and Embers, 1982. Directed by Haile Gerima.

Baldwin, Bridgette. 2010. "Stratification of the Welfare Poor: Intersections of Gender, Race, and 'Worthiness' in Poverty Discourse and Policy." *The Modern American* 6(1): 4–14.

The Blind Side. 2009. Directed by John Lee Hancock.

Bogle, D. 2003. *Toms, Coons, Mulattoes, Mammies & Bucks: An Interpretive History of Blacks in American Films*. 4th ed. New York: Continuum.

Bush Mama. 1975. Directed by Haile Gerima.

Child of Resistance. 1973. Directed by Haile Gerima.

Dangerous Minds. 1995. Directed by John Smith.

Django Unchained. 2012. Directed by Quentin Tarantino.

Freedom Writers. 2007. Directed by Richard LaGravenese.

Gerima, Haile. 1989. "Triangular Cinema, Breaking Toys, and Dinknesh vs. Lucy." In *Questions of Third Cinema*, edited by Jim Pines and Paul Willeman, 65–89. London: British Film Institute.

Hilliard-Nunn, Patricia. 1998. "Representing African Women in Movies." In *Afrocentric Visions: Studies in Culture and Communication*, edited by J. D. Hamlet, 175–94. Thousand Oaks, CA: Sage Publications.

Linder, Douglas O. 2011. Celia, A Slave, Trial (1855): An Account, http://www.famous-trials.com/celia.

Lincoln. 2012. Directed by Steven Spielberg.

McCormack, Karen. 2005. "Stratified Reproduction and Poor Women's Resistance." In *Gender & Society* 19:5, 660–79.

12 Years a Slave. 2013. Directed by Steve McQueen.

Mypheduh Films. http://www.sankofa.com/about.php.

Phaff, F. 1988. *Twenty-Five Black African Filmmakers.* Westport, CT: Greenwood Press.

Red Tails. 2012. Directed by Anthony Hemingway.

Reid, Mark A. 2005. *Black Lenses, Black Voices: African American Film Now.* New York: Rowman & Littlefield Publishers, Inc.

Safford, T., W. Triplett, and H. Gerima, 1983. "Haile Gerima: Radical Departures to a New Black Cinema." *Journal of the University Film and Video Association* 35, no. 2 (Spring): 59–65.

Sankofa. 1993. Directed by Haile Gerima.

She's Gotta Have It. 1986. Directed by Spike Lee.

Taylor, C. 1988. "The Birth of Black Cinema: Overview." In *The Birth of Black Cinema: A Symposium on the New Black Cinema Film Viewing Guide*, 1–4.

Turner, D. D., and M. Kamdibe. 2008. "Haile Gerima: In Search of an Africana Cinema." *Journal of Black Studies* 38, no. 6 (July): 968–91.

Willis, W. B. 1998. *The Adinkrah Dictionary: A Visual Primer on the Language of Adinkrah.* Washington, DC: The Pyramid Complex.

Woolford, P., and H. Gerima, 1994. "Filming Slavery." *Transition* 64: 90–104.

Yearwood, G. L. 2000. *Black Film as a Signifying Practice: Cinema, Narration and the African–American Aesthetic Tradition.* Trenton, NJ: Africa World Press, Inc.

10

DECOLONIZING MAMMY AND OTHER SUBVERSIVE ACTS

Directing as Feminist Praxis in Gina Prince-Bythewood's *The Secret Life of Bees*

Kimberly Nichele Brown

The sexual dimension of American racism is reflected in the motion picture portrayal of the black woman. Her film image has been defined by herself. When she is not the figment of white male fantasy, she is a product of white female thinking. Few black female writers have gained employment in the film industry. The result is a tragic history of stereotyping and steady procession of mammies, maids, miscreants, matriarchs, madams and assorted 'make-it-for-money' types.

—Edward Mapp, "Black Women in Films" (1973).

A GRADUATE OF UCLA's film school, Gina Prince-Bythewood had already established herself as an independent filmmaker concerned with black women prior to being asked by Fox Searchlight to direct and write the screenplay for *The Secret Life of Bees* (2008); her most notable credits are *Disappearing Acts* (2000) and *Love and Basketball* (2000).[1] The subsequent positive response to these two films on the part of African American female audiences served to prove Norma Manatu's assertion that "Black women still need public reaffirmation of the self, they still need images of hope. . . . Realistic narratives that truthfully reflect the self are embraced because such narratives acknowledge black women as fully functional persons" (2003, 118). As products of a *black female gaze* produced with a corresponding audience in mind, in their exploration of black heterosexual romance, both films defy the "tragic history of stereotyping" of which Edward Mapp speaks.

In the above epigraph, Mapp makes ample use of alliteration to express his displeasure with the Hollywood film industry's rampant practice of type-casting black women in roles that reinforce our position as societal outlaw or depict us in servitude to whites in terms of domestic, emotional, and sexual labor. Mapp also bemoans the dearth of filmic adaptations of novels written by black women—a lament that still resonates well into the new millennium. Although black female novelists have saturated the publishing industry since the eighties, to this date only a modest number of their novels have been adapted for film, and fewer still of these adaptations have been scripted or directed by blacks, irrespective of gender. While the decision to adapt *The Secret Life of Bees* (2002), a novel written by white southern female writer Sue Monk Kidd, does nothing to reverse this trend, the fact that an African American woman wrote the screenplay and directed the subsequent film presents an interesting conundrum with regard to who controls the filmic gaze.

At first glance Kidd's original story seems to mirror Hollywood practices, since the tale centers around four black women and their maternal relationship to a young white girl (two of these women were at one time employed by the girl's family). The novel is set in South Carolina during 1964, the year the Civil Rights Act was passed—the landmark legislation prohibiting discrimination on the basis of race, ethnicity, national origin, religion, or sex—and the year before the passing of the 1965 Voting Rights Act. Thus, readers are introduced to Lily Melissa Owens (later played by Dakota Fanning), a fourteen-year-old white girl coming of age as the nation undergoes a paradigmatic shift in regard to race relations.

Lily leads a life straight out of an American gothic, where, as Patricia Yaeger might argue, "traces of trauma fashion a regime of haunting" (2005, 90). She has had to live with an abusive and sullen father, T. Ray, who fatally shot Deborah, Lily's mother, when Lily was a toddler. Prompted by her father's revelation that Deborah intended to abandon her, Lily runs away with her maid, Rosaleen, in tow to Tilburon, South Carolina, to learn more about her mother's past and her reasons for leaving Lily to T. Ray's devices. Once in Tilburon, Lily and Rosaleen meet the Boatwright sisters. The eldest

Lily Owens (Dakota Fanning) and her father, T. Ray Owens (Paul Bettany) in *The Secret Life of Bees*.

of the three women, August, makes a living as a beekeeper and sells the honey locally in jars carrying the label of a black Madonna, a symbol readers later learn is emblematic of the religion the women practice. Lily soon learns that August used to be her mother's nursemaid when Deborah was a child, and the plot unfolds from there.

Given the novel's content, it is not a stretch to condemn it as a product of "white female thinking," since it is essentially about a white girl's desire to use black women's bodies for surrogacy in order to squelch her longing for her own biological mother. In fact, some scholars have questioned the extent to which *The Secret Life of Bees* accurately reflects the experiences of black women. For example, in her article "Teaching Cross-racial Texts: Cultural Theft in *The Secret Life of Bees*," Laurie Grobman accuses Kidd of appropriating black culture and, more specifically, the lives of black women. She asks, "On what ethical grounds does Kidd have the right to use a culture that is not her own as a plot device to help her fictional Lily develop spiritually, emotionally, and artistically?" (2008, 22). Nevertheless, *The Secret Life of Bees* obviously struck a chord with readers; the novel sold over six million copies and was on the *New York Times* best-seller list for over two and half years. Fox Searchlight, the studio responsible for the novel's subsequent adaptation, wanted to capitalize on the novel's success by targeting the same female demographic that made the book a best seller.

Prince-Bythewood's previous box office success, as well as the sensibility she brought to the book's subject matter as an African American female

Left to right: Rosaleen Daise (Jennifer Hudson), Neil (Nate Parker), June Boatwright (Alicia Keys), Lily Owens (Dakota Fanning), and August Boatwright (Queen Latifah) in *The Secret Life of Bees.*

filmmaker, seemed to make her the optimal candidate to adapt Kidd's novel into a movie. However, in multiple interviews, Prince-Bythewood reveals it took her seven years to accept Fox Searchlight's initial offer to oversee the film adaptation of Kidd's novel. Although she cites a busy work life and the birth of two children as the reason for the delay, one has to wonder if Prince-Bythewood struggled with how she would transform the story of four black women's relationship with a little white girl, set in the Deep South during the turbulent sixties, into a product that "acknowledges black women as fully functional persons." That these black women were the creation of a white southern woman had to give her pause.

Although *The Secret Life of Bees* encompasses an all-star cast of black female actresses and singers whom I admire—Jennifer Hudson, Alicia Keys, Queen Latifah, and Sophie Okonedo—I was reluctant to see the film or to read the book upon which it was based.[2] Even as trusted friends encouraged me that both had merits, I assumed that black female experiences, and by extension our bodies, would be used as background fodder or catharsis for white female audiences. Hollywood had conditioned me to expect as much, given its penchant for whitewashing history and deemphasizing black agency, and its privileging of contemporary "noble savages" over more radical depictions of blacks.[3] As Robert Stam and Ella Shohat have indicated, "The sensitivity around stereotypes and distortions largely arises . . . from the powerlessness of historically marginalized groups to control their own presentation" (184). Additionally, as an African American woman who understands that oftentimes black women paid to provide care to white children do so at the expense of spending time with their own biological children, my knee-jerk reaction is to reject up front any celebratory praise of black domestics on the part of whites.

However, there is no denying that black female domestics have played a significant role in the development and maturation of numerous white children, from slavery through Jim Crow segregation and beyond. For example, during the interviews she conducted for her article, "A Complex Bond: Southern Black Domestic Workers and Their White Employers," Susan Tucker explains:

> A recurrent sentence in the interviews with white women was, "She was closer to me than my own mother." This was probably accurate; in homes that employed full-time help, black women domestics were the more active caregivers. They were the ones who were there in day-to-day emergencies. They were often the ones who told girl children about menstruation, about sex, about relationships with men because they were often with these children at crucial times in their lives. (1987, 6–13)

Therefore, is it possible to give credence to this sentiment, to corroborate the affection of a white woman, let's say, for her black caregiver, and still validate the experiences of black female domestics by acknowledging the exploitative conditions under which this affection most likely fomented?

While on the surface Gina Prince-Bythewood's film seems to be a faithful adaptation of Sue Monk Kidd's novel, I argue that as the film's screenwriter and director, Prince-Bythewood offers black women viewers and mainstream audiences alike a space to grapple with complex intimacies that recognizes the connection that white southern women have to the black women who raised them, while also insisting that this fictive kinship not take precedence over a holistic treatment of black female subjectivity. Through a complex manipulation of the book's original matriarchal theme, one that speaks to the linguistic and tangible slippage between "Mammy" and "Mommy," Prince-Bythewood works to *decolonize* the black female domestic archetype from its long-standing role as catharsis for white girls and women. Using Alice Walker's concept of *womanism* as a methodological approach and the recent phenomenon of *The Help* (the fervor spawned by both the book and the film) as antithesis, in this chapter I examine the methods by which Prince-Bythewood seeks to recoup and reclaim the image of "Mammy" and by extension that of black female domestics in general. Her subtle acts of subversion ultimately push all viewers toward a truer vision of integration and empathy than do other movies with similar relationships and power dynamics.

My initial impetus for analyzing *The Secret Life of Bees* as a womanist film came during the question and answer portion of a lecture I gave criticizing both Kathyrn Stockett's novel *The Help* (2009) and its subsequent film adaptation, directed by Tate Taylor in 2011. Perhaps fearing that my racial allegiance compromised my critique, one audience member questioned whether or not it was possible for me to consider *any* film adapted from a novel written by a white female southerner as an ethical representation of the kinship felt between white charges and their black domestics. Although I positioned *The Help* as a contemporary maternal melodrama and relied heavily on the work of white feminists such as Sarah Arnold, Lisa Cartwright, Gwendolyn Audrey Foster, Ann E. Kaplan, Barbara Klinger, and Linda Williams to bolster and elucidate my thesis, the audience member posited that I was doing a *womanist* rather than a *feminist* reading of the film. I countered by stating that I did not think it possible to use womanism as a methodological approach to a text like *The Help*. Although *The Help* purports to be about *the help*, the plot foregrounds the white female protagonist, Skeeter, as a "white savior" who enables black domestics to find their voice through her efforts. Furthermore, I reasoned, the narrative is predicated on and consumed with the *lament* for both the lost Mammy and a bygone era; how black women felt about and fared under domestic servitude is somewhat inconsequential—whiteness is still central, which is antithetical to the very definition of womanism.

Tuzyline Jita Allan explains, "Each of Walker's three core womanist claims—audaciousness, woman and community-centeredness—finds support in the exigencies of life lived outside the privileged aegis of whiteness

Black Womanist Communalism. *Left to right*: Rosaleen Daise (Jennifer Hudson), August Boatwright (Queen Latifah), and June Boatwright (Alicia Keys).

and maleness" (1995, 439), while at the same time, "womanism has helped to fortify the long-standing discontent over white feminists' appropriation of womanhood, prompting active rather than reactive forms of criticism" (437). At its core, then, womanism is about black female self-actualization and resistance against our marginalization on multiple fronts. A black womanist *film* then, by extension, "centers Black women's voices and experiences; employs strategies of resistance, accommodation, and assimilation; and seeks intrapersonal, interpersonal, and community healing . . ." (Dawkins and Ryder 2013, 259).

Even though Grobman raises some valid concerns about Kidd's probity with regard to black female experiences in the Jim Crow South, I would argue that, to a large degree, *The Secret Life of Bees* is more conducive to the aims of womanism as a novel on its own merits than is Stockett's novel. Lily, Kidd's protagonist, eventually achieves self-actualization *with the aid of* rather than *at the expense of* black women. This distinction is important because it offers the possibility of real empathy, rather than a token gesture, by shifting the racial and class power dynamics between Lily and the Boatwright sisters. As somewhat affluent and self-sufficient African American women, the care the Boatwright sisters bestow on Lily is not mediated or muddled by the tenets of employment; in fact, Kidd insists upon the parental designation of "mother" throughout the narrative. Additionally, rather than position Lily as the "white savior" archetype, the novel puts the black women in the position of offering tutelage in healthy expressions of love, teaching Lily how to deal with her grief, and showing Lily how to find the divinity that resides within—in essence, they teach her how to be *her own savior* rather than perpetuate a potentially parasitic connection to black women.

The Secret Life of Bees lends itself more readily to an adaptation that would appeal to black female spectators, as well as to a womanist analysis, because of Kidd's deliberate intertextual dialogue with African American female writers, which underscores a potential desire on her part for true empathy between Lily and the blacks she encounters throughout the novel. For example, when T. Ray stumbles upon Lily lying on the ground in a secluded part of his peach grove, he mistakenly assumes that she has been making out with boy. Instead, T. Ray, leaving her flush as she frantically attempts to hide sacred items that once belonged to her mother, has startled Lily. Lily's connection with nature in this scene, coupled with T. Ray's angst regarding his daughter's budding puberty, call to mind the infamous masturbation scene with Janie under the pear tree in Zora Neale Hurston's *Their Eyes Were Watching God* (1937).

Kidd's gastric metaphors and tendency to conflate the act of ingestion with maternal or sexual desire is reminiscent of Toni Morrison. When describing Lily's feelings about Rosaleen, Kidd writes, "Water beaded across her shoulders, shining like drops of milk and her breasts swayed in the currents. . . . I couldn't help it, I wanted to go and lick the milk beads from her shoulders" (Kidd 2002, 55). Here Lily could easily be Pecola from *The Bluest Eye* (1970), who believes that she is ugly and unloved because she does not fit the white beauty ideal for girls and women. Pecola attempts a ritual of transformation by ingesting Mary Jane candies that have a picture of a cute white girl on their wrappers, because "To eat the candy is to somehow eat the eyes, eat Mary Jane. Love Mary Jane. Be Mary Jane" (50). Or is Lily, Beloved, in Morrison's same-titled novel, Sethe's reincarnated baby who eventually grows fat off of her mother's excuses for her act of infanticide; while Beloved becomes engorged, Sethe becomes emaciated. And finally, Kidd's use of honey as a symbol of love throughout the novel is resonant with Morrison's use of syrup to describe the love in the MacTeer household: "Love, thick and dark as Alaga syrup, eased up into that cracked window. I could smell it—taste it—sweet, musty with an edge of Wintergreen in its base—everywhere in that house" (*1970*, 12).

In any event, each daughter's longing for the love of her mother precipitates the hunger, which is akin to Lily's own sense of loss. Lily's desire to lick the milk from Rosaleen's shoulder (and she is much darker than the actress, Jennifer Hudson, who plays her in the movie—which conjures up a striking contrast for readers) is not only homoerotic; it also evokes the image of a child suckling at her mother's breast. The fact that Lily hungers for and lusts after Rosaleen rather than the reverse, her desire to consume Rosaleen like Pecola consumes Mary Janes candies, also serves to invert the long-standing beauty hierarchy that positions blackness as subordinate to whiteness.

Translating a novel into a film, even if it were possible to follow the original text verbatim, still requires much effort and imagination on the part of the filmmaker to transform the written narrative into a visual one. Therefore, it is important to evaluate the film version of *The Secret Life of Bees* not only for its fidelity to Kidd's novel but on its own merits and for what it communicates about Prince-Bythewood's vision and political motivations. Although one might argue that Kidd's original novel is rife with womanist connotations, it takes Gina Prince-Bythewood to make manifest the womanist potential inherent in the original text. Prince-Bythewood explains her process of adaptation as follows:

> My process for adaptation is just reading the book and start highlighting key lines for characters, key structure points. The hardest thing is figuring out what not to put in, how to condense it and give it the same amount of depth as the book. . . . The hardest thing is how do you visualize the things that are talked about in the book. In the book Lily is telling us her feelings. That is probably the hardest thing to show. Giving yourself the freedom to break apart from the book is also difficult. It is my bible not my blueprint.

The distinction Prince-Bythewood makes between a bible and the blueprint in reference to her approach is instructive because it implies that, while narrative fidelity is important, it can be achieved by an adherence to the thematic elements that are central to the novel's moral integrity, rather than a strict chronological visual representation of the plot.

In her book *A Theory of Adaptation*, Hutcheon takes issue with traditional theories of adaptation that privilege fidelity to the original text. Instead, she encourages viewing adaptation as both a product that has been transcoded to fit the parameters of the new medium and a process, one of both "creation" and "reception." As a *"process of creation,"* an adaptation involves both "(re-)interpretation" and "(re-)creation," while as a *process of reception,"* an adaptation relies on memory, repetition, and intertextuality (1996, 8). As Hutcheon contends, adaptation as process is dependent upon a symbiosis between the filmmaker and her viewers. This symbiosis is analogous to Mark A. Reid's employment of the term "black womanist film." For Reid the term "black womanist film" refers to films that generate a "spectatorial space" for black women whose "narrative constructions," "viewing positions," and "reading strategies . . . permit polyvalent female subjectivity" (1995, 57). Reid contends, ". . . black womanism, as a theory of reception and production, requires an 'interested' spectator to decode the plurality of (con)texts, which includes intra- as well as interracial forces that dehumanize the community. Equally, black womanist critical strategies deconstruct narrative systems and viewing positions which reduce racial, sexual, and class differences to one of gender" (59). In contrast to the average moviegoer, regardless of race, the interested spectator possesses acute racial acuity and is well educated in both black canonical visual and print media, as well as being a savvy deconstructionist.

The subversive scrutiny of Reid's "interested spectator" bears much in common with Manthia Diawara's "resistant spectator" and bell hooks's notion of the "oppositional gaze." Just as the Inuit and Yupik peoples (aka Eskimos) are purported to have ninety-nine words for snow as a result of their environment, the racist terrain of Hollywood has resulted in ninety-nine ways to describe the side-eyed looks blacks give to the institution's representations of us. As Ed Guerrero contends, ". . . Hollywood's unceasing efforts to frame *blackness* are constantly challenged by the cultural and political self-definitions of African Americans, who as a people have been determined since the inception of commercial cinema to militate against this limiting system of representation" (1993, 3).

In order to unpack what is "womanist" about Prince-Bythewood's adaptation, rather than focus on spectatorship like Diawara, Guerrero, hooks, Hutcheon, and Reid, I want to employ black womanism as a theory of woman-centered filmmaking praxis. Although I believe spectatorship is a crucial component to black feminist film scholarship, I have grown skeptical about the essentialist nature of this scholarship that often presupposes that black audiences have at our ready disposal a critical lexicon and cultural lens that is inherently oppositional. My skepticism is based on the growing fascination with "post-blackness" as a celebratory embracing of multivariate expressions of blackness even as it offers very little in the way of political mobilization for postsegregationist generations. Therefore, I am ultimately interested in the work of postsegregationist black films.

What Guerrero found indicative of black-focused and independent films sprouting up in the late eighties and early nineties is also true about the intervention Gina Prince-Bythewood has made in commercial cinema with this adaptation; *The Secret Life of Bees* reflects "an insistent black social consciousness and political activism" (Guerrero 1993, 3). I contend that Prince-Bythewood's ideas about using film as a consciousness-raising tool were influenced in a large part by the legacy of the black filmmakers who graduated from the film school at University of California at Los Angeles, such as Abdosh Abdulhafiz, Melvonna Ballenger, Charles Burnett, Ben Caldwell, Larry Clark, Julie Dash, Haile Gerima, Pamela Jones, Alile Sharon Larkin, Bernard Nichols, John Rein, and Bill Woodberry. Ntongela Masilela explains,

> The intellectual and cultural coordinates of this Black inde-
> pendent film movement are inseparable from the political and
> social struggles and conclusions of the 1960s. For these African
> and African-American filmmakers, imagination was inescap-
> ably wedded to political and cultural commitment. The Civil
> Rights Movement, the anti-war movement, and activities in
> America in support of national liberation movements in Africa,
> Asia, and Latin America informed the political consciousness
> of members of the group. ("The Los Angeles School of Black
> Filmmakers," 107–8)

This group of filmmakers has been lovingly nicknamed "the black insurgents" by Toni Cade Bambara because they "engaged in interrogating conventions of dominant cinema, screening films of socially conscious cinema, and discussing ways to alter previous significations as they relate to Black people" (Martin 2010, 2).

Although she graduated from UCLA's film department in 1991, Prince-Bythewood shares similar predilections. And even though she has achieved a modicum of success in Hollywood, the conditions under which she works do not seem to have changed much. For example, when questioned about whether or not Hollywood has become more receptive to making films for black audiences, UCLA Film School alum Julie Dash stated,

> With the success of Tyler Perry, F. Gary Gray, Gina Prince-Bythewood, Will Smith, Tim Story, Mara Brock Akil, and Shonda Rhimes, one wonders why it is still so difficult to convince the powers that be that we do, in fact, have an audience. It's a constant fight. . . . We need to be dedicated, with a concerted and focused effort to demand more balanced images of ourselves out there. People say things have changed. They have changed, but in many ways they have not. (Martin 2010, 11)

Prince-Bythewood's experiences with Hollywood corroborate Dash's comments:

> . . . for the most part, I feel like my choices are discriminated against in that a lot of things I want to focus on are female-driven or black female driven and those are the toughest things to get made. I have dealt with racism pretty face-to-face. But for the most part, I'm able to just push them aside and focus on what I'm trying to do and continue to believe that talent has no race or agenda, and that I have every right to be here. (Carnevale n.d.)

Prince-Bythewood's struggle with Hollywood and her need to voice her right to work within the institution is mirrored in *Dancing in September* (2000), a film by her husband, Reggie Rock Bythewood. Offering a commentary on Hollywood's stereotypical representations of African Americans similar to that of the satirical *Hollywood Shuffle* (1987) and *Bamboozled*, which was also released in 2000, its story line centers on an African American female television producer's struggle to portray blacks in an ethical manner within the confines of the Hollywood film industry. While *Hollywood Shuffle* tackles the theme from the vantage point of a black actor, *Bamboozled* and *Dancing in September* focus on the complicity of black television executives in perpetuating these stereotypes as they use black actors to produce modern-day minstrel performances. The moral of *Dancing in September*, along with Prince-Bythewood's and her husband's combined filmography, demonstrates an acute awareness of the accountability and responsibility they have to black viewers. Their social commitment to the black filmgoer also demonstrates their belief that beyond independent films, black filmmakers and media personnel must also make representational changes *within* Hollywood and mainstream venues.

Such a feat is more readily accomplished with a film like *The Secret Life of Bees* that defies easy demographic classification. In one interview, Gina Prince-Bythewood explains, "No one thinks of this as a black book and that is how we are viewing the film. It is a true ensemble film. The core audience is women. In this day and age people may assume this is a black film but it shouldn't matter." Prince-Bythewood was very strategic in how she marketed *The Secret Life of Bees*. In more mainstream venues, she emphasized the universal qualities of the film, while in magazines like *Ebony* and *Essence*, she highlighted the film's appeal to black audiences.[4] Her duplicity can be read as an act of subversion, in that her code switching enabled Prince-Bythewood to foreground black women even as she touts the movie's universal appeal.

And yet, as Prince-Bythewood surmises, in many ways *The Secret Life of Bees*, much like a movie such as *The Color Purple* (1985), *is* still seen as a black film despite that it is based on the novel of a white woman (*The Color Purple* was directed by Steven Spielberg). Richard J. Powell explains,

> . . . one could . . . argue that a film or video with a black cast and a well-crafted screenplay based on the experiences, narratives, and emotional states of black peoples . . . cannot escape being anything except a black cultural statement, regardless of the race or ethnicity of the [filmmakers] involved [additionally,] . . . Viewer responses to these works—if not a

precise measure of aesthetics, [are] certainly an indicator of a modicum of black cultural connectedness—would suggest that the race or ethnicity of the . . . [writer] alone does not make a film or video production black. (Powell, *Black Art: A Cultural History*, 204)

The characteristics and definition of what makes a "black film" have been debated and theorized widely by film scholars such as Thomas Cripps, Manthia Diawara, James Murray, Powell, Mark A. Reid, and Gladstone Yearwood.[5] In these debates, it would seem that with commercial films the label is even more ambiguous because these films are a complex conglomeration of adaptation, production, and reception.

The combination of the license Prince-Bythewood takes with the adaptation, the investment the lead black female actresses and producers (Will and Jada Pinkett Smith) had in the film, as well as the audience response persuade me to think of the film as "black." Having sat on the script for nearly seven years before making a decision to direct *The Secret Life of Bees*, Prince-Bythewood recalls, "And then I was talking with an actor friend of mine who said she was reading for the film. It was going to be directed by a male director. I just got incredibly jealous. In my mind I said, 'that is supposed to be my movie'" (Rosen 2008). Her possessiveness about the screenplay and her initial reluctance to embark on the adaptation partially derive from the ways in which the plot resonated with Prince-Bythewood's real life: "I connected to Lily's story. I was adopted. There is a line in the [book], 'there was a hole in me.' I felt the same way. I wanted to find my birth mother and find out why I was given up. What was wrong with me? What could make a mother give up her child?"[6]

Prince-Bythewood was also drawn to the characters Kidd had created because they did not correspond to monolithic or stereotypical conventions of black women: "And then these Boatwright sisters, I've never seen black women portrayed like that, it just kind of smashed every stereotype. Just the opportunity to bring them to life I thought would have been a gift."[7] The script and the characters also resonated with the cast; the lead black actresses are reported widely to have taken a pay cut in order to participate in the film. When asked why she decided to play the role of August, the eldest Boatwright sister, Queen Latifah replies, "I've purposefully chosen not to play slaves and certain roles where they just show us as victims. . . . There are a bunch of scripts that I have not done because I don't want to be that person on the screen" (*Ebony* 80). While I can point to several questionable roles that comprise Queen Latifah's repertoire, her aversion to being seen as a victim speaks volumes about why these characters resonate with black women.

The testimonials of Prince-Bythewood and the lead black actresses of the film serve as a stark contrast to Grobman, who argues that the novel "reinforces stereotypes of black women and desexualizes them; [Kidd creates] black women characters whose roots in black literature are unacknowledged; she whitens her black women characters; and she appropriates the black feminine divine to heal and nourish her white protagonist" (2008, 12). If Grobman is correct in assuming that Kidd's Boatwright sisters have no parallels in African American female literary traditions, I would suggest that the reason has more to do with the predilection of the publishing industry (both literary and popular culture) for stories of working-class and poor black women that has created a canon in which Grobman herself might be vested. As evidence of their "whitened" affect, Grobman points to the lack of a heavy southern dialect, their middle-class status, and their gentile predilections (June plays the cello). However, I would suspect that the Boatwrights' mannerisms seem derivative of whites to Grobman because of the ways in which blackness is often coded as working class, while the inverse is true for whiteness. I would also add that Grobman might not go far enough back or search widely enough within annuals of black literary traditions; literary foremothers to the Boatwrights can be found in the work of Pauline Hopkins, Jessie Redmon Fauset, Nella Larsen, Wallace Thurman, or Dorothy West or in the work of more contemporary writers such as Carolivia Herron, Gloria Naylor, or Emily Raboteau.

What makes Prince-Bythewood's adaptation distinctly womanist is the way she depicts the Boatwrights' (and Prince-Bythewood's own) allegiance to Black Nationalist discourse, as well as her affirmation of the black community as a site of healing. These gestures toward a politics of racial uplift and middle-class culture, one that does not simply mimic whites of a similar standing, are evident in things as subtle as costuming, vocal syntax, cast selection, and the lengths that Prince-Bythewood goes to enculturate the actors to the era.

In one interview, Prince-Bythewood empathizes her decision to make the Boatwright sisters don natural hairstyles, which, given the time period, would automatically signal a black nationalist leaning. She implies that this decision reflects the black actresses' commitment to the film's integrity, "We never say it out loud but our Boatwright sisters all have natural hair and the women were fine with that. Sometimes you'll ask an actor about it and they'll say no" ("Gina Prince-Bythewood: 'The Secret Life of Bees'" 2009). In addition to hairstyles, the other costume choices also serve to demonstrate Prince-Bythewood's political investments. In one scene June (Alicia Keys) dons an NAACP T-shirt; this image does not appear in Kidd's original novel.

The casting choices were also deliberate. Queen Latifah's initial entry into the hip-hop scene was based on marketing herself as a female rapper vested in Black Nationalist politics predicated on raising the consciousness of her listeners. Similarly, Caroline A. Streeter explains that Alicia Keys's style "points toward an aesthetic popularized by neosoul female artists like Lauryn Hill, Erykah Badu, Angie Stone, Jill Scott, and India Arie. These women self-consciously embody 'positive' representations of blackness that both derive from black cultural nationalist discourses and constitute a more contemporary feminist challenge to the gendered aesthetic that dictates that the body become progressively thinner and lighter-skinned and the hair straighter with fame" (2005, 197).

In one interview, Prince-Bythewood states that she "wanted the film and the actors to be saturated in the sixties rather than the sixties be a prop."[8] This saturation entailed providing cast members with a fuller understanding of the racial politics of the period. To this aim, Prince-Bythewood provided all actors with what she called a "Sixties Care Package." She shares:

> Each character had something a little different but everyone got *Coming of Age in Mississippi*, which is a brilliant autobiography. They all got this photo-biography on Freedom Summer that helped them just visually. They all got *Four Little Girls*, the documentary by Spike Lee. They all got *Eyes on the Prize*. And

then [for] Paul Bettany I found this great book written by a white man growing up at that time in the 60s. It just had a great perspective I hadn't read before. Again, no one thinks they're a racist. It's just they're reacting to the times and again, we didn't want Paul to be this redneck racist. I mean he believed what he believed because that's how he grew up. Dakota, same thing. Sue Monk actually wrote a great essay called, "The Slave Chair" and it was about her experiences with her nanny growing up and how complicated the relationship was and that was really big for Dakota and for Jennifer.[9]

It was important to Prince-Bythewood that she let actors, black and white, experience first-hand what it would have been like to live in the Jim Crow South and deal with overt racism as a cultural way of life. Dakota Fanning was only fourteen at the time of the shooting, however, and none of the featured black actresses, nor the director herself for that matter, had grown up under segregation. Therefore, Prince-Bythewood sent Jennifer Hudson and Fanning into a drugstore together without alerting either actress of her intention:

I hired some actors and put them in the drugstore and gave them each a character. Then I told Dakota and Jennifer . . . "Just don't hit anybody." But going in there, [Jennifer Hudson] didn't realize that they were actors. They were pretty rough with her, but they were treating her the way that they would have treated her back then. . . . I remember I was sitting in the corner watching because I didn't want to break the wall. I remember the guy at the counter. I had given him a specific thing. If she sits down next to you, tell the guy that you don't want to sit next to any niggers. I couldn't hear what he said, but I saw her head whip over to him and it was like okay, okay. . . . That was really great for her and also Dakota too to have to go through that with Jennifer and see the way that she was treated.[10]

When Prince-Bythewood asked Hudson what had been the hardest thing about the experience, she remarked on being taken aback by being ignored by the salespeople as if she were invisible, while "they would turn to Dakota and answer Dakota."

Although *The Secret Life of Bees* is set during the sixties, its filming also occurred during a significant historical juncture. Prince-Bythewood recalls:

> It was a phenomenal thing to shoot this film in North Carolina at the same time that Barack Obama was in South Carolina, winning over Hillary Clinton. It was so precarious. It could've gone either way. It was such a great way to tie things together for the actors, because when this movie was taking place, people were saying that we'd get the right to vote someday, but probably not in our lifetime. ("Gina Prince-Bythewood: 'The Secret Life of Bees'" 2009)

Prince-Bythewood equates this feeling of anticipation about the impending right to vote on the part of blacks during the sixties with the new millennium milestone of the anticipation of the country's first black president. In the same interview, Prince-Bythewood also recalls being told that the film's subject matter and the time of its release could also aid in Obama's election: "The coolest thing that has come out of these screenings is people saying that this movie could help Barack get elected. To have just a tiny part in [this historic election] would be amazing" ("Gina Prince-Bythewood: 'The Secret Life of Bees'" 2009).

Prince-Bythewood's general focus on community struggle and racial politics, as well as on the interior lives of black women, is more pronounced than in Kidd's original text:

> What was important to me was to tell [the narrative] in a different way. One of the changes I made from the book is that I pushed the civil-rights movement a little more to the forefront. What was important for me was all of the research that I did. My husband's family is from South Carolina, so I talked to all of his aunts that grew up during this time, and what I heard that struck me that then I pushed into the script and the film was, you know, when we think of '60s and black folks, every time we're portrayed, it's *only* about the struggle—that's our life.

And what these women were telling me was that while that was going on, it was also this time of hope when people could see some brightness, finally. And they're living their lives—they have businesses, they're falling in love, they're going to church, they're playing outside. Their life was not solely dominated by one thing. And that, again, was something I hadn't seen before and that I really wanted to do with the story.[11]

Prince-Bythewood foregrounds and reclaims the underlying womanist themes of Kidd's original novel as part and parcel of black female cultural practices. She makes manifest Kidd's emphasis on the communal over the individual, her valorization of black female divinity, her acceptance of anger as a logical response to racist oppression, and her rejection of sacrificial modes of maternal conduct. Additionally, Prince-Bythewood perhaps mitigates some of the problematic elements of Kidd's original story. For example, Kidd's description of Rosaleen seems emblematic of the Mammy figure. She describes Rosaleen as having a "big round face and a body that sloped out from her neck like a pup tent, and she was so black that night seemed to seep from her skin," while her breasts are said to be "big and soft as couch pillows."

Prince-Bythewood, in contrast, participates in the decolonization of the black female domestic from her infamous role as "Mammy" by taking ownership of and poetic license of Kidd's original material to make it more palpable for black audiences, while instructing white audiences in the proper way to make genuine and sincere connections with black people.

Although Melina Abdullah's scholarship is concerned with how black women mother their biological children, I find her employment of a womanist praxis of mothering useful for analyzing the maternal dynamic between Lily and the Boatwright sisters within the film. She explains, "Motherhood inarguably shapes the ways in which one interacts with power structures; it mediates relationships with social, economic and political structures and shapes ideology" (2012, 60). So while both *The Help* and *The Secret Life of Bees* rely on the maternal theme to tease out the complex and often close-knit relationships between the southern white female charges of black domestics, *The Help* demonstrates little desire to dismantle the hierarchy implicit in this fictive kinship arrangement. In contrast, Prince-Bythewood's version of

The Secret Life of Bees ensures that Lily will evolve beyond an unhealthy dependence on a black Mammy to developing a healthy relationship with black maternal role models and black people in general.

While August emerges as the primary maternal role model for Lily, Prince-Bythewood sets upon the task of decolonizing Mammy even before we are introduced to August. Prince-Bythewood explains that one of the biggest changes she made to the script was to make Rosaleen's character (played by Jennifer Hudson) much younger: "In the book she's in her forties. I thought it was important that Lily not have any maternal influence at all" (Morales 2008). By changing the dynamic between Rosaleen and Lily, Prince-Bythewood ensures that Lily comes to August without any firsthand or preconceived notion of what sort of nurturing a Mammy is supposed to give a young white girl. The new dynamic also changes how Rosaleen and Lily relate to one another; while in the novel Lily often comes off as somewhat impertinent, considering the age difference between the two characters, the change makes their interactions seem more sisterly and egalitarian, rather than demonstrating a white girl's impudence and failure to recognize Rosaleen's status as an adult.

Casting Rosaleen with a younger actress also eliminates the jealousy Rosaleen has in the novel as she competes with August for Lily's affection. This change enables Prince-Bythewood to highlight the black female camaraderie that emerges in the film. Additionally, the change in age helps to demarcate the line between expectations for black fictive kin and that for white. For example, when May commits suicide due to the daily pressures of racism, it is Rosaleen who is playfully rechristened by the remaining sisters as "July" and moved into May's room in the main house, while Lily remains in the honey shed.

Prince-Bythewood's decisions to foreground black anger in instances where their rights and humanity are up for question is a crucial step in Lily's tutelage in developing healthy relationships with blacks. Elsewhere I have argued that collective unmasking of black anger is one of the steps toward decolonizing black audiences (Brown 2010). In one scene, after Lily "rescues" Rosaleen from jail, Lily accuses Rosaleen of being ungrateful. Rosaleen denies Lily the opportunity to play the savior, which can be seen as an intertextual nod to Huckleberry Finn.

Referencing Kidd's novel, Grobman argues,

> Like the archetypal Mammy, August is stronger emotionally
> and spiritually than Deborah, and for nine years she devoted
> herself to raising Deborah and caring for Deborah's emotion-
> ally frail mother. August was Deborah's most significant mother
> figure, and Deborah's emotional reliance on August continued
> through her adult life. After her mother died, Deborah moved
> to Triburon to be near August, and, years later, when Deborah's
> marriage fell apart and she needed emotional support and
> guidance, Deborah lived with August and her sisters. (2008, 12)

However, because the reader interprets all scenes through Lily and Lily herself is in the process of development, it is sometimes difficult to separate
stereotypical depictions that are the fault of the novelist from those that are
deliberately written to highlight Lily's own need for maturation and a degree
of awareness of her own racism. Lily's views on maternal love are based on
consumption or the desire to reinhabit the womb, both of which are problematic when the figure is a black woman, given the connotations to economic exploitation and imperialism. Kidd suggests that continuation along
this path will lead to permanent infancy and is therefore a barrier to Lily's
self-actualization.

Grobman takes issue with the centralization of Lily's character within
the narration, and rightfully so; she explains how Lily's voice is foregrounded through Kidd's decision to use her as the frame narrator for the
novel: ". . . Lily is the central character; she narrates the novel, and, like so
many literary characters before her, she is transformed by and through the
black women and their community and culture. The black women's stories
are filtered not only through their white creator but through Lily's narrative
consciousness" (2008, 10). Prince-Bythewood's reduction of Lily's running
commentary to a frame narration that dissolves Lily's centrality in place of
the Boatwright sisters' experiences better enables one to see the shift from
Mammy to role model, especially on the part of August.

The subtle shift from how Kidd understands August's function as a role
model to Prince-Bythewood's understanding of feminist tutelage pushes

the audience to an intersectional analysis of the Black Madonna figure and the black women who worship her. Grobman argues that "Kidd exploits the black feminine divine as universal; [Lily] uses it to construct a new identity" (15). Both the novel and the film make it clear that August wants to offer up the Black Madonna as Lily's salvation in place of herself. In both versions, August explains to Lily that Mary can be "like a stand-in mother for you" (Kidd 2002, 287). Grobman unpacks the exploitative appropriation of black female divinity as follows:

> After Lily telephones her father, only to be rejected again, Lily, alone in her room, connects with the Our Lady statue. She asks the black Mary for love, comfort, and answers, and she presses her hand against the statue's heart: "*I live in a hive of darkness, and you are my mother,* I told her, *You are the mother of thousands*" (emphasis in original). Lily imagines herself being enclosed within the black Mary, as in a picture that she saw in one of August's books: "a little door in the black Mary statue would open up, just over her abdomen, and I would crawl inside to a hidden room." (Grobman 2008, 15)

Here, it would appear that August's wish that Lily transfer her maternal yearnings to Mary have worked; rather than see August (played in no coincidence by *Queen* Latifah) as the supreme ruler, Lily undergoes a spiritual awakening and therefore chooses to inhabit the Black Madonna's body instead of August's.

If we remove race from the equation, Lily's yearnings are reminiscent of Plum's desire to return to the womb after being traumatized serving in War World I in Morrison's *Sula* (1973). This re-habitation, then, replicates patriarchal expectations of maternal obligation to the offspring over one's own self. This re-habitation is doubly problematic when race is once again considered, as it inevitably replicates the black women's exploitation.

Catherine Emanuel points to Kidd's spiritual autobiography, *The Dance of the Dissident Daughter* (1996) to demonstrate the connection Kidd herself makes between female self-actualization and an imperative toward social justice. Kidd writes, "When she finally lets herself *feel* the limits and injustices of female life and admits how her own faith tradition has contributed to that, when she at last stumbles in the dark hold made by the absence of the Divine Feminine presence . . . this woman will become pregnant with herself, with the symbolic female-child who will, if given a chance grow up to reinvent the woman's life" (quoted in Emanuel 2005, 115). On the one hand, Kidd takes Christianity to task for its patriarchal practices, and yet her inability to *particularize* the ways in which the "injustices of female life" are intersectional lends credence to Grobman's accusation that Kidd is exploiting black female divinity for her own purposes.

It is not until Gina Prince-Bythewood reworks the scene to demonstrate June Boatwright's resistance to Lily's spiritual growth and use of the Black Madonna to prioritize her individual pain over the ancestral pain of Africans lost during the Middle Passage and those who suffered in slavery that we see Lily on a more egalitarian path to find the "Divine Feminine presence" within. The scene in the movie during which Lily achieves her initial spiritual awakening during an unconventional prayer meeting held in the Boatwrights' parlor with other women from the town is instructive. Prince-Bythewood places Lily on the periphery of the prayer circle, signifying Lily's outsider status. Although the parlor is clearly a woman's space, proximity to Our Lady is clearly demarcated by race, in that black women are prioritized. June solemnly plays "Amazing Grace" on the cello as the women, moved by the spirit and the music, rise to lay their hands on Mary's wooden chest. The diegetic musical selection is important, since the song was written in 1767 by John Newton, a former slave ship captain who repented his earlier sins, denounced slavery, and joined the priesthood.

Prince-Bythewood focuses the camera on the women's hands, while Lily is out of focus in the background. Lily, too, succumbs to the intensity of the music and the call of the spirit—the scene is undercut with flashbacks depicting Lily's tortured past. When she rises to touch the statue, June, out of breath and in a confused rage, stops the music—in the silence, what sounds like a whip cracks as June glares at Lily. Lily, frozen by her stare, does not touch the statue. When August asks, "June, what's gotten into you," Lily faints. What has gotten "into" June is her anger and her refusal to share the Black Madonna with Lily, who, unlike John Newton, has yet to truly repent.

Prince-Bythewood demonstrates that Lily's desire to colonize the bodies of either living or spiritual black women, then, is not the answer.

Of Kidd's original narrative, Emanuel argues that Lily's confrontation with systemic racism through witnessing the experiences of her black friends' failed attempts to seek justice on the local and national levels forces her to rethink what social justice really means. However, I would argue that this is somewhat more pronounced in the film than in Kidd's novel. After Zach Taylor (Tristan Wilds), Lily's black love interest, is arrested for sneaking Lily into the black section of the segregated movie theater for a date, Lily finally touches the statue of the Black Madonna for the first time. Touching the wooden chest, she prays, "Please let it be okay." Shortly thereafter, the scene cuts to Zach's mother praying to the same statue while she cries hysterically, overcome by the fear of what might happen to her son. This scene is important because in it Prince-Bythewood foregrounds the very real consequences of breaking Jim Crow mandates. Prince-Bythewood allows Lily to touch the statue because her prayer is on behalf of someone else, rather than for herself. Lily has already learned lessons of selflessness from May, who writes all of her prayers for others on a piece of paper to place in her version of the "Wailing Wall" that the sisters have constructed to help May cope with her empathetic nature.

Shortly after May commits suicide out of her own grief at hearing of Zach's arrest, Lily decides to reveal who she is to August, in part because she feels responsible for May's death. Envisioning the Boatwright household as a utopian space, she cries, "I brought the outside in" and conflates her complicity in May's death with the accidental murdering of her mother by her own hand. Prince-Bythewood takes this scene as another opportunity to decolonize Mammy. August reveals to Lily what Lily already knows, that she was her mother's nursemaid, and explains to her that June's initial resentment toward Lily was because they all knew upon seeing her that she was Deborah's daughter; June disliked the fact that her work in Deborah's family home took August away from her own family. August tells Lily about how her mother met T. Ray, but also explains that even though they fell out of love, they married because she was pregnant. August also confirms that Deborah initially abandoned Lily, just as T. Ray surmised.

The next time August and Lily discuss Deborah, Lily asks August if she loved her mother. August responds, "It was complicated, but yes I did." When pressed for further clarification, she says, "I was her nanny. Things were different in her world and mine. We like to think that love is pure and limitless, but love like that can't exist in a hateful time. But she made me love her anyway. There is no perfect love, Lily." This answer is a key departure from the original text. In Kidd's novel, August is essentially *mammified* as she volunteers a profession of love for Deborah, thereby prioritizing her feelings for Deborah and Lily over those for her own kin and kind.

Miki McElya explains that Mammy has become an iconic figure because "so many white Americans have wished to live in a world in which African Americans are not angry over past and present injustices, a world in which white people were and are not complicit, in which the injustices themselves—of slavery, Jim Crow, and ongoing structural racism—seem not to exist at all" (2007, 3). August's pensive response in the movie conveys a more nuanced assessment of a black domestic's feelings about her white charges. Even more than Kidd's novel, Prince-Bythewood's decision to give voice to this complex relationship, to say that pure love cannot exist in "a hateful time," counters the sentimentality associated with the lament for Mammy. However, when Skeeter poses a similar question to Aibileen in *The Help*, "what is it like . . ." Aibileen responds, "It's like . . ." and her voice trails off. Viewers never do get to hear her answer, and very few care because her answer, like her feelings, are secondary to that of, say, Mae Mobley, the little white girl who cries inconsolably as Aibileen leaves her after having been fired by the girl's biological mother.

Lily's fictional journey to find maternal love has real-life precedents. Most notably, it calls to mind the Delbridge case of 1916 when, at fourteen, Marjorie Delbridge was removed from the house of Camilla Jackson, the black woman who had raised her since infancy.[12] One could speculate that while whites deemed it permissible for Jackson to care for Marjorie when she was little, a black woman was determined to be ill equipped to guide a white girl into respectable womanhood.

At the end of the movie Lily declares, "I have more mothers than any three girls off the street. They are the moon shining over me." Kidd's and

Prince-Bythewood's insistence upon conferring the title of "mother" over that of "Mammy" for the women in Lily's life gives hope that true empathy between blacks and whites is possible if both are vested in dismantling white privilege. With such dismantling, the black subject is no longer seen as a static and reactive figure, but instead can also be an agentic force in the lives of whites and still remain centered in his or her own life experiences.

The Secret Life of Bees begins with Lily's voice articulating her despair while flashes from her past disrupt her present. In contrast, the movie ends with a sense of calm. Sunlight streams in between the tall trees as Lily explains what her life has been life since T. Ray officially left her in the care of the Boatwright sisters. Where the real-life Marjorie Delbridge faltered in Camilia Jackson's absence, the fictional Lily blossoms. As the scene dissolves into a montage sequence, we see Lily writing, praying to the statue of Mary, and placing her troubles in the Wailing Wall. The Boatwright sisters have taught her not only how to forgive her father but also to forgive herself. While Lily acknowledges that forgiveness is a process, she reckons, "But Mary is always there, I feel her at unexpected moments. She will suddenly rise, and when she does, she does not go up into the sky, but further inside of me." The Boatwright sisters, in teaching Lily about love, also opened several vistas to self-actualization, and therein is Prince-Bythewood's true act of subversion. The filmmaker offers Lily as a model of what a healthy maternal devotion to black women might look like. Prince-Bythewood encourages white viewers who pine for images of Mammy to consider an alternative to suckling at her black teat.

Notes

1. Prince-Bythewood won an Independent Spirit Award for Best First Feature and a Humanitas Prize for *Love and Basketball.*

2. Although she is relatively unknown by US audiences, I was familiar with Okonedo's work from films such as *Young Soul Rebels* (1991), *Dirty Pretty Things* (2002), and *Hotel Rwanda* (2004).

3. "Noble savages" is my tongue-in-cheek label for performances of blackness that are more palpable for mainstream white audiences. Rather than act out in anger or violence (no matter if such actions would typically be deemed logical or appropriate responses to the transgression in question) or even through or-

ganized protest, noble savages brave their oppression alone and with so-called dignity. Even though there is much to admire about some of these movies, as well as the talent of the very black actors I call into question, I am referring to recent movies such as *The Help* (2011), *The Butler* (2013), and *42* (2013).

4. This strategy is perhaps reflective of the type of racism and sexism Prince-Bythewood has faced as a black female filmmaker. She states, "for the most part I feel like my choices are discriminated against in that a lot of things I want to focus on are female-driven or black female driven and those are the toughest things to get made. I have dealt with racism pretty face-to-face. But for the most part, I'm able to just push them aside and focus on what I'm trying to do and continue to believe that talent has no race or agenda, and that I have every right to be here." See Carnevale n.d.

5. See Cripps's *Black Film as Genre* (1978), Murray's *To Find an Image* (1973), Reid's *Redefining Black Film* (1993), and Yearwood's *Black Cinema Aesthetics* (1982).

6. https://speakerpedia.com/speakers/gina-prince-bythewood.

7. http://madamenoire.com/230631/bet-you-didnt-know-secrets-behind-the -secret-life-of-bees/2/.

8. http://www.wildaboutmovies.com/behind_the_scenes/secretlifeofbeesmovie -behindthescenes/.

9. http://www.wildaboutmovies.com/behind_the_scenes/secretlifeofbeesmovie -behindthescenes/.

10. http://www.wildaboutmovies.com/behind_the_scenes/secretlifeofbeesmovie -behindthescenes/.

11. Munoz, Lorenza. 2008. "Interview: Gina Prince-Bythewood (*The Secret Life of Bees*)." *Issuu* October 15, 2008, 7. https://issuu.com/filmindependent/docs/ october_newsletter.

12. This case is foregrounded in "The Line between Mother and Mammy," which is chapter 3 of McElya's book.

References

Abdullah, Melina. 2012. "Womanist Mothering: Loving and Raising the Revolution." *Western Journal of Black Studies* 36, no. 1 (Spring): 57–67.

Allan, Tuzyline Jita. 1995. *Womanist and Feminist Aesthetic: A Comparative Review*. Athens: Ohio
University Press.

Brown, Kimberly Nichele. 2010. *Writing the Black Revolutionary Diva*. Bloomington: Indiana University Press.

Carnevale, Rob. n.d. "The Secret Life of Bees: Gina Prince-Bythewood and Lauren Shuler Donner Interview." indieLondon. Accessed April 16, 2018. http://www.indielondon.co.uk/Film-Review/the-secret-life-of-bees-gina-prince-bythewood-and-lauren-shuler-donner-interview.

Dancing in September. 2000. HBO. Directed by Reggie Rock Bythewood. DVD.

Dawkins, Marcia Alesan, and Ulli K. Ryder. 2013. "Passing as a Woman (ist)?" In *Interpreting Tyler Perry: Perspectives on Race, Class, Gender, and Sexuality*, edited by Jamel Santa Cruz Bell and Ronald L. Jackson II, 257–69. New York: Routledge.

Emmanuel, Catherine B. 2005. "The Archetypal Mother: The Black Madonna in Sue Monk Kidd's *The Secret Life of Bees*." *West Virginia University Philological Papers* 52: 115–22.

"Gina Prince-Bythewood: 'The Secret Life of Bees.'" 2009. *Essence*, December 16, 2009. https://www.essence.com/2008/10/17/gina-prince-bythewood-the-secret-life-of.

Grobman, Laurie. 2008. "Teaching Cross-Racial Texts: Cultural Theft in *The Secret Life of Bees*." *College English* 71, no. 1 (September): 9–26.

Guerrero, Ed. 1993. *Framing Blackness: The African American Image in Film*. Philadelphia: Temple University Press.

The Help. 2011. Touchstone Home Entertainment. Directed by Tate Taylor. DVD.

hooks, bell. 2003. "The Oppositional Gaze: Black Female Spectators." In *The Feminism and Visual Culture Reader*, edited by Amelia Jones, 94104. New York: Routledge.

Hurston, Zora Neale. 1937. *Their Eyes Were Watching God*. Philadelphia: J.B. Lippincott.

Hutcheon, Linda. 1996. *A Theory of Adaptation*. NY: Routledge.

Kidd, Sue Monk. 2002. *The Secret Life of Bees*. New York: Viking.

Manatu, Norma. 2003. *African American Women and Sexuality in the Cinema*. Jefferson, NC: MacFarland.

Mapp, Edward. 1973. "Black Women in Films." *The Black Scholar*. Black Women's Liberation Issue. 4, no. 6/7 (March–April): 42–46.

Martin, Michael T. 2010. "'I Do Exist': From 'Black Insurgent' to Negotiating the Hollywood Divide—A Conversation with Julie Dash." *Cinema Journal* 49, no. 2 (Winter): 1–16.

Masilela, Ntongela (1993). "The Los Angeles School of Black Filmmakers." In *Black American Cinema,* edited by Manthia Diawara, 107–8. New York: Routledge.

McElya, Miki. 2007. *Clinging to Mammy: The Faithful Slave in Twentieth-Century America.* Cambridge, MA: Harvard University Press.

Morales, Wilson. 2008. "The Secret Life of Bees: An Interview with Director Gina Prince-Bythewood." Blackfilm.com. October 15, 2008. http://www.blackfilm.com/20081009/features/qpb.shtml.

Morrison, Toni. 1970. *The Bluest Eye.* New York: Washington Square Press.

Morrison, Toni. *Sula.* 1973. New York: Knopf.

Munoz, Lorenza. 2008. "Interview: Gina Prince-Bythewood (*The Secret Life of Bees*)" *Issuu,* October 15, 2008, 7. https://issuu.com/filmindependent/docs/october_newsletter.

Norment, Lynn. 2008. "A Moment in Time." *Ebony* 64, no. 1, (November): 72–80. EBSCOhost, lp.hscl.ufl.edu/login?url=http://search.ebscohost.com/login.aspx?direct=true&db=aph&AN=35548792&site=eds-live.

Powell, Richard J. 2002. *Black Art: A Cultural History.* London: Thames and Hudson Ltd.

Reid, Mark A. 1995. "Dialogic Modes of Representing Africa(s): Womanist Film." In *Cinemas of the Black Diaspora: Diversity, Dependence, and Oppositionality,* edited by Michael T. Martin, 59–69. Detroit, MI: Wayne State University Press.

Rosen, Lisa. 2008. "Learning to Adapt." *Los Angeles Times,* October 12, 2008. http://articles.latimes.com/2008/oct/12/entertainment/ca-gina12.

Shohat, E. and Stam, R. 2014. "Stereotype, Realism and struggle over representation." In Shohat, E. and Stamm, R. *Unthinking Eurocentrism.* Routledge. http://readingtheperiphery.org/shoatstam.

Stockett, Kathryn. 2009. *The Help.* New York: G. P. Putnam's Sons.

Streeter, Caroline A. 2005. "Faking the Funk? Mariah Carey, Alicia Keys, and (Hybrid) Black Celebrity." In *Black Cultural Traffic: Crossroads in Global Performance and Popular Culture,* edited by Harry J. Elam Jr. and Kennell Jackson, 185–207. Ann Arbor: University of Michigan Press.

Tucker, Susan. 1987. "A Complex Bond: Southern Black Domestic Workers and their White Employers." *Frontiers: A Journal of Women Studies* 9, no. 3: 6–13.

Yaeger, Patricia. 2005. "Ghosts and Shattered Bodies, or What Does It Mean to Still Be Haunted by Southern Literature?" *South Central Review* 22, no. 1: 87–108.

11

BLACK WOMEN AND THE NEW MAGICAL NEGRO

Chesya Burke

"GENRE" IS THE TERM for any group of art—including film—based on some set of presumed characteristic individual to its category. Genres are formed by conventions that change over time, and as scholars say, they are "easier to recognize than to define" (Bordwell and Thompson 2012, 94). Although genre can represent a large body of divergent work, for the purposes of this chapter, I use the term "genre" to represent science fiction, fantasy, horror, and any subset within this group. These genre communities are often considered outside of the mainstream populace—and therefore claim to be as much, or more, tolerant of differences within their respective communities. Though each have different themes and plot points, films such as *The Exorcist* (1973), *Alien* (1979), and *Legend* starring Tom Cruise (1985) all fit under this genre umbrella. Over the past few years, however, there has been a noticeable impetus by genre filmmakers and producers on inclusivity and diversity within these films, which coincides with the broader push toward inclusion within society. This has led to several roles for black actors such as Will Smith in *I, Robot* (1997), Idris Elba in *Prometheus* (2012), and Idris Elba as the Greek god Heimdall in *Thor* (2011). However, this tolerance and movement toward acceptance has often not translated into acceptance for black women within the genre. Instead, the idea of the "other" is still often explored through an alien or foreign figure, and the black woman is more often than not ignored or relegated to a submissive role that combines two long-standing stereotypes that, when combined, work simply to contain her.

The two stereotypes in question are the Magical Negro and the Strong Black Woman.

While speaking to students at Yale University, Spike Lee criticized the "phenomenon" of the "magical, mystical Negro" character, which he contends "is just a reincarnation of "the same old" stereotype or caricature of African Americans as the "noble savage" or the "happy slave" that has been presented in film and on television for decades" (Yale Bulletin 2001). The term has since become popularized as the "Magical Negro" (MN), which references the stereotype of the magical black character who is written into fiction and films to help the white protagonist on his journey, but yet has no story of his own.

Likewise, in her essay Sheila Radford-Hill says that due to the constant negative images that are portrayed of black women, black girls find it difficult to "create self-images that liberate their spirits and ignite their creativity" (Radford-Hill 2002, 1085). One of the most damaging images, Radford-Hill admits, is of the Strong Black Woman. She goes on to explain that "Young women are right when they say that the "Strong black-woman" (SBW) stereotype demeans them in order to justify [black women's] collective marginality" (1086). Unfortunately, within the speculative genre it seems that the real-life stereotype of the "Strong Black Woman" is often conflated with the Magical Negro to create a character henceforth called the Negro Spiritual Woman (NSW). This character is endowed with magical powers that not only are used for the good of the broader white society but are also not powerful enough to change her status in the world, thus keeping her subdued and contained. Likewise, when these films do not sexualize the black female character, the public often corrects what it sees as the black woman moving outside of her constructed space, or being too "uppity," and thus the public works to sexualize her itself to ensure she remains contained.

For the purposes of distinction, I differentiate the NSW image from its predecessor, the MN, because of the presence of three important factors: submissiveness, mysteriousness, and sexuality. Although the MN trope includes the first two, it is the third aspect that separates the NSW from its antecedent. As a construct, both images work to affirm society's ideology and current structure, but only the Negro Spiritual Woman image uses the sexuality of black women as a way to defend her current social status. Using Sheila Radford-Hill as an example, I argue that much like the SBW real-life stereotype, the NSW image not only justifies the marginalization of black women but it is an acceptable fantasy for white society, much like the MN stereotype, and it attributes a sort of heroism to the black woman character that does not translate to actual autonomy for her and instead allows white audiences to uphold racial supremacist philosophy and ideology. In other words, the image of the real-life Strong Black Woman combined with the Magical Negro opens the way for the Negro Spiritual Woman genre image, which relegates a controlled type of heroism within the genre world to black women that does not translate into the real world and that justifies the current treatment of them.

Review of Literature

BECAUSE THE SPECULATIVE GENRE often appeals to people outside of the mainstream society, it is not widely discussed in academic circles unless the work is considered "literary" and is able to break out of the genre label.[1] Therefore there are fewer articles focused solely on works that do not fit into this literary label. Likewise, because of the "outsider" feeling among fans of the genre, many tend to group together in factions online, where they often discuss relevant topics. Although there may be little significant, broad-based critical analysis of genre films in relation to black women specifically, I will examine the fan culture in connection to the mainstream society and their similar ideology of "controlling images" in relation to black women in these works.

As Patricia Hill Collins says, "Race, class and gender oppression could not continue without powerful ideological justifications for their existence. . . . Portraying African American women as stereotypical mammies, matriarchs, welfare recipients and hot mommas has been essential to political economy of domination fostering black women's oppression" (P. H. Collins 2000, 67). However, the speculative genre has not been content to use old, worn-out stereotypes and chooses instead to create newer, although sometimes seemingly positive, ones. An example of this, as mentioned earlier, is the Magical Negro, which has found a place within the genre as a magical character who helps the white protagonist in his journey. Evolution for the black women has not been any better within the genre. Instead, black women have often been relegated to a confluence of several of these images, which upholds society's current racial ideology.

Scholar Dorothy Roberts touches on this as well: "The social order established by powerful white men was founded on two inseparable ingredients: the dehumanization of Africans on the basis of race and the control of women's sexuality . . ." (Roberts 1997, 23). Here, it is important to acknowledge that society has always needed to control black bodies, and controlling black women's sexuality and their images has become particularly paramount. Likewise, Robin Means Coleman's book, *Horror Noire*, quotes Ellen Holly as saying the following in the *New York Times* in 1974: "One of the penalties of being Black and having limited money is that we seldom control our own image. We seldom appear in media as who we say we are, but rather as who whites say we are" (Means Coleman 2011, 119). In other words, blacks have historically been misrepresented within white works for the benefit of white audiences. Taking into account older genre films such as *The Creature from the Black Lagoon* (1954), *Frankenstein* (1931), and *King Kong* (1933), which are each predicated on the imagery of the savage black man, it's easy to see that this has been the case for genre films throughout history.[2]

However, it is important to recognize the significance that racial myths' affect popular cultural forms as evidenced in the history of American entertainment. In his book, Maurice Berger (2000) states:

> Despite the visual sophistication and supposed vigilance of a media-oriented culture . . . Western commentators, critics, and academics seem not to realize how duplicitous words and images can be. They simply do not understand how myths work, how myths hold us hostage to their smooth elegant fictions. The subject of race, perhaps more than any other subject in contemporary life feeds on myth. . . . Myth is the book, seamless narrative that tells us the contradictions and incongruities of race and racism are too confusing or too dangerous to articulate. Myths provide the elegant deceptions that reinforce our unconscious prejudices. Myths are the white lies that tell us everything is all right, even when it is not."

For the genre, these myths are predicated on the idea that race and gender issues are not important to a functioning society. If minority peoples are not present in the future, it is because prejudice has been eliminated and not because race, class, and sex discrimination still exist in the world and movie producers could not be bothered to represent minorities within that futurist society.

The construction of stereotypes has always functioned to keep certain groups subordinate to the white populace. Hazel Carby explains that stereotypes are not meant "to reflect or represent a reality but function as a disguise, or mystification, of objective social relations" (Carby 1989, 69). Specifically, the objective of stereotypes is not only to make race, class, and gender biases acceptable but to make them necessary for the society to function as it does. This is often the case for works of genre. Although the field often explores different species and groups as a way to understand our own humanity and the human condition, black women are usually absent from these present and future explorations, leaving the genre oddly absent of her presence.

As black women move outside of their perceived roles, however, genre fans often level anger and resentment toward them. An example of this is with the controversy of *The Hunger Games* (2012) movie. Although the character of Rue is described within the book as having "dark brown skin and eyes," many fans directed racist insults at the young black actress playing the role and tweeted that they were unable to connect to the character after being confronted with her black presence in the film (S. Collins 2008, 45).[3] Examining these issues within the genre, the collaborative weblog Racialicious, which "discus[ses] media coverage of the multiracial community," argues that the idea of black identity within the genre is difficult to reconcile within a xenophobic society. "Black women cannot live vicariously through [many black female genre characters]. She is the Black Fantasy [the white creator] spent more than two decades telling us we could never be. The fantasy is useless, for there is no comfort in engaging it. The character only serves to remind us of how short Black women fall from the racist norms society demands we aspire to" (Lynn 2009). Although these images have not been widely examined, they highlight that the issue of the presence of black women is a routine battle within the speculative genre.

Kee (Clare-Hope Ashitey) and Theo Faron (Clive Owen) in *Children of Men*.

In her book of literary criticism, Toni Morrison argues that the "'Africanist presence" is placed in fiction according to the needs and desires of its "white creator," and its presence has been there since the creation of the construct of race—or at least the beginning of the American slave trade (Morrison 1995, 6). Most notably, though, she says that the black presence is there even if it's ignored and especially if it is unrecognized. In other words, blackness is a part of our social consciousness (in binary opposition to whiteness) and to ignore it shows more about the society than about the people the society hopes to alienate. This is no less true for the presence of black women within our society.

As Hood, and to some degree Morrison, suggest, it is the depiction of these images through genre that can enable the much-needed discourse about the "white creator" and the prevalence of problematic, negative images that don't fully examine the black woman image within genre, but that instead uphold the racial ideology of the broader society, despite surface appearances.

Antiheroism and the Negro Spiritual Woman

FROM THE INCEPTION OF the modern film, images of oversexed black women have permeated the screen. In the seminal film *Birth of a Nation* (1915), a blackface maid flutters onstage, swinging saucy hips while attempting to

The birth of a new nation through the loins of a black woman.

manipulate white men into sexual relations with her. Since that time, this image of the highly sexualized black woman has not diminished. Both off- and on-screen black women, likewise, are often categorized as strong and fiercely independent, in the image of the Strong Black Woman. This archetype describes a black woman who is unusually strong in comparison to her white female counterpart and sacrifices her own happiness for others—whether they are her children, the community, or the white employers for whom she works. Within the speculative genre, the image of the Magical Negro has evolved as a type of silent hero of (mostly) black men. However, for the black woman in the genre, these two images have evolved into a seemingly powerful representation of strong, self-assured authority: The Negro Spiritual Woman.

Using several examples of recent blockbuster genre movies, I will examine how the endowment of supernatural powers to black women characters often does not bestow real power to black women, and instead does the opposite by only offering just enough authority to maintain the current societal structure, so as not to upset the racial and gender hierarchy within the films or society. In this way, the mystical powers granted to black women by these films, as written by white creators, are quite possibly *antihero* powers, as they are in fact meant to offer her no hope or freedom from an oppressive society.

The real-life stereotype of the Strong Black Woman is depicted within society as a woman who willingly suffers quietly without help, supporting others selflessly and without reward to herself. In her book, Tamara Beauboeuf-Lafontant explains that a "discourse of strength is deployed to render Black women into self-disciplining bodies who uphold the social order" (Beauboeuf-Lafontant 2009, 36). Supposedly a positive image, this stereotype is constructed as an example of true black womanism. The Strong Black Woman does not complain about her place in society and is held up as an example of how others should be. She is content and accepting, and although not necessarily happy, she is proud of the society she supports.

The Strong Black Woman, like the Magical Negro, suffers quietly, without condemning the society that has oppressed her. The character is supportive of whites, doesn't normally have a family of her own, and is seemingly empowered. Likewise, within the genre, the Negro Spiritual Woman supports white society and is usually depicted as sexually provocative, solely for the benefit of white males.

Tia Dilma's Containment within *Pirates of the Caribbean*

A NOTABLE EXAMPLE OF the Strong Spiritual Black Woman genre image is in the character Tia Dalma from two of the popular *Pirates of the Caribbean* films. Introduced as Davy Jones's ex-lover, Dalma is a flirty seductress who is more than willing to help the white characters for little or no reward. Originally the powerful goddess Calypso, she once held control over the seas and everything within them. Now she is "bound" into human form because she rejected her white male lover, Davy Jones, and her power is reduced to only aiding the heroes on their journey, as she has been denied one of her own.

Dalma's character within the two Pirates of the Caribbean films *Dead Man's Chest* (2006) and *At World's End* (2007) is focused on sexual innuendos and resurrecting several of the dead white male characters in the films. We are first introduced to Dalma as the hero, Captain Jack Sparrow, tells his men not to worry or to be afraid of the black woman, as the two of them "go way back" (*Pirates of the Caribbean: Dead Man's Chest*). After greeting Sparrow seductively—"Jack Sparrow. I always done known the wind would blow you back to me one day"—Dalma sets about flirting with another young white male character, Will Turner, advising him that he "holds a touch of destiny" (*Pirates of the Caribbean: Dead Man's Chest*). Although Dalma has been cursed and bound into human form by white men, it seems she cannot resist using her mystical powers to help them secure their fates, as she immediately gives the group the information they need through her special crab-claws-reading abilities.[4] When the crew returns after Jack has fallen to the Kracken, Dalma, having predicted his demise, produces a resurrected Barbossa (another white male captain) to save Jack Sparrow. Though Dalma has perfected the ability to resurrect the dead, she cannot resurrect herself so easily. It is soon learned that Dalma brings both men back to life to free herself from her current form, but it is a complicated process that requires "Pieces of Eight," two of the talismans of which Sparrow and Barbossa carry. It's important to note that although it seems relatively easy for white men to reclaim their past lives as if this is deserved, it is intrinsically more difficult for the black female character. She must bargain, accepting the value of white male life, before she can value her own. It is as if the world, and by extension life itself, belongs to white men, and more powerful black female beings, such as Tia Dalma, must work harder to prove they are deserving.

Dalma vows that when she is returned to her natural form, "the last thing [that Sparrow and Barbossa] will learn in life is how cruel [she] can be," and she offers to "give [Davy Joes] her heart" again (*Pirates of the Caribbean: Dead Man's Chest*). However, when Calypso is free, she discovers that Davy Jones is responsible for enslaving her into human form.[5] Angry, Calypso grows to six feet tall, then collapses into thousands of crabs, which escape into the sea and causes a giant storm that overtakes the ships. In the end, the newly returned Calypso does not take her revenge on the two characters that she has vowed to punish. Instead, the white male protagonist, Jack Sparrow, is left to continue his journey as the black woman returns quietly to the sea, where she has rightfully learned her lesson. For this character, the message is clear. Black women are meant to support white men. If they are unwilling to do this, the punishment is swift and uncompromising. Dalma is, however temporarily, relegated to a mere shadow of her former self until she is thoroughly contained, and the society is better for it. Without Dalma's submissive state, the journey of the white men would be in jeopardy and all of the fictional society would be threatened by the presence of her black superpowers. Instead, she is depicted as an overly strong, sexual woman, who is rightly regulated to a submissive role for the benefit of this wider fictionalized world.

Children of Men and the Representation of Future Black Motherhood

CHILDREN OF MEN (2006), based on the novel of the same name, is about a futuristic society where women have stopped being able to bear children. The world's youngest child has just been murdered, and all of the societies across the globe are distraught and in ruin, "because really, since women [have] stopped being able to have babies, [there's nothing] left to hope for." (*Children of Men*). The main character, Theo, is tasked with taking care of seemingly the last pregnant woman on earth. The woman, Kee, a West African refugee, is on the run because many people are after her and her unborn child.

In the film, Kee exposes her pregnancy to Theo by completely disrobing and showing her naked body. In a barn full of cows and milking equipment belying the fertile world in which the characters live, Kee's dark skin and plump belly expose her otherness within the society. Not only are immigrants, such as Kee, routinely rounded up and placed in concentration camps but she is the only known fertile woman in the world. Standing naked in the stall, Kee is, as all of the other animals, simply another creature to be herded and milked for the contributions that her offspring will bring to the world. She has very little value on her own, other than the fact that she can reproduce. Her sexuality, like many other controlling images of black women, is constructed for the benefit of the movie, and by extension, society. Like a slave woman at auction, Kee exposes her body to the white male character so that he can take control of her. Unlike a slave, however, Kee's character willing gives herself over to Theo in exchange for his protection. Theo's whiteness acts as a shield for Kee within the movie, and through him she is able to move more freely as long as her pregnant body, and thus her sexuality, is not exposed.

This image is further exacerbated when the young woman is asked who the father of her child is: "Whiffet! I'm a virgin," she responds. And then, right away, revealing the joke: "Nah! Be great, though, wouldn't it? Fuck knows. I don't know half the wankers' names. You know, when I started

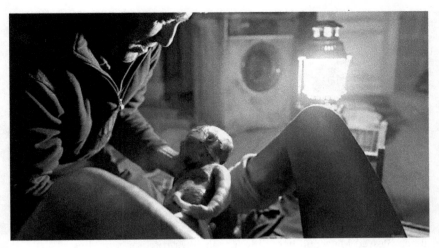

Kee and her baby in *Children of Men.*

fucking, thought I'd catch the pest, but my belly started getting big" (*Children of Men*). The joke here is not that the idea of a virgin is archaic or outdated in 2027 society (there is much Christian symbolism within the film[6]) but seemingly that the idea that a black woman could ever represent the virgin is itself absurd. Instead, Kee is pictured as society has constructed black women since well before the advent of film, as a sexually aggressive deviant who does not care about herself or her child. It is revealed that Kee has had sex with many men without thought to her future or her body. This is reinforced in the end, when Theo protects Kee and her newborn child and he issues her a stern warning before he dies, having sacrificed himself for the mother and child. "Keep her close, Kee," the man says, "keep her close" (*Children of Men*). Theo's advice for her to take care of her daughter is cemented in the idea that black women, and by extension Kee, cannot be good mothers. As far as the audience is concerned, Theo is probably correct in warning Kee, as her character has been all but infantilized and constructed through the negative image of black motherhood, and the audience is left unsure of her ability to take care of her own child.

Although it is easy to argue that Kee does not have supernatural powers within *Children of Men*, and thus she is not contained through them within the film, I suggest that Kee, more than any of the other characters, is directly subjugated through her sexuality and more specifically the power of her womb.

Black Blessed Mary and her white Joseph-like protector, who dies.

Kee's power, as with Mary from the Bible, comes from being the mother of the new, burgeoning world. Unlike Mary, however, Kee is constructed as a hypersexed vixen who is incapable of mothering the new world. Instead, as the film ends, she is waiting to be taken into custody by government forces so that she is rightfully contained. Considering that Kee is always within the control of whites within the film, it's easy to see that her unique power to bear children does not protect her, but instead contains her fully.

It is important to note that being gifted with the ability to bear the last child on earth is not enough to change Kee's position in life. In fact, this ability is oppressive for her, as it compounds the racism she already receives as a black woman in futuristic, apartheid Britain. As a black woman within the racist, dying society, Kee is oppressed with very little hope of overcoming this position. However, by the end of the movie, viewers are contented, as she has been contained and put safely away from the society at large. In the end, they are able to ignore her position, comfortable in the idea that her powers bring her no real freedom from even this fictional oppressive society.

Hushpuppy's Uncontrollable Beast in *Beast of the Southern Wild*

BEAST OF THE SOUTHERN *Wild* (2012) is a magical realism movie about a six-year-old young black girl, Hushpuppy, who lives in the southern Louisiana bayou in a community called the "Bathtub." The little girl lives with her father, who disappears for days at a time, leaving Hushpuppy to fend for herself. Her father eventually returns wearing a hospital gown and arm band and acting confused. In school, the children in the community, including Hushpuppy, are taught about the melted ice caps, which, they are told, released prehistoric creatures called "Aurochs." Within the story, Hushpuppy conflates the levees breaking during hurricane Katrina with the release of the Aurochs, which she imagines chasing her throughout the film. To protect her community, Hushpuppy eventually confronts the Aurochs that have been causing her and her community distress, while the people watch and support her. In the end, the giant beasts nod their acceptance and leave Hushpuppy and her community to bury her dead father.

Hushpuppy is a tough character, often taking care of herself (despite her age) for days at a time, due to her missing, ill father, and there is no question that she is the embodiment of the Strong Black Woman archetype. In her article "No Love in the Wild," bell hooks says, "Hushpuppy has a resilient spirit. She is indeed a miniature version of the 'strong black female matriarch,' racist and sexist representations have depicted from slavery on into the present day" (hooks 2012). At one point during the film, the six-year-old punches her father for slapping her and causes him to pass out, as if due to her strength alone. The message, of course, is that Hushpuppy is capable of taking care of herself and so the audience need not sympathize with her. Although her father is abusive, and a six-year-old is not normally expected to defend herself from an adult who has attacked her, this is expected of Hushpuppy. Her black skin is not obviously damaged from the attack, and she is "resilient." Because Hushpuppy is strong on her own, the viewers are content in the knowledge that she does not need their help, as, for instance, a young white girl in this position would, because she is fully capable of doing it herself. Strong Black Women always are. Instead, the girl is charged with taking care of the community and "mothering" them, as she protects them from the savage beast plaguing the broken town. Since Hushpuppy is expected to mother, instead of be mothered, in the end, when her father dies, the audience does not question how the young girl will survive. We are instead secure in the understanding that she is going to endure the trials of her future life, if not completely overcome them, as is usually desired for white characters in her position.

Although Hushpuppy is, as bell hooks says, "eroticized [as a] child, [in] all manner of dirt and filth," she is not completely sexualized within the film, as the previous characters have been (hooks 2012). She wears baggy clothes, including a loose T-shirt and shapeless boy briefs. In this way, Hushpuppy is, unmistakably, a child—though she is a particularly mature one. At one point in the film, Hushpuppy goes to a brothel to find her mother. Although the male patrons are present as the women of the brothel "mother" Hushpuppy and her friends, it is clear that the young girl does not belong in this place. When the woman Hushpuppy has chosen as her mother holds her in her arms, the girl whispers: "I can count on two hands the times when I've been lifted up" (*Beast of the Southern Wild*). Like any young girl of her age, Hushpuppy does not notice the availability of scantily clad women and simply seeks out the one that she can call mother. Unfortunately, however, although the film does not sufficiently sexualize her, the public reacts differently, as if to correct what they see as the black child moving outside of her constructed space, or being too "uppity."

Quvenzhané Wallis, the young nine-year-old actress who plays Hushpuppy, arrived at the 2013 Oscars showing her "guns" to mimic the character in the movie, a smile splashed across her face.[7] Obviously this offense of being "full of herself" is not to be forgiven, as the feminist weblog Jezebel posted an image of the girl and the comments exploded in response. They include: "Am I the only one who saw this [little girl] and was disgusted? I immediately decided I didn't want her to win because I don't want her to get any more full of herself than she seemed right there," "it just seemed like a tacky thing to do. I realize she's just a little kid—but even little kids should show some class," and "Sorry this Quvenzhane kid annoys the fuck outta me. She's insufferable. Ever see her on a talk show? She is dangerously carried away with herself—way past the point of cute. You're never too young to learn humility" (Jezebel). Many replies rightly suggest that this strong reaction has everything to do with race, as young white actresses such a "Dakota Fanning or Emma Watson" never received such hatred. Ms. Wallis is simply "insufferable" because her black skin does not inspire adoration and thus she is perceived to be stepping outside of her designated submissive role. In fact, the message for the young black actress seems clear: she is too uppity and needs to behave more like white America's idea of how a "good" black girl should act. Because the audience cannot reconcile the cute little humble black child of their imaginations with the confident, willful one that they see before them, they begin to objectify her, placing her within a more stereotypical sexualized role with which they are more familiar.

During the same awards show, the host Seth McFarlane cracked a joke at the actress's expense: "So let me just address those of you up for an award. So you got nominated for an Oscar, something a nine-year-old could do! . . . To give you an idea how young she is, it'll be sixteen years before she's too old for Clooney." Another joke aimed at Wallis is from the satirical site The Onion, which tweeted, "Everyone else seems afraid to say it, but that Quvenzhané Wallis is kind of a cunt, right?" Both of these "jokes" center on the nine-year-old actress's sexuality. Not only does McFarlane suggest that it is no big deal to be nominated for an Oscar, because, well, even this nine-year-old black girl could do it, but he directs the audience to picture her as sexually available for older white men. The latter joke, of course, is more direct. It outright states that Wallis is nothing more than her female genital parts, as if to say, like the Jezebel posters, that the black girl has moved outside of where The Onion believes she should be. Thus this term is meant, unmistakably, to not only put Wallis in her place but ensure that she does not have movement outside of where the white populace imagines her. There is nothing in the movie to suggest that Wallis is either sexually available for men old enough to be her grandfather or a "cunt." Unlike other black women in the genre, Hushpuppy is not sexualized on screen, although she is the representation of the Strong Black Woman and the Magical Negro, as she is the only one with the power to exorcise the Aurochs. But this is not enough for society, as they seem to need to contain Wallis as the other images of black women in the genre have been contained. For this reason, the public sexualizes Quvenzhané Wallis themselves, as if they are adding to the script what is missing: the domination and sexual humiliation of this young black woman.

Conclusion

DESPITE THE DIFFICULTY FOR black women in the genre, they have long worked to combat the negative images of themselves. Radford-Hill explains why this is important:

> Black women must develop identities that will not destroy them, but the broader society does not give us much with which to work. For example, history hands us identities built on racist stereotypes like mammy, auntie, prissy, jezebel, sapphire, bitch, video ho, and welfare queen. The social movements of the 1960s and 1970s handed us identities that appeared radical but required an odd combination of activism against racism and submission to sexism (Radford-Hill 2002, 1085).

In order for black women to be fully represented, they have begun to form their own identities within a genre that has been shown to be hostile toward their presence. Notable black women film directors are Kasi Lemmons, director of *Eve's Bayou* (1997) and Julie Dash, director of *Daughters of the Dust* (1991). Each of these movies has a black women protagonist and can easily be placed in the genre category. A more recent example of community support within the genre is with *Danger Word*, the 2014 short film by black woman writer Tananarive Due and her husband, Steven Barnes. Fully funded through crowd sharing, the film raised nearly $15,000, surpassing their original $12,500 goal. The film is directed by black woman director Luchlna Fisher and follows a thirteen-year-old black girl, Kendra Brookings, and her grandfather during a zombie apocalypse. Unlike the previous characters, Kendra does not accept the abuse of white society, doesn't put aside her own needs, and finds strength within her family, particularly her grandfather, who does not sexualize her. Although empowered, Kendra is not simply a Strong Black Woman or the Magical Negro, and she is not endowed with superpowers that don't offer her hope. In the film, when Kendra's grandfather is bitten by a zombie, she must use the sharpshooting skills that he has taught her to save herself and her future. It is clear, upon watching, that Kendra is not submissive, mysterious, or overly sexual. For Kendra, and many of the other characters directed by black women, society

Kee (Clare-Hope Ashitey) in *Children of Men.*

does not offer protection; instead they choose to protect themselves, subverting the status quo. Because of this, I would argue that Kendra, as a black woman genre protagonist, does not have antiheroic powers, but instead actually crosses over into full heroism.

IN THE END, POWERFULLY created supernatural characters, such as heroes in genre movies, often live within a society that has created them or that is their own culture, so they fight for the society that supports and accepts them. These powerful characters uphold the oppressive laws because they are mutually beneficial for the society and for the heroes themselves. But for black women, who are often alienated within the society, the speculative genre creates a world in which, not so different from ours, the Negro Spiritual Woman has no option other than to uphold the status quo. However, as Morrison states about the absence of the black presence, the lack of black women within the genre shows their lack of value within the hierarchy of the genre. Likewise, the image of the Negro Spiritual Woman is created simply to fit into the world of the white creator, despite the appearance of acceptance within the genre. Instead, these genre conventions very well may create a space where black women are more subjected through the bestowment of supernatural powers, as that appearance leaves the mostly white audience unthreatened in their patriarchal and racial positions in society. Ultimately, however, the most detrimental facet of this problem is not that there are negative images of black women within the genre, but that instead there are rarely any positive contrasting images to combat the hurtful ones.

Notes

1. A popular essay published in *The New Yorker* in 2012 titled "It's Genre. Not That There's Anything Wrong With It" resurfaced the popular debate that genre is a lesser medium than highbrow literature or movies. The author, Arthur Krystal, expounded on the long-held belief that "literary fiction is superior to genre fiction" (Krystal 2012). Although this debate was about fiction, the belief stands for movies and other forms of genre as well.

2. Means Coleman says of each, respectively: The Creature from the Black Lagoon "bodily . . . resembles a racist caricature—its lips are large and exaggerated, its skin is dark" (98); "[Frankenstein] Monster's entrance into the world reveal[s] that [he], whether he knows it or not, possesses a reliance on his (White) master" (27); "King Kong extended the assault to metaphorically implicate Black men through the imagery of the big Black ape in pursuit of White women" (41).

3. The feminist blog Jezebel (http://jezebel.com/5896408/racist-hunger-games -fans-dont-care-how-much-money-the-movie-made) has a cache of the offending tweets, which include: "why does rue have to be Black not gonna lie kinda ruined the movie"; "EWW rue is black?? I'm not watching"; "KKK call me racist but when I found out rue was Black her death wasn't as sad"; "Sense [*sic*] when has Rue been a nigger"; "How in the world are they going to make Rue a freaking Black bitch in the movie?!?!?!?!?!" among many others.

4. As with most clichéd black Hoodoo princesses on film, Dalma reads the future through mystical charms in a small hut on what resembles a haunted cinematic depiction of the Louisiana Bayou. Unlike others, who have used rocks or other trinkets, Dalma uses crab claws to see the future—more than likely because she is from the sea or because crabs give her special power (later, she will turn into a legion of crabs). In this scene Dalma shakes the claws in her cupped hands and then throws them on the table, as if they were a pair of dice. The scene instantly shifts to another location in the ocean, where the sea rocks are laid out in the exact pattern in which the crab claws had spread out on the table.

5. Speaking in a form of French Creole, Calypso curses the group of men on the ship, saying: "Malfaiteur en Tombeau, Crochir l'Esplanade, Dans l'Fond d'l'eau!" Translated, the phrase means: "To your graves, wrongdoers, I bend your path, to the depths of the sea!"

6. Examples of this are when Kee reveals her pregnancy to Theo in the barn as Mary of Nazareth has Christ in a barn; British terrorists who support the refuges are called "Fishes"; and critics such as Dana Stevens have called the movie a "modern-day Nativity story," comparing Theo and Kee to Joseph and Mary.

7. In the movie, Hushpuppy's father tells her: "show me them guns," and the girl proceeds to do a strong man pose, which consists of pumping her arms up and down, flexing her muscles.

References

Beauboeuf-Lafontant, Tamara. 2009. *Behind the Mask of the Strong Black Woman: Voice and Embodiment of a Costly Performance.* Philadelphia: Routledge.

Berger, Maurice. 2000. *White Lies: Race and the Myths of Whiteness.* New York: Farrar, Straus and Giroux.

Bordwell, David, and Kristi Thompson. 2012. *Film Art: An Introduction.* New York: McGraw Hill.

Carby, Hazel. 1989. *Reconstructing Womanhood: The Emergence of the Afro-American Woman Novelist.* New York: Oxford University Press.

Collins, Patricia Hill. 2000. *Black Feminist Thought, Knowledge, Consciousness, and the Politics of Empowerment.* New York: Psychology Press.

Collins, Suzanne. 2008. *The Hunger Games.* New York: Scholastic Press.

Cuarón, Alfonso. 2006. *Children of Men.* Strike Entertainment.

hooks, bell. 2012. "No Love in the Wild." NewBlackMan (in Exile). September 5, 2012. http://www.newblackmaninexile.net/2012/09/bell-hooks-no-love-in-wild.html

Jezebel. 2013. "The Only Oscar GIF You Need, Starring Quvenzhané Wallis." June 12, 2013. http://jezebel.com/5986598/the-only-oscar-gif-you-need-starring-quvenzhane-wallis.

Krystal, Arthur. *2012. "It's Genre. Not That There's Anything Wrong with That."* October 24, 2012. http://www.newyorker.com/online/blogs/books/2012/10/its-genre-fiction-not-that-theres-anything-wrong-with-it.html.

Lynn, Cheryl. 2009. *Trinity: The Black Fantasy.* http://cheryllynneaton.com/2009/05/07/trinity-the-black-fantasy/

Means Coleman, Robin. 2011. *Horror Noire: Blacks in American Horror Films from the 1890s to Present*. New York: Routledge.

Morrison, Toni. 1995. *Playing in the Dark: Whiteness and the Literary Imagination*. New York: Vintage.

Radford-Hill, Sheila. 2002. "Keepin' It Real: A Generational Commentary on Kimberly Springer's Third Wave Black Feminism?" *Signs Journal of Women in Culture and Society* 27, no. 4 (Summer): 1083–1190.

Roberts, Dorothy. 1997. *Killing the Blackbody: Race, Reproduction, and the Meaning of Liberty*. New York: Vintage Books.

Singer, Bryan. *X-Men*. 2000. 20th Century Fox.

Verbinski, Gore. 2006. *Pirates of the Caribbean: Dead Man's Chest*. Walt Disney Studios.

Verbinski, Gore. 2007. *Pirates of the Caribbean: At World's End*. Walt Disney Studios.

Yale Bulletin. 2001. "Director Spike Lee Slams 'Same Old' Black Stereotypes in Today's Films" May 2, 2001. http://archives.news.yale.edu/v29.n21/story3.html.

Zeitlin, Benh. 2012. *Beast of the Southern Wild*. Film. Fox Searchlight.

V

SEXUAL AND
RACIAL POLYPHONY
IN NEW BLACK FILMS

12

FROM QUEER TO QUARE

The Representation of LGBT Blacks in Cinema

Anne Crémieux

IN THE SEMINAL *BLACK Queer Studies* (2005), Rinaldo Walcott argues that black studies and queer studies need each other to grow and draw meaningful conclusions, and hopes to reveal "the potential of a black queer diaspora studies to rejuvenate the liberatory moments of the black studies project" (Johnson and Henderson 2005, 91). In the same volume, Roderick A. Ferguson argues that sociology's forays into sexuality studies and later queer studies have always been related to race studies, since white migrants were in the privileged position of being able to intermarry into the dominant white society. He adds that today, white same-sex couples can assimilate in very much the same way, excluding other working-class and nonwhite queers (52–66), so that race is equally always a factor in queer studies. In his literary study of white supremacist texts, *The Color of Sex* (2001), Mason Stokes quotes black activists who accuse whiteness and homosexuality of being equally "sick" (190), most famously Eldridge Cleaver, who denounced the black gay man's fantasy of being impregnated by the white man's semen, harking back to the great American taboo of interracial sex.

All of this scholarly work points in the same direction, one of greater inclusion and mutual collaboration that resonates in the Black Lives consciousness era and its attempts at fostering alliances to confront long-standing racial issues that affect the black community as a whole, including its LGBT members. In the same way, the study of black queer representation in cinema can only enrich both black film studies and queer film studies, and push them both to be more inclusive. This was Mark Reid's attempt in *PostNegritude Visual and Literary Culture* (1997), which features on the cover the famous intertwined black male bodies of *Looking for Langston* (Isaac Julien, 1989), alongside screenshots of Spike Lee's *Jungle Fever* and a photograph of a black gay man by white gay photographer Alex Hirst, bringing together queer and nonqueer productions.

One great lesson from Donald Bogle's ever enlightening writings is that because marginalized communities are both stereotyped and rendered invisible by the mainstream media representation, it is only through a diverse and repetitive on-screen presence that they can eventually overcome the burden of representation. (Imarisha 2001)

As Catherine Saalfield notes in *Queer Looks* (Gever and Greyson1993, 23), nonwhite queers "live with a double-edged invisibility of being people of color in various queer communities and being queer in various communities of color." Many filmmakers are fully aware of this phenomenon and increasingly unapologetic, with black queer characters who take center stage on both accounts.

1. A Short History of Queer Black Characters in Film

BEFORE THE BLAXPLOITATION ERA, queer black characters are few and far between. In "Birth of a Notion: Towards Black Gay and Lesbian Imagery in Film and Video" (Gever and Greyson 1993, 234), Michelle Parkerson notes that in "mainstream media, gay men and lesbians of color are either woefully present or predictably absent," reading "like its own form of blackface." She then lists the "burly, black 'bulldagger' as whorehouse madam in the 1933 film, *The Emperor Jones*," "the predatory lesbian vamp in Spike Lee's 1983 *She's Gotta Have It*," "Eddie Murphy's ultra-camp Miss Thing hairdresser on NBC's *Saturday Night Live*," and "the snap queen duo on Fox TV's *In Living Color*." This list gives a good sample of black LGBT characters in popular movies up to 1993, when *Queer Looks* was published. There is very little to be found before the 1970s, and the black film wave of the late 1980s and early 1990s made little room for queer characters.

Spike Lee himself confessed that Nola refusing her predatory lesbian friend while juggling her three male lovers was not the most realistic development of her character, but judging that he was "going to be in mud as it is with black women," having Nola "going to bed with another woman" was not an option (Lee and George 1987, 44). Clearly, he shies away from portraying lesbians for the sake of not offending—even more than he already does—straight black women, and one may wonder how satisfied lesbians might have been with Spike Lee's representation of Nola's lesbian experimenting. His later incursion into female sexuality, *Girl 6* (1996), also chooses not to broach the subject, while *She Hate Me* (2004) was widely criticized for creating lesbian characters–eighteen of them!—desiring sexual intimacy with their sperm donor.

The strongest presence of queer characters in black films is found during the Blaxploitation era, though not always in the best of lights. *The Celluloid Closet* critically attempts to record all such occurrences:

> The black exploitation films *Cleopatra Jones* (1973) and *Cleopatra Jones and the Casino of Gold* (1975) used lesbians (played by Shelly Winters and Stella Stevens) as dope pushers and gang leaders. *Mandingo* (1975) and *Drum* (1976) saw male homosexuality as a white man's disease visited on black men to enforce a racist powerlessness. In *Drum*, John Colicos played an evil white slaver that raped and mutilated black men. His character was no less a cartoon than Snowflake, the black transvestite in Ralph Bakshi's animated feature *Coonskin* (1975). Snowflake, described in the script as a "lousy, no good queer," likes to get beaten up by real men and spends his time having sex in the back of a trailer truck on the waterfront. Such films said not only that the homosexual life was synonymous with sex and violence but that this was the norm, that homosexuality *belonged* in the sexual ghetto because it was an abnormal manifestation of love. (Russo 1987, 214–15)

Such heavy criticism of queer representation in Blaxploitation films should, however, be qualified by the equally homophobic white films of the same period.

Additionally, instances of not-so-negative portrayal of queer characters can be found in major Blaxploitation films. One minor character in *Shaft*

(1971) is Rollie, a white gay bartender working across from John Shaft's apartment. He calls him "Johnny" and admires his leather jacket, and because "there's nothing he wouldn't do for twenty dollars," Rollie lets Shaft take over the bar so he can get two mobsters arrested. They actually discuss how two women at a table have expressed interest in them, and joke how they want to "straighten out" Rollie. Being comfortable with a gay man clearly adds to Shaft's general coolness. Another major Blaxploitation hero shown to be unanxious in homosexual surroundings is *Foxy Brown* (1974) who, during an all-white lesbian bar brawl, is referred to as "a friend of ours" that should be left alone. Though clearly exploitative, with a lot of hair pulling and name-calling, the scene is more complex than it seems, implying again that a self-confident straight black heroine is not threatened by homosexuality. Although some Blaxploitation films have been reclaimed by queer audiences for their subtext (particularly female action films), they include no openly queer black characters (Hankin 2002, 85).

Two very different 1976 films, *Next Stop, Greenwich Village* and *Car Wash*, include a black gay character played by Blaxploitation star Antonio Fargas, among an otherwise straight ensemble cast. Though condemning *Next Stop* for being "depressing as hell," Vito Russo singles out Antonio Fargas, "brilliant as Bernstein, a black homosexual of 1950s Greenwich Village. Here is a good example of a stereotype treated in an interesting and inoffensive manner" (1987, 228). Bernstein is gay, but in no way more eccentric, or self-centered, or lonely, than the rest of the otherwise white artist community he is fully part of. He does seem to have no connection to the mainstream black community that is simply absent from the film, as is often the case when a black character appears in a white film. Fargas is further praised in *The Celluloid Closet* for portraying "another memorable gay character in *Car Wash*," Lindy, showing "uncharacteristic militancy that is both funny and challenging." When insulted by black militant Abdullah (Bill Duke) for being a "sorry-looking faggot," Lindy takes offense at being called "sorry-looking." Abdullah continues using feminine pronouns, telling the others "she's just another poor example of how the system has been destroying our men," to which Lindy famously quips—"Honey, I'm more man that you'll ever *be* and more woman than you'll ever *get*," punctuated by a dramatic snap. Vito Russo aptly notes that such self-affirmation is only ever voiced in comedies rather than dramas (no such empowering lines turn up in *Next Stop*) but should nevertheless be commended (229).

The sympathetic, unthreatening, most often comical-in-spite-of-a-tragic-past black queen is in fact a recurrent character in white cinema, whether Lady Chablis playing herself in *Midnight in the Garden of Good and Evil* (Clint Eastwood, 1997) or Chris Tucker as frenzied, intergalactic drag-queen deejay Ruby Rhod in *The Fifth Element* (Luc Besson, 1997). More over-the-top than offensive, Lady Chablis's character is often read as empowering in hindsight. Admittedly a blatant caricature, she is also very much at ease with who she is, although not always appropriate about it. She forces protagonist John Kelso (John Cusack) to flirt with her, demanding flowers, car-door service, and a date at the Alpha Phi Cotillion, all in exchange for agreeing to testify. Most of her scenes are of dubious taste and could certainly have been shortened, but if the film was not over two hours and thirty minutes long, Lady Chablis's excellent sassy drag queen cabaret stage number would probably have been cut out, too.

Two years earlier, *To Wong Foo Thanks for Everything Julie Newmar* (1995), literally riding on the success of the Australian drag-queen road movie *Priscilla, Queen of the Desert* (1994), mainstreamed the drag-queen figure with a multiracial trio played by testosterone-packed actors Wesley Snipes (Noxeema), John Leguizamo (Chi-Chi), and Patrick Swayze (Vida), with special appearances by Ru Paul and, of course, Julie Newmar. Although hardly convincing in drag, the film's protagonists reflect the racial diversity of drag-queen culture. Although the white character Vida is undeniably more levelheaded than her Latina and African American acolytes, and while Chi-Chi is stereotyped as dippy, man-obsessed, jealous, and volatile, Noxeema is sassy and smart, referring to African American history in a comical, educated way as she refuses to "drive Miss Daisy" or be "mistaken for Ms. Rosa Parks" and ride a bus. The seemingly well-intended production never departs from its clownish, cabaret aesthetics, constantly playing on the freak-show thrill of watching three unlikely actors in drag who, in total disregard for verisimilitude—they are fugitives, after all—never take off the makeup they patiently put on in the very first scene.

Although not perfect, all of these attempts are a step up from Eddie Murphy's *Saturday Night Live* gay hairdresser Dion (1980–84), reincarnated in *Beverly Hills Cop* (1984) when Eddie Murphy—who wrote the sequence—manages to get into an exclusive men's club by passing off as a gay man who needs to inform the man he is looking for that he might have infected him with "herpes simplex 10," a particularly offensive dialogue at a time when AIDS was starting its terrifying death count. Eddie Murphy's stand-up comedy tours *Delirious* (1983) and *Raw* (1987) were even more offensive, as he was responding to being shunned by the LGBT community. The same kind of humor can be found in Robert Townsend's *Hollywood Shuffle* (1987)—which ironically includes a great caricature of Eddie Murphy as Hollywood's buffoon. Robert Townsend plays an aspiring actor who refuses to play stereotypical gay gangsters and addicts for stereotypical Jewish directors. The scene implies that calling a black man gay is the highest insult. The same is true in Spike Lee's *School Daze* (1988), in which rival black college fraternities taunt each other in a casually homophobic call and response routine: "When I say Gamma, you say Fag. Gamma—fag, Gamma—fag . . ."

The emerging black film wave of the late 1980s and early 1990s proved particularly sexist and homophobic, inspiring independent black queer artists to respond with political films that influenced the representation of black queer characters in mainstream 1990s movies and beyond.

2. New Black Queer Cinema

African-American independents Marlon Riggs and Cheryl Dunye, black British filmmaker Isaac Julien, and white feminists Lizzie Borden and Jennie Livingston are all part of the "New Queer Cinema" as defined by B. Ruby Rich in 1992. Among other things, their films are direct responses to direct and indirect accusations by various black cultural and political agents that homosexuality is a white phenomenon that is not to be tolerated in the black community.

These independent efforts also aimed at making black queers visible when they were being erased by productions like *The Color Purple* (1985), in which Celie's love for Shug is toned down to one innocent kiss on the lips and a sisterly friendship (Weiss 1992, 79–80).

As America's cultural funding was being hit by the Reagan-Bush administration, the impact of the black queer wave of the late 1980s was uncertain (Gever, Parmar, and Greyson 1993, xv). Michelle Parkerson lists as responses Isaac Julien's *Looking for Langston* (1989) and *Young Soul Rebels* (1991), Marlon Riggs's *Tongues Untied* (1989), *Affirmations* (1990), and *Anthem* (1991), as well as videos by Dawn Suggs, Thomas Harris, Sylvia Rhue, Cheryl Dunye, Jacqueline Woodson, Jack Waters, Aarin Burch, Jocelyn Taylor, and Yvonne Welbon, to which must be added Michelle Parkerson's own independent documentary films. She also acknowledges the importance of white-women-directed films such as *Portrait of Jason* (Shirley Clarke, 1967), *Tina and Ruby: Hell Divin' Women* (Greta Schiller and Andrea Weiss, 1987), and *Paris Is Burning* (1990), as well as the New York City 1989 "How do I look" conference, the nonprofit Women Make Movies organization, Third World Newsreel, and Frameline (see Gever, Parmar, and Greyson 1993, 235).

Marlon Riggs's documentaries still remain among the most provocative black queer productions to this day. In limited time and with an even more limited budget, they seem to encompass everything, from interracial homophobia to AIDS, history, arts, and politics.

Riggs's posthumous documentary *Black Is . . . Black Ain't* (1994), uses gumbo as a metaphor for the black community, with "a little bit of everything in it." Two earlier documentaries, *Ethnic Notions* (Riggs, 1986) and *Color Adjustment* (Riggs, 1992), had already explored the representation of blacks in popular culture. *Black Is . . . Black Ain't* truly incorporates the queer dimension, while not focusing solely on it, allowing for a reflection that brings together race and sexuality using Riggs's usual hybrid form, with performances by choreographer Bill T. Jones and poet Essex Hemphill, interviews of bell hooks, Michele Wallace, Barbara Smith, Cornel West, Maulana Karenga, and Angela Davis. Personal testimony, musical interludes, and historical archives come together in a film dominated by Marlon Riggs's hospitalization and growing weakness.

3. The Changing Representation of Queer Black Characters

UNTIL RECENTLY, BLACK GAY men were almost exclusively portrayed as effeminate or pathetic, and rejected by or cut off from the black community.

This is at least partly true of Jason in *Portrait of Jason* (Shirley Clarke, 1967), Bernard in *The Boys in the Band* (1970, although no more effeminate or pathetic than most of the other boys in the band), Lindy in *Car Wash* and Bernstein in *Next Stop Greenwich Village* (1976), the drag queens of *Paris Is Burning* (1990), or Will Smith in *Six Degrees of Separation* (1993).

In her contribution to *Queer Looks* entitled "When Difference is more than Skin Deep," B. Ruby Rich looks at a number of black characters featured in white lesbian films and concludes that unlike in *Mala Noche* by Gus Van Sant (1986), *Born in Flames* (1983) features "uncomplicated race relations" while Joy Chamberlain's *Nocturne* (1990) "brings to the foreground, more than any other recent films, the pitfalls into which queer white filmmakers can fall in creating characters drawn from other races or cultures (. . .) [demonstrating] the limits of any "color-blind" approach to cinema or lesbian relations" (Gever, Parmar, and Greyson 1993, 327–28). Indeed, the plot involves a female threesome in which the black character is gradually pushed into the submissive role, without the slave/master dynamic ever being questioned in racial terms. For Rich, McLaughlin uses the racial elements for "mise-en-scène more than narrative" (322), as acknowledged by the director herself in a *Screen* interview (Autumn 87, 24, reprinted in *Queer Looks*).

It could be argued that the situation has indeed changed since 1987, and that white filmmakers today have more examples to follow when attempting to create interesting, race-conscious queer characters of color. *Tongues Untied* (1989) is indeed part of the queer canon and can be safely assumed to have been seen by most queer filmmakers today, whether when originally made available to everyone on PBS (and greatly publicized by Pat Buchanan during the 1992 presidential campaign as proof that George Bush was allotting tax money to pornography) or today on the internet. In addition, *Black Is . . . Black Ain't* (1994), Riggs's final film, is a documentary questioning the black community's sexism and homophobia, but also the racism of the white queer community, as illustrated by a repeated scene in which black men keep getting carded to get into a gay club. On the main poster for the film, Marlon Riggs is embraced by an emaciated Essex Hemphill standing behind him, fists clenched, both shirtless, looking straight at the camera. Knowing that Marlon Riggs loved a white man who saw him through his fatal illness, and who is deliberately absent from both his autobiographical films, only complicates issues of sex and racism for black and white filmmakers alike to draw from when writing black queer characters.

Two productions stand out in that respect: *Boy Culture* (2006) by gay Filipino filmmaker Q. Allen Brocka and *Tru Loved* (2008) by white gay director Stewart Wade. *Boy Culture* is narrated by the main white character, X, who is a professional prostitute living with two gay roommates, Andrew, who is African American, and Joey, a white teenager with drama-queen tendencies. X is in love with Andrew, a "good boy" who, unlike him, is somewhat new to the gay life. X jealously watches him develop a taste for one-night stands and three-ways. When his ex-girlfriend gets married, Andrew asks X to be his date. But Andrew is afraid of telling his parents, because "a middle-class black family from Oregon" is "different." Andrew's mother greets X with open arms, telling her son she's known he was gay since he was eight, putting a happy spin on the stereotypical black homophobia expected by characters and audiences alike. The racial issue ends up a nonissue, but without being denied either, while playing with stereotypes. X and Joey are typically fascinated by Andrew's male attributes, and Andrew is enjoying taking X to an event where he will be the only white person. When the three roommates discuss terrible pickup lines, Andrew quotes the very line X used to introduce him in voice-over—"I'm not normally into black guys"—to which he answers, "Oh, this must be my lucky night, you're feeling abnormal, and I'm black," unknowingly pointing out X's racial prejudice. *Boy Culture* is a typical coming-out/coming-of-age comedy, with a racial twist that is significant without being overbearing.

Tru Loved features a very similar character, Lo, short for Lodell, or perhaps "down low," which is the way he lives his life, making sure everyone at school and at home believes he is straight. He is the football team's quarterback and very much used to the coach calling the team "pansies" and "ladies" to keep them in line. The main character, Tru, is transferring from San Francisco to a new school where she is immediately labeled as "gay," "queer," and a "dyke," because she is raised by her two moms (one of whom is black) and on great terms with her two dads. Lo immediately spots her as the perfect beard, hoping she will need him as much as he needs her. His grandmother, however, disapproves, asking whether there "aren't any nice black girls in that school you go to?" Quickly enough, Tru understands Lo is gay and urges him to come out, which he eventually does when it becomes obvious that everyone will accept him. When he finally introduces his white boyfriend to his grandmother, she shakes her head and says, "Aren't there any nice black boys at that school you go to?"

Because both *Boy Culture* and *Tru Loved* are comedies, the inter- and intraracial tensions, and the difficulty of coming out, are played down, portraying black families that are no more homophobic than your average white family, with the contrast coming from the white character's family not being traditional (*Tru Loved*) or being completely absent (*Boy Culture*, in which X says his family never noticed when he left). Both films set the black characters in a believable, nonstereotypical family situation and voice their awareness of the racial, geographical, and class difference (Lo explains that "this ain't San Francisco, and I ain't some privileged white boy").

Unsurprisingly, both films are the product of a multiracial, race-conscious creative team. *Tru Loved*'s first-billed producer, Antonio Brown, who acted as story consultant, is African American and has always been an activist for social change, representing racial and sexual minorities. *Boy Culture* is based on a novel by Matthew Rettenmund, who explains in a joint interview (2007) with Filipino director Q. Allan Brocka how surprised and upset he was to find out Andrew would be black:

> I saw casting calls for black actors . . . and I assumed that meant you didn't see any of the criticisms I was playing with in the novel, since they were aimed at white, gay male culture. Of course, since then I've seen the film and realized the change of Andrew's race only expanded on what I was saying.

Brocka explains he insisted on casting a black man—"I just don't see people of color in queer films and didn't want to make another one without one."

Although Brocka points to the absence of people of color in queer films, there are other examples, including from white directors. In many ways, just like liberal white filmmakers made black films in the 1960s and 1970s, LGBT white filmmakers made black LGBT films in the 1990s and 2000s. A case in

point is *Strange Fruit* (2004), the low-budget race-gay thriller by white director Kyle Schickner, whose production company, FenceSitter Films, according
to their Facebook and Twitter accounts, specializes in "Cinema for the rest of
us! Founded on the belief that films & TV don't need straight white men as
heroes in order to be Successful & Entertaining." Kyle Schickner is a bisexual
rights activist whose films and TV series always feature nonwhite and non-
straight characters. *Strange Fruit* tells the story of a successful gay black New
York attorney, William Boyals, who visits his childhood Louisiana bayou for
the funeral of his gay cousin, who was found hanging from a tree outside a
gay bar. The plot is awkwardly similar to Norman Jewison's *In the Heat of
the Night* (1967), in which Sidney Poitier's character, detective Virgil Tibbs
from Philadelphia, comes down for his mother's funeral. First picked up as
a suspect, he reluctantly helps local police investigate what looks like a racist
crime but turns out to be a theft gone wrong. In *Strange Fruit*, Boyals's aunt
begs him to investigate what she believes is a hate crime, which he does,
only to uncover that the local white racist homophobes he suspected are not
involved in the murder, which was perpetrated by a black gang. *Strange Fruit*
denounces the same extreme bigotry in similar terms, with a complex end
that does not erase the rampant racism and homophobia of the South that
pervades the film. Like Tibbs, Boyals is proud and competent, must face his
own prejudice that led him to false conclusions, and fears for his life. *Strange
Fruit* certainly anchors its queerness in black history, if only through its title,
but also in black film history, with the strong parallel with Jewison's film.

4. Black Queer Production Today

QUEER BLACK INDEPENDENT FILMMAKERS have been producing films at the
intersection of race, class, gender, and sexuality, and in particular address
issues of race in a more direct fashion than white queer filmmakers who
include black characters in their films. In *Black Queer Studies* (Johnson and
Henderson 2005), the editors introduce the notion of "quare," coined as the
black pronunciation of "queer," and which questions both white racism and
black homophobia, with a sense of black history.

Movies such as *Brother to Brother* (Rodney Evans, 2004) and *Brother
Outsider: The Life of Bayard Rustin* (PBS POV TV series, 2003) are perfect

examples. The first is a fiction about a black college student facing homophobia in his black literature class. *Brother Outsider* focuses on Bayard Rustin, whose life is presented through the lens of his homosexuality. Although not at the center of his political life—Bayard Rustin never fought for gay rights—homosexuality is at the center of this historical biography, as a key element to understanding his position as the background, marginal leader who quietly organized the March on Washington.

Another example of quare cinema is the documentary about intraracial rape, *NO!* Started in 1995 and released in its final version in 2006, *NO!* includes a historical, literary, and political perspective. Director Aishah Shahidah Simmons weaves together testimonies of black women rape survivors, community and human rights activists, theologians, sociologists, and historians, interspersed with spoken word by poet Essex Hemphill and others, dance performances, archival footage, and historical reenactments. In both form and content, Aishah Simmons's documentary is a direct emanation of the groundbreaking productions of the 1980s and 1990s, providing a compelling educational documentary for the community at large.

In fact, it can be argued that black queer films have always been quare, as previously quoted critics bell hooks, B. Ruby Rich, Kobena Mercer, and Michelle Parkerson very well show, becoming acutely aware of their quareness in the 1990s. *Black Nation/Queer Nation?* (Shari Frilot, 1995), shot during the March 1995 CUNY conference on lesbian and gay sexualities in the African diaspora, explains how both the conference and the documentary aim at "bringing race and sexuality together to question the notion of nation."

Cheryl Dunye, who was the production manager on *Black Nation/ Queer Nation?*, personifies the strong connection between queer black fiction cinema and academic productions. In *The Watermelon Woman* (1996), Cheryl's efforts to uncover black lesbian presence in films from the 1930s directly echo the *Black Nation/Queer Nation?* interogations about black queer identity, while quaring black queer identity through grounding it in history.

The Watermelon Woman, Cheryl Dunye's first feature film, incorporates black film history both in form and in content. It tells the story of Cheryl, a film student and video-store clerk who gets involved with a white woman,

Diana, while making a documentary about a black actress of the 1930s cast in Mammy roles and billed as "the Watermelon Woman." Cheryl discovers her real name, Fae Richards, and that she was romantically involved with Dorothy Azner–like Hollywood director Martha Page. As soon as Cheryl meets Diana (Guinevere Turner from *Go Fish*), her best friend Tamara questions her internal racism ("Don't you like the color of your skin?") and is answered by a profound interrogation about the politics of blackness: "Who's to say that dating someone white does not make me black?" As detailed in Stefanie Dunning's *Queer in Black and White* (2009), the film interlaces a number of black-white relationships in which the black characters are strongly anchored in the black community, through friends and family. Cheryl is out to her mother (Irene Dunye, playing herself) and close to her, as her inclusion in her fake documentary about the Watermelon Woman implies, both within and without the film. *The Watermelon Woman* offers a vision of queer blackness and black queerness that goes against both stereotypes that queerness is "a white thing" and that the black community is particularly homophobic.

Cheryl Dunye's production since her groundbreaking debut feature film has been diverse. The generally well-received HBO prison drama *Stranger Inside* (2001) is centered on a complex mother-daughter relationship within prison walls, with a minor lesbian subplot, not unlike the generally very poorly received Miramax *My Baby's Daddy* (2004), about three straight black men dealing with fatherhood. Dunye's two most recent productions, *The Owls* (2010) and *Mommy is Coming* (2012) have taken her back to the LGBT festival circuit, with interracial queer comedic dramas.

The Owls is Dunye's most experimental film, with its split screens and nonlinear storytelling, interspersed with reality TV–like interviews of the characters. It tells the story of four middle-aged lesbians who used to be in a rock band together (the actors were actually together in *Go Fish* and *The Watermelon Woman*). They must cover up for a murder one of them has accidentally committed, which they do successfully until the victim's black girlfriend, Skye (Skyler Cooper), returns from Iraq to investigate.

The Owls is revealed in the final credit sequence to be a collective that welcomed input from every member of the cast and crew, among which is black British filmmaker Campbell, a.k.a. Fag daddy, who explains that "the dominant theme of *The Owls* seems to be age, not race, and not ethnicity." Although it is true that Carol is not defined by her race, she does express angst about aging in racially marked political terms: "I began in my spiritual journey to sisterhood, to empowerment, to building community, I'm lost, . . . I'm alone, and I only have, Lily," her white lover.

Cheryl Dunye's *Mommy Is Coming*, once more features an interracial relationship. It is set in queer Berlin and its underground leather S/M culture, featuring a number of famous queer porn stars, including Jean Seberg impersonator Dylan, and Papi Coxxx as the black lover. Just like *The Owls* included an interview of queer theorist Jack Halberstam, *Mommy Is Coming* is steeped in very contemporary queer performance and theory, with a cast assembled by former porn star and regular guest of academic performance events Annie Sprinkle. It reprises the split screen, reality TV–like actor and character interviews, and concludes with the cast sharing their incest fantasies. Perhaps because it is set outside of the United States, race is never addressed as such and is limited to the visible presence of black lesbian and transgender characters.

Although Cheryl Dunye's very strong connection to queer theory is certainly an exception in the entertainment world, many black queer filmmakers produce aesthetically and narratively challenging work. Documentaries such as *The Aggressives* (Daniel Peddle, 2005) and recent fictions such as *Pariah* (Dee Rees, 2011), *Money Matters* (Ryan Richmond, 2011), and the web TV series *The Lovers and Friends Show* (Charmain Johnson, 2008–10) are a refreshing reminder that black lesbian identity is alive, if not always well. Indeed, all present lesbianism as a somewhat dangerous path to follow, with the violence coming mostly from unaccepting parents.

The Aggressives is a drag-king version of *Paris Is Burning*, featuring six lesbian or transgender drag kings of color presented in their everyday life as well as their performance persona. None of them are interested in labels. They call themselves "aggressive," with an added "fem" or "butch." Their lives are complicated by lack of money, breakups, and loving yet disapproving mothers (fathers are either not present or not interviewed). The traditional final sequence telling what the six main characters have become is neither

Alike (Adepero Oduye) and Arthur (Charles Parnell), Alike's understanding father who shelters her from the wrath of her homophobic mother in *Pariah*.

bleak nor rosy: *The Aggressives* presents complex characters with ordinary lives and ordinary dreams, some of which come true, like getting your GED, moving in with your girlfriend, reuniting with your mother, or landing a part in a Spike Lee film. The documentary strongly asserts a black, queer, lower-class identity that is not interested in being labeled as such.

Equally seeking to escape preset categories, Monique "Money" Matters gets away from her violent neighborhood and irascible mother by writing free-verse autobiographical poetry during her private Catholic school classes, a mostly white environment that she in turns escapes by spending time with the 8th Street Angels, a group of queer black girls from her own neighborhood. She becomes good friends with teenage dropout Braids, who happens to participate in local poetry events. They become close, even intimate, with Money ironically answering every "how are you?" and "are you cool?" with "Yeah, I'm straight." Although words like "butch," "dyke," "gays," and "girl gang" are used in the film, Braids never labels herself. It all comes down to confused, adolescent feelings that cut across adult categories.

Pariah is also a coming-of-age story, starring Alike, a troubled teenager who is doing well in school and writes in her spare time. She is a friend of a very butch, very out lesbian. Both Alike and Laura are perfectly clear about their sexuality. Alike is transgender, changing clothes and looks on the bus

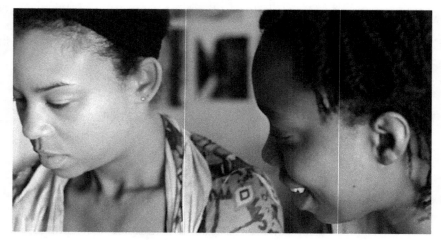

The coming-out of Alike (*right*) to her best friend, Bina (Aasha Davis), who only wants to experiment with lesbianism and not companionship.

to and back from school, as she is not out to her family. Laura is struggling to get her GED now that her mother has thrown her out, a decision Alike's own mother seems to approve of. Her father, a policeman, hears word on the street that his daughter is a "bull dyke," but makes sure to give Alike a chance to deny it, until a climactic scene between the three, in which Alike insists she is a "dyke" and a "lesbian," not afraid to use words that make her mother explode in violence. Although her father supports her, it is not clear whether her churchgoing mother will come around, and the film ends, like *Money Matters*, on a much more ambivalent note than *Boy Culture* or *Tru Loved*. *Pariah* is strongly held together by its clearheaded, charismatic main character, making B. Ruby Rich (2011) say about the film being compared with *Precious* (Lee Daniels, 2009) that "*Pariah* is a film about coming into agency, not about abjection," and that it compares better with another filmmaker's work: "Rees has got Scorsese in her blood."

One feature that all of these black lesbian films have in common that also differentiates them from *Precious* is that the self-identified black queer characters are all distinctly butch, while the fem characters they often sleep with do not voice their identity. In *Precious*, however, the lesbian school-teacher and role model, Ms. Rain, is very fem, along with her partner, in contradiction to the novel *Push*, on which the film is based. Gay director

Lee Daniels explains in the DVD bonus that she was a much-needed "breath of fresh air," because "people equate literacy with beautiful," so that Paula Patton's beauty was needed to lighten the film. And indeed, most people do equate women's beauty with femininity, whether they are straight or queer. Black lesbian characters still tend to be masculine and gangster-like, tapping into the same African sexual stereotype of power and performance assigned to black men. This stereotype is perhaps not inaugurated but certainly most strongly impersonated by lesbian-icon Queen Latifah in *Set It Off* (F. Gary Gray, 1996). She plays Cleo, the most fearless, hotheaded, and uncontrollable of the four black female bank-robber protagonists. She is butch with a gangsta attitude, pulling out a gun on Stony (Jada Pinkett) and ultimately choosing to get shot by the police in true Tony Montana fashion. Her very sexy, very fem girlfriend, Ursula (Samantha MacLachlan), only adds to her butch persona.

The Lovers and Friends Show (2008–10), which is hard to not read as a black version of *The L Word* (2004–9), tips the excessively fem and upper-class representation of the predominantly white lesbian friends over to a primarily butch representation of a mostly black, middle- and lower-class lesbian community. In comparison, the black gay series *The DL Chronicles* (2007 and 2012) and *Noah's Arc* (2005–6, starring *Boy Culture* costar Darryl Stephens) are just as diverse in terms of gender representation as the exclusively white *Queer as Folk* (2000–2005). These shows also benefit from much higher production value and larger audiences, and are somewhat bound to follow in the footsteps of very well known and notoriously black gay TV series characters that include Keith in *Six Feet Under* (2001–5) and Omar in *The Wire* (2002–8), two complex, well-rounded characters that certainly set a new standard in terms of narrative development. Again, in comparison, the equally interesting lesbian characters from *The Wire*, detective Kima Greggs and gang killer Snoop, are both butch and identified as such by their collaborators, who praise them for acting like one of the guys. Whether this difference is due to the reality of a strong butch/fem black lesbian culture, as opposed to a less polarized black gay culture, is very difficult to assess, and it is telling that even the relatively fem black lesbians of *The L Word*, Bette and Tasha, take on the butch role in their relationships with white women (in contrast, Bette is the fem one when she cheats on Tina with an

African American carpenter, who wears overalls and prefers to be on top). But while this strong predominance of the butch lesbian is more than a little suspect, it takes nothing away from the political strength and complexity of contemporary black lesbian characterization in film and web and TV-series, quite the contrary.

5. Conclusion

KOBENA MERCER THEORIZES THE position of African American queer people as such:

> precisely because of our lived experiences of discrimination in and exclusion from the white gay and lesbian community, and of discrimination in and exclusions from the black community, we locate ourselves in the spaces *between* different communities—at the intersections of power relations determined by race, class, gender, and sexuality. (Gever, Parmar, and Greyson 1993, 239)

The conscious effort from queer and black filmmakers to represent this position has been having a diffuse, yet lasting impact on film production at large. Two unequally successful films, *Naz & Maalik* (Jay Dockendorf, 2015) and *Moonlight* (Barry Jenkins, 2016), by including Muslim characters and actors, incorporate a religious and political dimension to post-9/11 black queerness. In *Naz & Maalik*, straight white director Jay Dockendorf tells the story of two Muslims outed by a suspicious FBI agent monitoring radical youths. In *Moonlight*, straight black director Barry Jenkins tells the story of Chiron, a gay inner-city child whose role model is Juan, a straight drug dealer played by notoriously Muslim actor Mahershala Ali. Ali's presence adds an unscripted dimension: he won the Oscar for best supporting actor, and the film won best picture in the wake of Donald Trump's travel ban efforts against seven majority-Muslim countries. Crossing race, class, gender, and religion, the two films result from a long history of fighting fixed identities and stereotypical representations.

In Justin Simien's satirical debut film *Dear White People* (2014), about four black students at an Ivy League college, one of the main characters,

Lionel Higgins, is a gay geek with a terrible sense of fashion. In one of many scenes in which lethargic Lionel wallows in self-pity, he observes a young black student who effortlessly moves from a black straight crowd to a white gay one, making a smooth change from a cool streetwise attitude to a hip and campy one. Lionel sits in admiration of such chameleon skills, seeing someone who does not stand *between* communities, like him, but instead navigates both.

Pratibha Parmar (Gever, Parmar, and Greyson 1993, 5) declares, "I do not speak from a position of marginalization but more crucially from the resistance to that marginalization," positioning herself in the "mode of disidentification" that José Esteban Muñoz borrows from French linguist Michel Pêcheux in *Disidentifications: Queers of Color and the Performance of Politics* (1999). A black queer character like Lionel Higgins seems marginalized yet disidentified from any stereotypical community, which does not protect him from racist and homophobic reactions within and without the film (Diaz 2014). Lionel, Naz, Maalik, Chiron, Alike, Cloe, and many others are black queer bodies at the mercy of racist or homophobic institutions and individuals in sometimes separate, sometimes connected ways, expanding Black Lives consciousness to include quare consciousness. Watching black films about race, sexuality, and everything else gives hope that the connection has been made and that the level of diversity and repetition Donald Bogle wished for is within reach.

References

Butler, J. 1993. *Bodies That Matter: On the Discursive Limits of "Sex."* New York: Routledge.

Carby, Hazel. 1989. *Reconstructing Womanhood: The Emergence of the Afro-American Woman Novelist.* New York: Oxford University Press.

Diaz, Evelyn. 2014. "Dear White People Sparks Homophobic Reactions." BET. com. October 27, 2014. http://www.bet.com/news/celebrities/2014/10/27/dear-white-people-sparks-homophobic-reaction.html.

Dunning, Stefanie K. 2009. *Queer in Black and White: Interraciality, Same Sex Desire, and Contemporary African American Culture.* Bloomington: Indiana University Press.

Gever, M., P. Parmar, and J. Greyson, eds. 1993. *Queer Looks: Perspectives on Lesbian and Gay Films and Video.* New York: Routledge.

Hankin, K. 2002. *Girls in the Back Room: Looking at the Lesbian Bar*. Minneapolis: University of Minnesota Press.

Imarisha, W. 2001. "Donald Bogle." *Philadelphia City Paper*. March 1–8, 2001.

Johnson, E. P., and M. G. Henderson, eds. 2005. *Black Queer Studies*. Durham, NC: Duke University Press.

Lee, S., and N. George. 1987. *Spike Lee's Gotta Have It*. New York: Fireside.

Muñoz, José Esteban. 1999. *Disidentifications: Queers of Color and the Performance of Politics*. Minneapolis: University of Minnesota Press.

Reid, M. 1997. *PostNegritude Visual and Literary Culture*. New York: SUNY.

Rettenmund, M. 2007. "Interview with *Boy Culture* Director, Q. Allan Brocka." April 7, 2007, accessed on September 27, 2012, http://www.myspace.com/boyculture/blog.

Rich, B. R. 1992. "New Queer Cinema." *Sight & Sound* 2, no. 5: 30–35.

Rich, B. R. 2011. "Park City Remix." *Film Quarterly* 64, no. 3 (Spring). http://www.filmquarterly.org/2011/03/park-city-remix/.

Russo, V. 1987. *The Celluloid Closet*. 2nd ed. New York: Harper & Row.

Stokes, M. 2001. *The Color of Sex: Whiteness, Heterosexuality, and the Fictions of White Supremacy*. Durham, NC: Duke University Press.

Weiss, A. 1992. *Vampires and Violets: Lesbians in the Cinema*. London: Jonathan Cape.

West, C. 1993. Race Matters. Boston: Beacon Press.

13

THE PAST, PRESENT, AND FUTURE OF BLACK QUEER CINEMA

James Smalls

ALTHOUGH BOTH TERMS IN the designation "black queer" are signifiers of difference, there are tensions that do exist between them. Blackness and queerness have historically made for antagonistic bedfellows and remain so for many activists and theorists of color who have expressed a sense of aliena-tion, or at least discomfort, with attempts to associate the two terms and con-cepts. "Black" and "queer" complicate more than complement one anoth-er. Perhaps no one knew this better than the African American filmmaker Marlon Riggs (1957–94), who, in 1989, released his groundbreaking and in-fluential documentary film on black gay identity called *Tongues Untied*. The title of his film was taken from an anthology of poems by five black gay poets published in England in 1987. In the film, Riggs combines poetry (including some of his own), performance, and personal testimony to reflect on and critique the situation of black gay men in the United States. His documentary became representative of a handful of films produced by black independent filmmakers in the 1990s and classified under the rubric *Black Queer Cinema* (BQC), itself a subcategory of what is known as *New Queer Cinema* (NQC). The latter was a term first coined by the film theorist B. Ruby Rich and hinted at a sense that lesbian and gay images and filmmakers had finally gained in-dependence and had freed themselves from their marginal status in society, having moved away from expectations of positive imagery.

This chapter discusses the when and why of BQC by surveying, examin-ing, and critiquing the historical legacy of selected films that fall under this

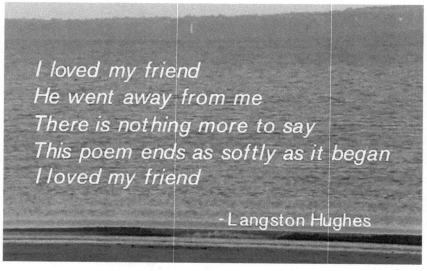

I loved my friend
He went away from me
There is nothing more to say
This poem ends as softly as it began
I loved my friend

—Langston Hughes

Langston Hughes's written homoerotic love poem.

rubric in the United States. It will provide a critical assessment of the past, present, and possible future of BQC as a filmic genre or theme, and proposes to provide some insight into the history and theory of the issues involved. It sets out to examine the continued viability of the genre by bringing together questions of racial and queer identities as these are inextricably linked in our past, present, and future histories.

Films in the NQC category were characterized as "radical and popular, stylish and economically viable," "irreverent," "energetic," and "unapologetic" (Aron 2004, 3). The majority of them, however, were primarily for and about Caucasian lesbians and gays, but some under the BQC heading did make it a point to broach the sentiments of identities along combined racial and queer lines. These included, in addition to *Tongues Untied*, Isaac Julien's *Looking for Langston* (1989), and Jennie Livingston's *Paris Is Burning* (1990). These films and their makers defied the sanctity of the homophobic past and challenged mainstream cinema history. They were very postmodern in their lack of respect for cinematic convention in form, content, and genre. Their defiance, rather than their conformity to status quo expectations, marked them as queer (Aron 2004, 4–5). Black queer films highlighted that uncomfortable and unstable space that has always existed between blackness and queerness. That space and the volatility of it have become part of the appeal and power of black queer visual culture.

Tongues Untied and *Looking for Langston* have become two iconic works of cinema that constitute the birth and optimistic goals of BQC. Although Julien is a black British filmmaker, his film is an acclaimed cinematic meditation on an American subject—the Harlem Renaissance and its premier literary figure, Langston Hughes. It is a film that casts Julien into the history of African American cinema. *Tongues Untied* and *Looking for Langston* are typically discussed together in terms of their differences in cinematic form and their similarities in engaging the urgent topics of the visibility of black male queerness and its plurality, all the while searching for the black queer voice as agency. That voice combines "the poetic with the political and the personal with the collective," as well as the past with the present (Wallenberg 2004, 129). As B. Ruby Rich has noted, these two films "set the framing for what queer films could be like: fresh, edgy, low-budget, inventive, unapologetic, sexy and stylistically daring" (Rich 2000, 23). As well, the two films "shared a simultaneous coming to terms with what have been referred to as diasporic or even hybridic experiences" (Wallenberg 2004, 128). Stress on the hybridic and the performative as means of dislodging racial and sexual binarisms, fixedness, and essentialisms constitutes a significant and consistent aspect of black queer strategies of representation.

Both Riggs and Julien bring together and affirm the ties between blackness and queerness, diaspora and (homo)eros, not in terms of an either/or but of an inclusiveness stressing that the two cannot be divided "so as to serve or represent different communities at different times." (Wallenberg 2004, 128–29) Because their works focus on the plural, rather than on the singular of race and same-sex sexuality, both filmmakers moved away from the simplistic negative/positive binary that framed earlier representations of blackness, queerness, and their theoretical analyses. Their works focus instead on the heterogeneity of black experience as part of a process of understanding and insight. The unfixed space that these films create and exploit is both critically black *and* critically queer.

As part of black visual culture, BQC operates as a means to explore and critique the parallel yet divergent historical and conceptual developments and intersections of black histories, theories, and lived experiences, while realizing that none of these are homogenous or monolithic. A look at the past, present, and future of BQC constitutes a project of recovery and discovery, in that it draws attention to the ways in which a visualizing of the interrelationship of blackness and queerness might inform black diasporic participation as well as disrupt black contributions to modernism and postmodernism.

The analysis of the construction and intersectionality of blackness and queerness in *Tongues Untied* is an important prerequisite for understanding the politics and aesthetics of 1980s and 1990s black queer culture in the United States (Dickel 2011, 54). That culture had its origins in feminism, specifically black and black lesbian feminism, for it was with feminism that questions were asked and challenges were made regarding racial difference and sexual identity. It should not, therefore, be at all surprising to learn that Riggs was a student of the renowned poet and black lesbian feminist scholar Audre Lorde (Smith 2009, 13). It is also important to note that it was black feminist critique that initially motivated the concept of "intersectionality," which has become indispensable to the historical unfolding of black queer politics and aesthetics.

The ideological foundation of black feminism in the BQC of the past is clearly seen in Cheryl Dunye's *The Watermelon Woman* (1996). This film is the first and only one by an African American lesbian filmmaker to be theatrically released. In it, Dunye (b. 1966) foregrounds black lesbian identity in order to work against marginalization both in front of and behind the camera (Sullivan 2000, 450). *The Watermelon Woman* stands out as "the first narrative feature film made by an out African-American lesbian" and has become part of the historical legacy of BQC (Braidt 2000, 181). It is a lighthearted mockumentary about a black lesbian filmmaker researching the life of Fae Richards, a relatively unknown black actress who played "mammy roles" in the 1930s. The main character, Cheryl (played by Cheryl Dunye), discovers that Richards, the actress dubbed "the Watermelon Woman," was actually in a sexual relationship with the white female director, Martha Page, and was part of a vibrant underground black lesbian community in Philadelphia throughout her life. The film sparked controversy because it had been partially funded by the National Endowment for the Arts, thus resurrecting the debate over the issue of federal funding of art deemed by some to be obscene.

According to film theorist Andrea Braidt, *The Watermelon Woman* is a prime example of how queer cinema radically changed various aspects of filmmaking, most notably by representing African American history as establishing a discourse of what Braidt calls queer ethnography. Braidt notes that Dunye uses interracial romance as a vehicle for "a deconstructive praxis of antiracist political rhetoric" that "powerfully demonstrates the political potential of queer filmmaking" (Braidt 2000, 182). Dunye herself has stated that she went into cinema because "sometimes you have to create your own history." By doing so, she has forged a unique genre, dubbed the "Dunye-mentary," which has been described as "[a] mixture of documentary, Dunye storytelling, and life itself" (Guenther 2010).

There were, of course, other, earlier black lesbian films, but none of them were as acclaimed as was *The Watermelon Woman*. These include *Storme: The Lady of the Jewel Box* (1987) by Michelle Parkerson, which tells the story of Storme DeLarverie, an emcee and male impersonator at the Jewel Box Revue, the first integrated gender-impersonation show, during the 1950s and 1960s. Parkerson also codirected with Ada Gay Griffin the documentary *A Litany for Survival: The Life and Work of Audre Lorde* (1995), an epic portrait of that famed black lesbian poet and activist.

As these titles indicate, the vast majority of black lesbian films made during the so-called golden age of BQC were documentaries. Others included Aishah Shahidah Simmons's coming-out short films *In My Father's House* (1996) and *Silence . . . Broken* (1993). Both films explore issues of race, gender, homophobia, rape, and misogyny. Jocelyn Taylor's *Like a Prayer* (1991), *Looking for LaBelle* (1991), and *Bodily Functions* (1995) and Yvonne Welbon's *Living With Pride: Ruth C. Ellis @ 100* (1999) were other black lesbian documentaries. Despite the appearance of these films, that of Dunye stood out because it was a feature-length fictional work that showcased a black lesbian protagonist and was also picked up for distribution by a reputable production company.

Since *The Watermelon Woman*'s release in 1996, there have been more than twenty feature films directed by black lesbians. However, like most women in Hollywood, black lesbian directors do not have access to the necessary networks, capital, or resources to have their films made and distributed for mass circulation.

The question of (in)visibility constitutes a guiding force behind the past of BQC, primarily due to a dearth of visual representations. Such a lack perpetuated a "silencing" of black queer voices and, even more specifically, as pointed out by Kara Keeling, black lesbian voices. Black lesbian cinema remains historically invisible, with a next-to-nil public presence. In her essay "Joining the Lesbians," Keeling attempts to place black queer filmmaking, specifically of the black lesbian variety, in the context of what she calls "regimes of visibility." However, Keeling cautions us to be careful in relying on "celebratory notions of visibility that is counterposed positively" to visibility's binary opposite—"invisibility" (Keeling 2005, 215). It is important to note, as she does, that celebratory visibility is not the same as political power. It is the potential of black queer cinema as political intervention and how it is done that, as Kobena Mercer has noted, gives importance to black queer filmmaking, and not "who or what the filmmakers are" (Mercer 1993, 238–56). Also, to presume that the mere fact of "visibility" is what constitutes a political force for black queer filmmaking allows the black queer subject to become a novelty rather than a profound intervention (Smith 2009, 44).

Tongues Untied, Paris Is Burning, and *The Watermelon Woman* all fall under the heading of documentary even though the approach and effect of each is definitely distinct. What is common in all three is that, as a genre of "truth" in its pure form, documentary has always played a seminal role in the political history of the LGBT community. None of these films is, however, documentary in the literal sense. Each adds varying layers of both optimistic and pessimistic metaphor to the struggle of black queers to be visible, to be liberated, and to be understood within the queer community, the black community, and the white mainstream.

Documentary film privileges itself by underscoring the impression that it is more politically efficacious than other genres due to its lesser reliance on narrative conventions like fiction (Nichols 1991, 191). The African American film scholar Kara Keeling believes that the use of documentary is largely based on economics, in that documentary films are less expensive to produce and so "a black queer documentary project has a more viable chance of reaching completion, and subsequent distribution." Economic concerns are not, however, the sole factor in the historical trend of black queer filmmakers opting for documentaries over other genres. Documentary film is a genre that offers greater autonomy to black queer filmmakers to produce images or content that Hollywood studios are wary of exploring, specifically explicit displays of racialized homoeroticism (Smith 2009, 21).

The Past of BQC

(In)Visibility

AFRICAN AMERICAN FILMS PRODUCED prior to the 1980s rarely incorporated queerness as a theme. If they did, they typically adhered to derogatory and negative stereotypes of gay men and lesbians, presenting the former as passive and weak antitheses to the idea of a strong, active, and independent black masculinity. Melvin Van Peebles's *Sweet Sweetback's Baadasssss Song* (1971) broke cinematic ground for African Americans. Ironically, it also helped pave the way for the genesis of BQC more than two decades later. Although most literature on *Sweet Sweetback* and the genre of Blaxploitation do not mention it, the film does have something to say about queers of different races (Wlodarz 2004, 10–25). *Sweet Sweetback* includes a very brief scene in which three effeminate looking and sissy-acting young men—one white, one black, and the other Hispanic—are questioned by the police (who represent the white power structure) as to the whereabouts of Sweet Sweetback, the film's protagonist, who is on the run. The dialogue here is revealing. The black man begins: "No, chile, I mean officer. I haven't seen Mr. Sweetback." The Hispanic man then chimes in: "If you see him, send him here." The black man then assertively declares: "I'm a militant queen." The white man finishes by questioning: "Won't I do, officer?" All three men then giggle and, while sipping their soft drinks, look coyly at the camera. Although the three men in this scene are negatively stereotyped as gay men, it is significant that Van Peebles made it a point to include them as part of a cross-racial "black" community, and who, as members, do not give up Sweetback's location to the white power structure. However, despite this inclusion and the film's radical and subversive position on the racial front,

Sweet Sweetback has unfortunately helped fuel homophobia—the view that homosexuality is pathology, a form of white racist oppression (the white man's disease) foisted upon the black community—and the subsequent marginalization of black queers, inadvertently reinforcing the laughable and taboo nature of queerness in American black communities. As a related aside, it is also important to point out that BQC, as part of the rise of independent filmmaking, ascended in popularity (or at least in its visibility) during the germination of the so-called hood film genre, in which homophobia and heterosexist hypermasculinity were seemingly unproblematically foisted upon the viewing and consuming black public. The relationship between the two film genres remains a rich area of future critical investigation.

Most scholars will agree that during the 1980s and 1990s, there arose a discernible body of cultural work (written, filmic, visual) that became constitutive of the interests of a definable black lesbian and gay culture. These texts set out to negotiate and politicize the categories of blackness and queerness as sources of empowerment. During the late 1980s and early 1990s, African American gay and lesbian artists became foot soldiers fighting in the trenches and on the front lines of the culture wars. This was a battle conducted on two simultaneous fronts: one, against resistant social and political forces from within (i.e., homophobia from black America) and two, from without (i.e., racism from white America). These decades saw a proliferation of black queer visual imagery in which black queer image-makers began to explore issues specific to gender, race, sexuality, class, and their intersections, as a form of identity politics. Using art as a transformative weapon, many black queer image-makers acknowledged the dramatic and traumatic history of the black body and focused in on its vulnerability in conjunction with accompanying desires that were all at once erotic, political, and otherwise.

The body as gendered, eroticized, and raced remains the primary focus for queer identity-formation strategies and critique in the realm of film in particular and in the visual arts in general. The eroticized or sexualized black body—male or female—has always been threatening to strategies of black liberation and to the development of subjectivity, thereby raising the question of whether it is at all possible for black queers to transcend a body that carries with it the denigrating mark of a double difference. When black queers retake control over the representation of their own bodies outside of prepackaged notions of family and nation-building—as demonstrated by many of the films that constitute BQC—it becomes dangerously provocative to Black Nationalists and afrocentrists. Indeed, for these constituencies the very term "black queer" might seem oxymoronic, in that "black" speaks supposedly to a preferred collective or group identity while "queer" has been interpreted (perhaps wrongly) as focusing on an individual or self-centered (and therefore selfish) identity (re)construction. For the Black Nationalist and afrocentrist, the black queer body manifests a "desire gone wrong"—a lamentable symptom of white racist coercion and domination. Black queer cinematic and visual artists used the black body to create new nonessentialist possibilities for a different kind of blackness that they saw as resistant and free, redolent of an "unbounded" desire put to the task of searching for and publicizing the myriad possibilities of black queer being and black queer experience.

Kobena Mercer has grappled with the issue of duality as a struggle for black queers. Duality, he notes, informs working against both the racist white gay front and the homophobic front of the black community at all times. Battling on both barricades creates a situation in which black queers are constantly "negotiating our relationships to the different communities to which we equally belong." Mercer notes that this dual struggle means that black queers are constantly locating themselves "in the spaces between different communities—at the intersections of power relations determined by race, class, gender, and sexuality" (Mercer 1993, 239). The attempt to convert "black or queer" into "black and queer" speaks to "a persistent state of being" always in negotiation with "a series of different positionalities" (Hall 1997, 129). It is the constant working out of these situations that becomes crucial to strategies of black queer visualizing. In *Tongues Untied* and *Looking for Langston*, gayness and blackness are brought together, forcing us to see the former as an inextricable part of the latter, and hence, to "queer blackness" (Wallenberg 2004, 128–29).

The hybrid and performative nature of black queer films critically locates black queers in a third or in-between space of self-discovery and provides testimony to the potential redemptive or sanctifying powers of homoeros. For the African American cultural critic Robert Reid-Pharr, the black queer body in the visual and literary frame represents a site of *boundarylessness* and *in-betweenness*. The black queer image-maker sees in unbounded desire the boundarylessness of black queer bodies, black queer desires, and black queer experiences. In other words, she or he sees the possibility for a homo-utopian fulfillment and salvation. Regarding black-on-black homophobia, Reid-Pharr has noted that "to strike the homosexual, the scapegoat, the sign of chaos and crisis, is to return the community to normality, to create boundaries around blackness . . ." (Reid-Pharr 2001, 103–4). Such boundaries are precisely what BQC of the past attempted to contest.

Tongues Untied makes artistic and politically strategic use of voices and visuals that overlap, intercut, and dissolve into one another rhythmically to make a collage of voices that speak the personal, yet together, reference and galvanize the collective. The film approaches racial and sexual identity as fluid and plural, never uniform, and shows that one can and must be both black and queer at the same time. Riggs stated it best in an interview: "The way to break loose of the schizophrenia in trying to define identity is to realize that you are many things within a person. Don't try to arrange a hierarchy of things that are virtuous in your character and say 'This is more important than that.' Realize that both are equally important; they both inform your character" (Simmons 1991, 190).

In addition to the focus on the overlay and unity of blackness and queerness, *Tongues Untied* also emphasizes the powerful connections between black gay men and black cultural traditions, black history, and links to the larger black community. The film highlights acts of resistance "rooted in black vernacular traditions" and, as such, resists the oppression black gay men face within the dominant culture as well as within the black community (Dickel 2011, 49).

Interracialism

RIGGS, ALONG WITH ISAAC Julien, are two exemplary black queer filmmakers who have not been afraid to broach the queer and the question of interracial desire in their works. The visible and affective expressions of interracialism are transgressive and, as such, have the potential for politically charged interventions in dismantling the boundaries around and between blackness and queerness. Black bodies and their histories in the West have always been seen in relationship to white bodies. That connection is a highly contentious one, forever rooted in a back-and-forth play of the erotic and the political.

The film theorist B. Ruby Rich has noted that

> queers have the potential for a different relationship to race, and to racism, because of the very nature of same-sex desires and sexual practices. . . . [In interracial relationships,] race occupies the place vacated by gender. The non-sameness of color, language, or culture is a marker of difference in relationships otherwise defined by the sameness of gender. Race is a constructed presence of same-gender couples, one that allows a sorting out of identities that can avoid both the essentialism of prescribed racial expectations and the artificiality of entirely self-constructed paradigms. (Rich 1993, 318–19)

Indeed, as Rich has so eloquently observed, "scenes of same-sex interracialism demonstrate the power to put into circulation a complex relationship of want, need, and desire, and have the potential to serve as a dialectic road map for the future of representation" (Rich 1993, 339).

Films such as *Tongues Untied*, *Looking for Langston*, and *The Watermelon Woman* attempt to use interracialism to unfix identities; this is their political power. Interracialism becomes a potent critical weapon in BQC against the fixity of identity. All of these films constitute political as well as aesthetic products of intervention in racial and queer matters. In them, the discourse of sexuality and that of race are tightly interwoven and become indistinguishable. To address one requires addressing the other. They grapple with racial and sexual essentialism in very ambivalent ways, "informed by contradictory desires, and giving voice to desires that are inter-racial." Interracialism constitutes one of many alternative "spaces in-between" for queers, creating what Benedict Anderson (*Imagined Communities* 2006) has called "imagined communities." Although both *Tongues Untied* and *Looking for Langston* regard interracial relations as a possible future of harmony among equals, in order for that future to come to pass, the films argue, black men must first turn to their own and find collective power among themselves at the exclusion of others. These and other films that attempt to confront black queer invisibility also have the potential of producing another silence by representing an exclusively black picture of gay and lesbian life, thus promoting a separatist gay and lesbian experience. Such films can unintentionally silence other racialized groups, such as Asians or Latinos.

Autography

MANY OF THE FILMS that fall under the rubric BQC make use of *autography* or "self-fashioning," as a means to critique blackness, the racial and sexual self, the community, politics, and aesthetics. As a subjective process, the artist takes "his or her own body as the 'canvas' . . . or 'screen,' so that the work of translation and re-appropriation is literally a 're-writing of the self on the body', a re-epidermalization of the body" (Fanon 1967, 20). Black queer filmmakers such as Marlon Riggs, Isaac Julien, and Cheryl Dunye oscillate between documentary, biography, memoir, and narrative fiction to produce new and subversive cinematic forms that redress prior disavowal of the existence and experiences of black gay men and lesbians (Smith 2009, 17). The politics of intervention through autography in film are important to the historical relevance of black queer cinema. Filmic texts (unlike paintings or still photographs, for example), because of their mobility, are more immediate and powerful, in that they enable an infinite range of possible audiences and responses. Films have the potential to shift social mores in part because they do more than simply confront academic discourse alone—they "engage actual bodies who hail their audiences to confront the material effects of one's positions such that the audience is called upon to question their implication in what can/cannot be rendered in the field of representation" (Smith 2009, 18).

The Present of BQC

AS THE 1990S PROGRESSED, BQC, in parallel with the NQC, began to mature as well as mutate. The genre journeyed from "radical impulse to niche market," with its range of "innocuous and often unremarkable films targeting a narrow, rather than all inclusive, new queer audience" (Rich 2000, 23). These films began to focus on bankable narrative forms, such as romantic comedies. More crossover films were produced and there was a transition to subjects and their treatment less informed by activism or identity politics. Radicalism had become co-opted by the mainstream. This phenomenon has been referred to as "gaysploitation," a queer riff on "Blaxploitation" (Aron 2004, 8). Most of these films were about white men and women. However, even in the limited subgenre that was BQC, romantic comedies and feel-good "coming of age" films such as *Punks* (Patrick Ian Polk, 2000), *Boy Culture* (Q. Allan Brocka, 2006), *Noah's Arc: Jumping the Broom* (Patrick Ian Polk, 2008), *Finding Me* (Roger S. Omeus Jr., 2009), and *Finding Me: Truth* (Roger S. Omeus Jr., 2010) were produced and found a ready-made audience. In this mix, black lesbian films were few and far between. On the one hand, such crossover works could be interpreted positively, as a way of re-introducing the idea of hope and social validation of queer experiences and relationships among men of all colors in the future. On the other hand, they could signal a willful move of a color-blind queer from the radical margins to the acquiescence of mainstream acceptance. There were underlying factors that facilitated these events. One was that there was a change in independent film distribution tactics during the first decade of the twenty-first century. Also, with the proliferation of DVDs, fewer films relied on theatrical releases. For some observers, this was a lamentable state of affairs, in that it signaled a loss of the communal experience of queers going to the movie theater en masse. On the other hand, gay and lesbian film festivals continue to play a seminal role in queer community building, for such events create an opportunity for queer folk to gather and commune around queer culture.

The present of BQC underscores the observation that "black" and "queer" are going through a process of commodification and consumption and are losing their meaning as once-efficient militant forms of resistance. Both sectors have reached a high saturation level of institutionalization and visibility (black culture through hip-hop and queer culture through the popular media of television, film, and fashion), and increasingly throw into question the oppositional power of black queer cultural forms and their production. This process renders most black, queer, and black queer forms of cultural production as more nostalgic (historic) than oppositional, and thus, more regressive than progressive. Perhaps one exception to this is Rodney Evans's 2004 narrative film *Brother to Brother*, a work that focuses on differences within the

Perry (Anthony Mackie) in search of a proud black masculinity within his homosexuality in *Brother to Brother.*

black community while at the same time operates in a tradition of reveling in a shared black culture and history. The film, written and directed by Evans and first presented at the Sundance Film Festival, presents a queer reading of the African American cultural period known as the Harlem Renaissance (c. 1925–35). Evans's film parallels Isaac Julien's *Looking for Langston,* in that both films not only deal with the Harlem Renaissance as historical backdrop but also confront the past and present of black queer experiences of racism and homophobia. Both films make use of nostalgia, but to different ends.

Evans's film "re-discovers" and takes the Harlem Renaissance beyond the focus on race and brings to public attention and recognition the intersection of homosexuality and race during this period. The existence and vibrancy of a black and gay Harlem of the 1920s and thereafter provide some evidence that African Americans and homosexuals had something in common—oppression by the majority culture based on difference. Louise Wallenberg has noted, "the Harlem Renaissance is understood to be an important epoch for the entire black community as it provided the Western world with images and words previously kept invisible and silent. It was also a period—and an art community—very much formed by queerness. Not to acknowledge this is to deny the fact that the Renaissance was 'as gay as it was

Perry after being beaten by a group of his homophobic classmates.

black,' [and] that many of its key figures . . . were known to be queer, one way or another" (Wallenberg 2004, 143; Mercer 1993, 249).

Brother to Brother's plot centers around an art student named Perry (Anthony Mackie) who befriends an elderly homeless man named Bruce Nugent (Roger Robinson), who was an important writer in the Harlem Renaissance and who had the reputation of an "out" gay man in 1920s Harlem. In the film, the aged Nugent character guides the young protagonist Perry on a flashback tour of 1920s Harlem. As invisible observers, they go to a rent party at "Niggeratti" Manor, the name given to the house where Nugent, the African American writer Wallace Thurman, and others resided during the 1920s. Nugent points out to Perry his past friendships with important Harlem Renaissance artists and writers, including Wallace Thurman, Langston Hughes, Aaron Douglas, and Zora Neale Hurston. The two men's odyssey chronicles some of the challenges Nugent faced as a young, black, gay writer during the 1920s. Perry soon discovers that the challenges of homophobia and racism he faces in the early twenty-first century are not all that different from those experienced during Nugent's youth.

Another exception and harbinger of the possible future of BQC is the film *Pariah*, which is indebted to a cadre of coming-out films and documentaries released between 1991 and 1996, the so-called golden age of BQC. *Pariah* is a 2011 feature-length narrative film directed by African American filmmaker Dee Rees. The film was well received and is much more than its classification as a women's "coming-out, coming-of-age" film or a meditation on African American identity. It goes beyond "issues" and gender binaries. Dee Rees's characters are black, queer, straight, self-doubting, and conflicted. They are poor and middle class. Refreshingly, we are shown flesh-and-blood, multidimensional characters in fraught and complex relationships. Although it is a mainstream film, the protagonists exhibit depth of character and complexity of experience. The principal character, Alike, played by Adepero Oduye, is a shy young black lesbian from the middle class who is just beginning to discover and come to terms with her "masculine" gender expressions. Her best friend, Laura (Pernell Walker), a confident black butch lesbian from a disadvantaged background, supports and encourages Alike on her journey to self-discovery and acceptance. Laura, disowned by her mother, is a symbol of black queer women's self-made communities and black lesbian self-making. She mentors Alike in the ways of the black aggressive woman, helping her to develop "the grand swagger" of hip-hop masculinity. This hip-hop identification is Laura's "male protective armor," and the gateway to her vulnerability as well (Sullivan 2012). Alike attempts to merge her own "Afro-punk" personality with the lessons learned from Laura, but she finds it difficult to fully identify with one or the other. Alike is constantly tossed back and forth between expectations of masculine and feminine physical appearance and behavior, as defined by heterosexuals and by black lesbians.

A phrase that is repeated throughout the film is "doing my thing." Dee Rees repurposes this hip-hop youth mantra to explore black gender across lines of sexuality and generation. Throughout the film, there are characters and plot lines that express a complex attitude toward black queer gender and sexuality. The film invites us to think about the intricacies of identity that many commercial films gloss over or altogether ignore, particularly when the characters are black. Blackness, sexuality, class, and gender are all at play. Homophobia, too, rears its ugly head within the context of the nuclear family and pressures from the black community taken as family. As with BQC of the past, *Pariah* showcases an unapologetic humanity, which

Alike (Adepero Oduye), an adolescent seeking her first sexual encounter in *Pariah*.

is perhaps the film's greatest strength and accomplishment. The film resists binaries vehemently, insisting on presenting an in-your-face story from a black social world where pressured ideas about gender, sexuality, and intimacy are either rejected or constantly negotiated. Ultimately, *Pariah* is about what it means to be a black queer woman as a complex human. This is a feat that many of today's commercial films have failed to accomplish.

The Future of BQC

As WE HAVE SEEN, the 1980s and 1990s witnessed a spate of films that highlighted a convergence of concerns about the formation and desired seamless joining of racial subjectivity (how we come to know ourselves as black people) with same-sex affective (erotic and sexual) desires. It was during these decades that the strategies for a politics of identity flourished. These were strategies borrowed from the civil rights movement and from feminism.

The past of BQC involved a small number of courageous filmmakers who created from the margins of mainstream visibility and understanding, and whose works challenged or subverted the mainstream. Through cinema, these individuals grappled with issues of race, sexuality, class, culture, and politics while trying to produce art (Hardy 2003). *Tongues Untied* interrogated the intersections of blackness and queerness—what Kathryn Stockton has called "switchpoints"—and rejected the premise of the mutual exclusivity of black and queer (Stockton 2006). The future of BQC would have to take into consideration how these "switchpoints" between blackness and queerness could open up new pathways of thought to stimulate thinking concerned with a host of issues relevant not only to black queers but to society at large.

A pertinent and timely question for the twenty-first century is this: What might a more expansive view of queerness and blackness look like and how might it be visualized on film? Have we come to a dead end of inquiry regarding the intersection of black and queer, and if so, how might a reinterrogation of both blackness and queerness reanimate a supposedly moribund mode of interrogation? Has the current situation fostered a desire for transcending or surpassing blackness and queerness, as is suggested by the contemporary notions of "post-black," "post-queer," and "post-black queer?" The affix "post" is suggestive of a want and need to move beyond the racialized and sexualized body, to ascend to a "higher" plane of existence and inquiry. It signals the future of our increasingly globalized world and its deleterious effects resulting from intensified commodification, consumption, and dehumanization. The dilemma of the "post" in post-black, post-queer, and post-black queer rests in the contradictions and discursive ambivalence found in postmodernism itself. Maybe "post" indicates a distrust of distinctiveness and the horrifying possibility of fading away and disappearing into the vagueness of the status quo. The "post" or afterlife of black queer may very well be the future of BQC.

Is the total abandonment of identity politics more ideal than practicable under today's current circumstances for blacks, queers, and black queers? If so, the result might be the evolution of new manifestations of the genre black queer not yet imagined. Indeed, the resurgent interest of various kinds of genre, such as cowboy films, detective dramas, romantic comedies, spy thrillers, and the like, could be a sign of a new wave of (black) queer filmmaking. The future of black queer cinema may in fact be rooted in its past—not a return to the identity politics of the 1980s and 1990s, but, rather, learning the lessons of such politics so to go beyond them. This future may, in fact, lead to an eradication of itself—an annihilation or perhaps transformation of the very terms "black" and "queer."

Whatever "post" is or ends up becoming, its definition will always call for redefinition and will be driven by the eternal query, "What's next?" or, as I like to phrase it, "W(h)ither black queer?" The rethinking or reconceptualizing of blackness, queerness, and black queerness will certainly rile things up and perhaps shake us out of any sense of complacency with the seemingly increased acceptance (or simply tolerance) of racial difference and queerness. However, the more important question, I think, for the future of black queer is how do we continue to empower black, queer, and black queer communities so that they become, in the future, examples of illuminating cultures for others? The remedy might lie in minimizing the dysfunctional and emphasizing the transformational. For the future of BQC, we must analyze what has or has not changed in the discursive ordering of race, sexuality, and gender in a "history of the present." What is needed today is a commitment by black queer filmmakers to offering different, as opposed to necessarily new, forms of black queer liberation, keeping well in mind that the cinematic and visual arts remain sites of "imaginative prospect and revolutionary force for transformative thinking about the nature of black queer" (Wallenberg 2004, 129). This is a tall order for both the producers and the consumers of visual culture, but it is a messy and ultimately rewarding piece of work that has to be done.

References

Abrams, Kathryn. 1999. "From Autonomy to Agency: Feminist Perspectives on Self-Direction." *William and Mary Law Review* 40(3): 805–46.

Anderson, Benedict. 2006. *Imagined Communities: Reflections on the Origin and Spread of Nationalism*. London: Verso.

Aron, M. 2004. "New Queer Cinema: An Introduction." In *New Queer Cinema: A Critical Reader*, edited by M. Aron, 3–14. New Brunswick, NJ: Rutgers University Press.

Braidt, A. B. 2000. "Queering Ethnicity, Queering Sexuality: A Paradigmatic Shift in the Politics of Cinematic Representation in Cheryl Dunye's *The Watermelon Woman* (1996)." In *Simulacrum America: The USA and the Popular Media*, edited by E. Kraus and C. Auer, 181–88. New York: Camden House.

Butler, J. 1993. *Bodies That Matter: On the Discursive Limits of "Sex."* New York: Routledge.

Lynn, C. 2009. Trinity: The Black Fantasy. http://cheryllynneaton.com/2009/05/07/trinity-the-black-fantasy/

Cripps, T. 1978. *Black Film as Genre*. Bloomington: Indiana University Press.

Diawara, M. 1993. "Black American Cinema: The New Realism." In *Black American Cinema*, edited by M. Diawara, 3–25. New York: Routledge.

Dickel, S. 2011. *Black/Gay: The Harlem Renaissance, the Protest Era, and Constructions of Black Gay Identity in the 1980s and 1990s*. Berlin: LIT Verlag.

Fanon, F. 1967. *Black Skin, White Masks*. New York: Grove Press.

Forgiarini, Matteo, Marcello Gallucci, and Angelo Maravita. 2011. "Racism and the Empathy for Pain on Our Skin." *Frontiers in Perception Science*. July 12. http://www.ncbi.nlm.nih.gov/pmc/articles/PMC3108582/

Harris, Trudier. 1995. "Genre." *Journal of American Folklore* 108, no. 430 (Autumn): 509–27.

Guenther, H. 2010. "Spike Lee ≠ Black Independent Cinema." http://eyecandy.ucsc.edu/archive/old-pdfs/2010_vol20.pdf.

Hall, S. 1997. "What Is This 'Black' in Black Popular Culture?" *Representing Blackness: Issues in Film and Video*, edited by V. Smith 123–33. New Brunswick, NJ: Rutgers University Press.

Hankin, K. 2002. *Girls in the Back Room: Looking at the Lesbian Bar*. Minneapolis: University of Minnesota Press.

Hardy, E. 2003. "Young Soul Rebels: Negro/Queer Experimental Filmmakers," http://mfj-online.org/journalPages/MFJ41/hardypage.html.

Hilliard-Nunn, Patricia. 1998. "Representing African Women in Movies." In *Afrocentric Visions: Studies in Culture and Communication*, edited by J. D. Hamlet, 175–94.

hooks, bell. 2012. "No Love in the Wild." NewBlackMan (in Exile). September 5, 2012. http://www.newblackmaninexile.net/2012/09/bell-hooks-no-love-in-wild.html.

JanMohamed, A. R. 1995. "The Economy of Manichean Allegory." In *The Post-Colonial Studies Reader*, edited by Bill Ashcroft, Gareth Griffiths, and Helen Tiffin, 18–23. London: Routledge.

Keeling, K. 2005. "Joining the Lesbians: Cinematic Regimes of Black Lesbian Visibility." In *Black Queer Studies: A Critical Anthology*, edited by E. P. Johnson and M. G. Henderson, 213–27. Durham: Duke University Press.

Lacan, J. 1978. The Four Fundamental Concept of Psycho-Analysis, edited by Alan Sheridan, New York: W. W. Norton 203–60.

Mapp, E. 1973. "Black Women in Films." *The Black Scholar*. Black Women's Liberation Issue. 4, no. 6/7 (March–April): 42–46.

Masilela, N. (1993). "The Los Angeles School of Black Filmmakers." In *Black American Cinema*, edited by Manthia Diawara, 107–8. New York: Routledge.

McCormack, Karen. 2009. "Stratified Reproduction and Poor Women's Resistance." Paper presented at the annual meeting of the American Sociological Association, Hilton San Francisco & Renaissance Park 55 Hotel, San Francisco, California. http://www.allacademic.com/meta/p108918_index.html.

Means Coleman, R. 2011. *Horror Noire: Blacks in American Horror Films from the 1890s to Present*. New York: Routledge.

Mercer, K. 1993. "Dark and Lovely Too: Black Gay Men in Independent Film." In M. Gever, P. Parmar, and J. Greyson (eds.), *Queer Looks: Perspectives on Lesbian and Gay Film and Video*, edited by M. Gever, P. Parmar, and J. Greyson, New York: Routledge, 238–56,

Lynn, Cheryl. 2009. *Trinity: The Black Fantasy*. http://cheryllynneaton .com/2009/05/07/trinity-the-black-fantasy.

Miller, Jacques-Alain. 1997. *The Ethics of Psychoanalysis 1959–1969: The Seminar of Jacques Lacan Book VII*. Translated by Dennis Porter. New York: Norton.

Morrison, T. 1993. *What Moves at the Margin: Selected Nonfiction*. Jackson: University Press of Mississippi.

Muñoz, José Esteban. 1999. *Disidentifications: Queers of Color and the Performance of Politics*. Minneapolis: University of Minnesota Press.

Munoz, Lorenza. 2008. "Interview: Gina Prince-Bythewood (*The Secret Life of Bees*)" *Issuu*, October 15, 2008, 7. https://issuu.com/filmindependent/docs/ october_newsletter

Murray, J. 1973. *To Find an Image: Black Films from Uncle Tom to Superfly*. New York: Bobbs Merrill.

Nichols, B. 1991. *Representing Reality: Issues and Concepts in Documentary*. Bloomington: Indiana University Press.

Newton, Huey P. 1971. "He Won't Bleed Me: A Revolutionary Analysis of 'Sweet Sweetback's Baadasssss Song.'" *The Black Panther* 6, June 19.

Norment, L. 2008. "A Moment in Time." *Ebony*, 64, no. 1, (November): 72–80. EBSCOhost, lp.hscl.ufl.edu/login?url=http://search.ebscohost.com/login .aspx?direct=true&db=aph&AN=35548792&site=eds-live.

Powell, R. J. 2002. *Black Art: A Cultural History*. London: Thames and Hudson Ltd.

Reid, M. A. 1993. *Redefining Black Film*. Berkeley: University of California Press.

Reid, M. A. 1997. *PostNegritude Visual and Literary Culture*. Albany: State University of New York Press.

Reid, M. A. 2005. *Black Lenses, Black Voices: African American Film Now*. Lanham, MD: Rowman and Littlefield.

Reid-Pharr, R. 2001. *Black Gay Man: Essays*. New York: New York University Press.

Rich, B. R. 1993. "When Difference Is (More Than) Skin Deep." In *Queer Looks: Perspectives on Lesbian and Gay Film and Video*, edited by M. Gever, P. Parmar, and J. Greyson, 318–39. New York: Routledge.

Rich, B. R. 2000. "Queer and Present Danger." *Sight and Sound*, 10, no. 3: 22–25.

Riley, Clayton. 1972. "Shaft Can Do Everything—I Can Do Nothing," *New York Times*, August 13.

Simmons, R. 1991. "Tongues Untied: An Interview with Marlon Riggs." In *Brother to Brother: New Writings by Black Gay Men*, edited by E. Hemphill, 189–205. Boston: Alyson Publications.

Smalls, J. 2006. *The Homoerotic Photography of Carl Van Vechten: Public Face, Private Thoughts*. Philadelphia: Temple University Press.

Smith, C. G. 2009. "Thinking Otherwise: The Politics of Black Queer Filmmaking." Master's Thesis, York University.

Stockett, Kathryn. 2009. *The Help*. New York: G. P. Putnam's Sons.

Stockton, K. B. 2006. *Beautiful Bottom, Beautiful Shame: Where "Black" Meets "Queer."* New York: New York University Press.

Sullivan, L. L. 2000. "Chasing Fae: 'The Watermelon Woman' and Black Lesbian Possibility." *Callaloo* 23, no. 1: 448–60.

Sullivan, M. J. 2012. "Black Queer Gender and Pariah's Grand Swagger." *The Feminist Wire*, January 3 2012. http://thefeministwire.com/2012/01/black-queer-gender-and-pariahs-grand-swagger/.

Wallenberg, L. (2004). New Black Queer Cinema. In M. Aron (ed.), *New Queer Cinema: A Critical Reader*, New Brunswick, NJ: Rutgers University Press, pp. 128–43.

Wells, Veronica. 2012. "Bet You Didn't Know: Secrets Behind The Secret Life of Bees," Madame Noire. November 5, 2012. http://madamenoire.com/230631/bet-you-didnt-know-secrets-behind-the-secret-life-of-bees/2/.

West, Cornel. 1993. *Race Matters*. Boston: Beacon Press.

Wlodarz, Joe. 2004. "Beyond the Black Macho: Queer Blaxploitation," *Velvet Light Trap* 53 (Spring): 10–25.

Yearwood, G. L. 2000. *Black Film as a Signifying Practice: Cine, Narration and African-American Aesthetic Tradition*. Trenton, NJ: Africa World Press.

CONTRIBUTORS

KAREN BOWDRE is an independent scholar. She is coeditor of *From Madea to Media Mogul: Theorizing Tyler Perry* (2016). Her essays have appeared in *Falling in Love Again: The Contemporary Romantic Comedy* (2009) and the journals *Black Camera* and *Cinema Journal*.

MELBA JOYCE BOYD is a poet, biographer, essayist, documentarian and Distinguished University Professor and Chair at Wayne State University's Department of Africana Studies. Her films include *The Black Unicorn: Dudley Randall and the Broadside Press* (1995) and *Austere and Lonely Offices: The Poetry of Robert Hayden* (2014).

KIMBERLY NICHELE BROWN is Chair and Associate Professor, Department of Gender, Sexuality, and Women's Studies, Virginia Commonwealth University. She is the author of *Writing the Black Revolutionary Diva: Women's Subjectivity and the Decolonizing Text*. Her current book-length project is "Incognegro Stances: Cross-racial Espionage in Contemporary Film and Literature."

CHESYA BURKE has published several books and written articles for the African American National Biography. She is interested in genre studies and has written in the field for many years. Burke's story collection, *Let's Play White*, is being taught in universities around the country. Presently, she is working on her Ph.D. in English at the University of Florida.

GERALD R. BUTTERS, JR. is a Professor of history at Aurora University. His publications include *Black Manhood on the Silent Screen* (2002), *Banned in Kansas* (2007), and *From Sweetback to Superfly: Race and Film Spectatorship in Chicago's Loop, 1970–1975* (2015). Dr. Butters's work focuses on the intersection of race and gender in film.

Anne Crémieux is Assistant Professor at the University of Paris West Nanterre's English department, where she teaches American cinema, TV series, and African American history. Crémieux is the author of *Les cinéastes noirs américains et le rêve hollywoodien* (2004). She has directed short films, documentaries, written books, and articles in French and English about minorities in American cinema.

Mark D. Cunningham received his Ph.D. in radio-television-film from the University of Texas at Austin. His dissertation considered narrative, race, and gender in John Singleton's hood trilogy: *Boyz N the Hood*, *Poetic Justice*, and *Baby Boy*. He has published in the areas of film, television, popular culture, and race studies.

Dan Flory is Associate Professor of philosophy at Montana State University, Bozeman. He is the author of *Philosophy, Black Film, Film Noir* (2008) and numerous essays on film and critical race theory, and the coeditor (with Mary K. Bloodsworth-Lugo) of *Race, Philosophy, and Film* (2013).

Patricia Hilliard-Nunn, Ph.D. with an M.F.A. in film is a Lecturer of African American studies at the University of Florida, where she is also an affiliate faculty member in the Center for Women's Studies and Gender Research. Hilliard-Nunn is a public historian and a filmmaker whose research focuses on African American history and culture and media. She studied with Haile Gerima as her film professor.

Jonathan Munby is Senior Lecturer in film studies and American studies at Lancaster Institute for the Contemporary Arts, United Kingdom. He is the author of *Public Enemies, Public Heroes: Screening the Gangster from Little Caesar to Touch of Evil* (1999) and *Under a Bad Sign: Criminal Self-Representation in African-American Popular Culture* (2011).

Charlene Regester is an Associate Professor in African and African American studies at the University of North Carolina-Chapel Hill. She is author of *African American Actresses: The Struggle for Visibility, 1900–1960*. Her articles have appeared in *Film History, Film Literature Quarterly, Jour-*

nal of Film and Video, Popular Culture Review, Popular Music and Society, Screening Noir, Studies in American Culture, and the *Western Journal of Black Studies.*

MARK A. REID is Professor of English at the University of Florida. His published works include *Black Lenses, Black Voices: African American Film Now* (2005), *PostNegritude Visual and Literary Culture* (1997), and *Redefining Black Film* (1993). He is the editor of *Spike Lee's* Do the Right Thing (1997) and the coeditor of *Le Cinéma noir américain* (1988). In addition to film, Reid has written on literature and photography.

JAMES SMALLS is Professor of art history and theory, and Affiliate Professor of gender and women's studies at the University of Maryland, Baltimore County. His research interests focus on the intersections of race, gender, and queer sexuality in the art of nineteenth-century Europe and the visual culture of the black diaspora. He is the author of *The Homoerotic Photography of Carl Van Vechten: Public Face, Private Thoughts* (2006) and *Gay Art* (2008).

INDEX

CPSIA information can be obtained
at www.ICGtesting.com
Printed in the USA
JSHW031257250922
30832JS00007B/270

9 780814 345481